Management Research

Management Research

Anshuman Sharma

RANDOM

RANDOM PUBLICATIONS

NEW DELHI (INDIA)

Management Research

ISBN 978-93-5111-349-2

Published in 2014 in India by

RANDOM PUBLICATIONS

4376-A/4B, Gali Murari Lal, Ansari Road
New Delhi-110 002
Phone : +91-11-43580356, +91-11-23289044
e-mail: randomexports@gmail.com, sales@randompublications.com, info@randompublications.com

Reprinted 2026

Type Setting by : Keystoneprintads, Delhi-110051

Preface

Why do we inquire into activities of wealth creation? At its most general, this inquiry is defined by its aim: to become more aware of and find meaning in, social experience. From such awareness comes the possibility of influence, both within the institutional structures and objects we encounter, create, and use, and over our own development in terms of character and conduct. Using this influence we can satisfy what Alfred Whitehead (1929a: 14, 23) calls our three-fold urge: 'to live, to live well, to live better'; and so to transform life into a potentially good and better life. Managerial research is a particular and increasingly important form of such influence; its concerns being those aspects of social life that are broadly concerned with the production and distribution of material wealth through some form of social organization, whether an entrepreneurial venture, a corporation, a public department, a profession, an occupation, etc.

Management research is in the throes of a healthy debate on both its ontological status and the appropriateness of various research processes. This debate has been prompted partly by a recurring concern that much of the management research appearing in top-rated academic journals is of little relevance to most practitioners. Management comprises planning, organizing, staffing, leading or directing, and controlling an organization or effort for the purpose of accomplishing a goal. Re-sourcing encompasses the deployment and manipulation of human resources financial resources, technological resources, and natural resources. Because organizations can be viewed as systems, management can also be defined as human action, including design, to facilitate the production of useful outcomes from a system. The present book entitled Management Research deals with all the aspects, concepts, and issues of management research. The text are arranged in lucid form and written in simple colloquial English.

I would like to thank my team for standing beside me throughout my career and writing this book. My special thanks go to "Random Publications" who have published the book.

— ***Anshuman Sharma***

Contents

1

Constraints on Developing Management Practices

The background to the study described was rooted in policy initiatives designed to remedy deficiencies identified in successive reports on management education and training during the 1980s and 1990s. In 1987 two reports were produced as part of a review of management education and training, prompted by the recognition that the UK still lagged behind other industrialized nations in terms of its formal management education. A few years later, the Cannon and Taylor Working Party Reports, arising out of the 1992 Institute of Management review of management development, noted that the challenges of organizational changes, especially contracting out, de-layering and empowerment, made the need for management development particularly acute. The situation was exacerbated by persistent structural unemployment, competitive pressures from low-wage economies, rapid technological change and standards in education that were inappropriate to the needs of employers.

The Handy Report recommended that a group of top companies form a Charter Group and establish a charter of good practice for management development. From these origins, the Management Charter Initiative (MCI) was established in 1988 as the operating arm of the National Forum for Management Education and Development and by the end of 1991 had the support of over 800 companies. Following the adoption of a competence-based approach to vocational training in the UK, MCI was recognized as the lead body for management and developed a generic set of occupational standards relating to areas of activity in which managers need to be competent.

In 1994, with renewed concern over developing the UK managerial workforce, the Employment Department decided to appraise the use of the Management Standards developed by MCI. The subsequent study that we undertook for the Department investigated the business benefits that could be attributed to competence-based management development in a range of sixteen organizations.

The Growth, Competitiveness, Employment White Paper from the European Commission (1994) argued that skills must be raised at all levels if European enterprises were to compete in global markets. At the same time the Teaching and Learning White Paper stressed the need to provide opportunities for continuous development in order to achieve this. The arguments resurfaced in successive Competitiveness White Papers in the UK during the 1990s and, after the Labour victory of 1997, in the work of the Skills Task Force and the emerging framework for lifelong learning. For UK managers, the need to increase the volume and quality of development is particularly acute given the dramatic changes taking place in the external environment and in organizations.

The study was therefore stimulated both by the need to increase management development and to evaluate the effectiveness of development that was competence based, the approach promoted under the reform of vocational education and training in the UK. If performance improvements could be identified and attributed to management development, managers would be more likely both to engage in development themselves and to make opportunities available for their subordinates. Moreover, if tangible benefits to business could be identified from the competence-based approach, more managers might use the NVQ/SVQ route to accredit their competence, thereby raising the overall level of managerial qualification.

The conceptual and theoretical underpinning of the study is first considered in relation to the literature on the role of HRD in general, and management development in particular, in improving performance. The empirical context, explaining the logic of the research design and briefly describing the sixteen organizations involved. Elaborating the design of the case-study protocol and the fieldwork that was involved.

The critical analysis that follows highlights the significance of the findings. Clear performance benefits were identified from management development, and these were more evident where management development was linked with organizational strategy and where HRD systems and processes adopted a coherent set of competence statements, such as the Management Standards.

Theoretical Context

There is an extensive literature supporting the crucial role of human resources in improving organizational performance and sustaining competitive advantage. Snell and Dean (1992) showed that effective management of human capital, especially in relation to building employee skills and commitment, was the key factor in releasing the productive potential of advanced manufacturing technology. Where organizational strategies have focused on replacing employees with physical capital, the effect of human activity on organizational performance is correspondingly minimized. However, investment in human resources as the ultimate source of competitive advantage is more plausible in the context of globalization, which weakens the advantages deriving from economies of scale and access to product markets and capital. Therefore, the optimum human resources policy, and the potential role of human capital, is contingent upon the relative importance of cost, quality and flexibility imperatives in the manufacturing strategy adopted.

Nevertheless, there is insufficient robust evidence concerning the effect of HRD on organizational performance, because relatively few organizations bother to evaluate the impact of training and development beyond the reaction level as defined in Kirkpatrick's (1967) typology. The paucity of evaluation of HRD initiatives is often explained by the difficulty of attributing causality: 'at best, management development and training must always be an act of faith'. Not only is it difficult to identify operational results that are amenable to improvement through training and development, causality is difficult to establish because often 'no single factor, including training, could by itself have brought about the change that has taken place'.

The problem is compounded by 'political' considerations which deter proper evaluation because of vested interests in demonstrating the effectiveness of MD opportunities for which individuals are responsible or to which they have committed time or money. Because of these practical difficulties in measuring the effects of developing people, reported benefits are often anecdotal and confined to a single aspect of performance.

Not only is the cumulative body of knowledge under-developed, it also lacks a coherent conceptual framework and an accepted structural model. In one of the pioneering contributions to the HRD and performance literature, Rummler and Brache distinguished three different levels of analysis: individual; process; and organisation. In the influential Analysis for Improving Performance, Swanson adopted the same framework of analysis, which was perpetuated in subsequent work.

This division of individual, process and organizational levels of performance has created conceptual confusion because it neglects the team or group level in the structure and conflates structures with processes. Performance at the team level links individuals with the organisation and therefore plays a pivotal role in translating individual performance improvements into bottom line results. Team level activities are important in facilitating the transfer between individual learning and organizational learning through the development of shared mental models and the adoption of routines that improve existing practices to develop core competence. However, as Russ-Eft (1996) has argued: 'We need more research on defining and measuring team performance.'

Individuals, groups and the organisation as a whole represent different structural levels, whereas processes (along with capacities and accomplishments) exist at each of these levels, as Fisher and Sleezer (1999) recognized. In advance of commissioning the research described here, the Department established an expert group to identify an appropriate methodology for assessing the business benefits of the Management Standards.

From the outset, the study group drew a clear distinction between levels in the organisational structure and work processes at each of these levels in exploring appropriate methodologies for tracing and measuring the business impact of management development, particularly that which was competence-based. Given the causal ambiguity concerning the mechanisms by which human resource practices translate into improved business performance, the expert group recognized that rigorous methods of analysis would be required.

The literature provided the expert group with some indication of the nature of performance benefits to be anticipated from management development. At the individual level, the literature demonstrates above all else the difficulties of measurement and attribution associated with identifying performance improvements arising from management development. In relation to team performance, the key message is the importance of developing collective knowledge so that when individuals change jobs, organizational capacity is not adversely affected.

With organizational performance, the literature links the achievement of critical success factors to the management capability of organizations. Strategies that recognize core competence as a key resource for gaining competitive advantage are prevalent in the recent literature. Clearly, if the development of core competence, including managerial competence, is a crucial determinant of improved organizational performance (as represented by competitive success), then improved performance of individuals and teams ought to be intervening outcomes. The need to link management development with organizational strategy is also prominent in recent literature, as is the need to justify individual development in terms of benefits to the organisation.

There is evidence that organizational performance is enhanced when there is a good fit between organizational strategy and employees' competences, whether employees are developed in line with strategy or strategies are designed to match employees' competences. Finally, recent literature contains claims that management development is more effective where HRD systems and procedures have adopted the MCI Standards. Having considered the literature alongside the evaluation needs of the Employment Department, the expert group proposed five testable hypotheses:

- Management development improves individual performance.
- Management development improves team performance.
- Management development improves organizational performance.
- Improvements in individual, team and organizational performance are more likely if management development is linked to organizational strategy.
- Improvements in individual, team and organizational performance are more likely if HRD systems and processes are based on a common, coherent integrated set of competence statements.

The expert group recommended to the Department that these hypotheses could best be tested using a case-study approach in a range of organizations.

The group drafted a preliminary case-study protocol identifying the evidence to be assessed in relation to the processes and performance outcomes to be investigated at each level. The draft protocol was included as part of the specification for the project when the tender was awarded to us with colleagues at PriME Research and Development of Harrogate.

Empirical Context

In order adequately to test all five hypotheses, it was necessary to include 'counterfactual cases'. We needed organizations that did not use the Management Standards as well as users, and to include organizations in which management development was not linked with organizational strategy as well as those where there was a clear link.

For each of the four categories defined by these two variables, the objective was to identify five organizations suitable for case study. Information therefore had to be gathered from potential case organizations before any fieldwork took place in order tentatively to allocate them to one of the four categories. Contenders for study were identified from discussions with MCI, the Department Steering Group, and from previous research. The organizations were to be drawn from a range of different economic sectors, and it was intended that one third of the organizations studied would be SMEs.

The MCI supplied details of twenty-five organizations known to have adopted the Management Standards and a second tranche of eighteen organizations, known to practise competence-based management development but not thought to be users of the occupational standards, was also identified. Initially, a letter was sent to each organisation by the Department, which the researchers followed up by telephone to arrange a meeting with senior managers and negotiate access. Difficulties in achieving access, particularly with SMEs, made it necessary to approach further organizations and out of a total of 126 organizations approached sixteen cases were selected for detailed study from those that agreed to collaborate.

The sixteen cases were tentatively allocated to the four categories on the basis of preliminary discussions with the contact in each organisation, and the cases appeared to be weighted in favour of Standards users, and especially in favour of those claiming that management development was closely linked with organizational strategy. There were early indications that using the double dichotomy as a basis for categorizing cases were an over-simplification and would prove less useful than intended. Each dimension was really a spectrum, with cases located somewhere along each continuum. Differentiating cases according to whether management development was linked to organizational strategy was especially problematic, since most respondents believed that development was linked to strategy. Clearly management development could be integrated with organizational strategy in some respects and not in others and the difficulty in establishing the extent to which the two were integrated was reflected in the different perspectives of individuals in the same organisation.

It was feared that these problems would impose limitations on the extent to which the first conditional hypothesis (concerning the impact of linking management development with organizational strategy) could be tested. Differentiating cases according to whether the organizations had adopted the Standards appeared less problematic, and cases were provisionally labelled as users and non-users (of the occupational standards developed by MCI). However, the case studies demonstrated that some organizations that were ostensibly users of the Standards had not, in fact, adopted them comprehensively.

The case reports and written evidence were evaluated by independent consultants and validated against the criteria established by the expert group. The cases were re-classified on the basis of this evaluation, producing the achieved cases. In this final classification, only four cases were defined as type A, while five were viewed as type D, and the remainder type C. Type B, in which HRD systems were based on the Management Standards but management development was not linked to organizational strategy, proved to be an empty cell. This finding confirmed empirically, for the cases studied, what, with the benefit of hindsight, might have been assumed a priori: that an organisation is unlikely to adopt the Management Standards and not link its management development to organizational strategy.

The sector, size and final classifications of the sixteen cases that were involved in the study and detailed information is provided in the extended account of the case studies. In terms of sectors involved, the cases were drawn from:

Methodological Issues

The Employment Department study group considered a variety of methodologies and recommended an embedded, multiple case-study approach to investigate the impact of CBMD and the adoption of the Management Standards.

The case study offers a distinct advantage in examining 'a contemporary set of events, over which the investigator has little or no control'. Case studies, whether exploratory, descriptive or explanatory, are by definition empirical inquiries that investigate a contemporary phenomenon within its real-life context, when the boundaries between phenomenon and context are not clearly evident, and in which multiple sources of evidence are used. Given appropriate research design, a series of case studies may be generalized to theoretical propositions, not to a universal population, as is the goal with statistical generalization from a sample. In recommending a case-study approach, the expert group recognized that observation would play a minor role in data collection and that case-study reports should be kept concise and focused on the issues relating to the hypotheses outlined above.

A multiple case-study approach was identified as most appropriate for this research. Multiple case studies offer the advantages associated with replication when cases are selected to offer either literal or theoretical replication, the theoretical framework establishing the conditions under which a phenomenon should be, and should not be, found. It was recognized that the research design for the case studies would have to embody the theoretical and conceptual underpinnings of what was being studied. As the elements of the design were developed, so the theory was more clearly articulated.

In formulating the research design, five areas were addressed:

- The research question to be explored: how does management development or the adoption of the Management Standards developed by MCI improve performance?
- Propositions or hypotheses: such as the hypotheses that management development improves both individual and team performance.
- Unit of analysis: the primary unit of analysis was the organisation, but within this sub-units such as functional areas and individuals were defined.
- Logic linking data to propositions: such as evidence of improved performance following the adoption of the Management Standards.
- Criteria for interpreting a study's findings: it was necessary to establish criteria to assess what constitutes a significant improvement in performance.

After the initial theory development stage, the cases for study were selected and the hypotheses operationalized by defining appropriate measures and identifying methods of data collection. An embedded design (involving more than one unit of analysis) was most appropriate for this research since each case involved a consideration of different functional areas and different levels of analysis. Each case was a self-contained study, and each case report sought to establish conclusions concerning the propositions to be tested. The cross-case analysis aimed to explain convergence and divergence between cases in terms of a priori predictions made as part of the replication logic at the design stage.

The expert group offered a tentative case-study design including the data collection protocol that specified the written evidence required and recommended detailed interviews with key respondents in each organisation. This initial case-study protocol was operationalized, piloted and refined by the authors once the research was commissioned. The protocol defined the written evidence to be examined in relation to each hypothesis and the range of measures of performance to be considered. It also comprised interview schedules that were to be used for in-depth, semi-structured interviews with senior strategic managers (chief executive, finance director and head of human resources), line managers and junior managers. The full case-study protocol is contained in the official report of the study.

As a minimum in each case, face-to-face interviews were conducted with the three senior strategic managers, four line managers and four team members.

Multiple sources of evidence were collected to increase the reliability of data through triangulation and interlocking questions in the interview schedules were designed to test for consistency between the views of managers at different levels. Details of improvements in performance and of HRD systems and processes were collected through an extensive range of written evidence. Managers' job specifications gave an indication of the extent to which responsibility for management development was a feature of their role, while company accounts were examined as evidence of improvements in organizational performance. A dossier was compiled of written evidence and interviews for each organisation studied, and a case report was written in accordance with the protocol. The case reports provided background details of the organisation, details of the organizational strategy, the HRD systems and processes, and the evidence of improvements in individual, team and organizational performance attributed to management development by respondents. Each case report was validated with two senior managers in the organisation and revised before being evaluated and used in the cross-case analysis.

To test the five hypotheses, a team of independent consultants was asked to rank the cases according to three criteria:

- The extent of improvements in individual, team and organizational performance attributable to management development;
- The degree to which management development was linked to organizational strategy;
- The extent to which the Management Standards had been adopted in HRD systems and processes.

The evaluation was co-ordinated by a consultant who had been involved in developing the Management Standards and had participated in the original expert group but had not been involved in the case studies; she was therefore familiar with the protocol but was not biased by knowledge of particular cases. The rank order of the cases according to the three performance measures and the two defining characteristics was used to structure the cross-case analysis. The rankings made it possible to test for any correlation between the defining characteristics and performance improvements measured at the three levels, as well as correlation and concordance between the three performance measures. In addition to the case-study evidence, therefore, the hypotheses were examined using robust non-parametric techniques.

The Research

The dossiers for each case study were too extensive to be included in the official report of the research although abbreviated case reports are included in the extended account of the study. A selection of the evidence is considered below in relation to the hypotheses outlined above.

In the cases demonstrating the most robust evidence of improvements in individual performance, the central importance of management development was demonstrated through written evidence and corroborated interviews.

The improvements included increased personal confidence, awareness of potential and continuous development of general managerial skills and competences. Managers reported having a better understanding of both organizational objectives and their individual responsibilities. A range of efficiency gains were attributed to management development, such as better planning and time management, more effectiveness in running meetings, and improvements in project management, change management and problem solving. Increased competence in managing people was also cited, especially through raising skills in communications, presentation, leadership and motivation. Middle management mentioned empowerment, faster individual career advancement and a more methodical approach to developing others.

Improvements in individual performance were clearly associated with the use of the Management Standards and the implementation of NVQs, which provided criteria for performance, facilitated best practice benchmarking and promoted new ways of conceptualizing work tasks. With the Standards, individuals take responsibility for, and can track, their own development, and this is associated with increased commitment and motivation.

In the organizations providing less robust evidence of improvements in individual performance, there were nonetheless examples of specific improvements attributed to management development activities. In other organizations, isolated examples of individual performance gains were cited, but these were more a consequence of ad hoc initiatives than the result of operating a coherent management development framework. Towards the lower end of the ranking, there was ambiguity in relation to reported improvements, difficulties of measurement and of attributing improvements to management development. In particular, there were difficulties in separating individual and team performance measures, and systematic measurement and evaluation was thought to be too costly. It was also noted that the outcomes of development vary between individuals and that the effects are difficult to isolate when other major changes are taking place.

Where there was most evidence of improvements in team performance attributed to management development, these typically related to process issues such as quality of service, better focus on customer needs, reduced queues, better telephone standards and improved customer relations. Managers in some organizations cited evidence of more strategic behaviour and identified better procedures and monitoring of actions. Cost reductions, efficiency gains and more effective debt control were also reported. Other examples of improved team performance arising from management development included improved procedures for controlling and handling materials as well as the identification of potential areas for improvement in the future such as new information systems.

Improvements in team performance attributed to management development initiatives designed to promote team working included greater flexibility, awareness of team responsibilities and more effective team working.

Both interpersonal and interdepartmental relations improved as a result of better communications, and individuals were also said to demonstrate increased commitment and motivation. In one case, managers identified improved team performance, such as more 'flexibility and commitment', as a result of management development introduced to support business process re-engineering. In another case, improvements in team performance as a result of management development initiatives were visible in the changes in team behaviour, including performance and the dynamics of work-groups.

Major difficulties of measurement of team performance and of attributing improvements to management development were encountered, especially where the same measures were used for individual and team performance, or where team performance was regarded as a function of a manager's performance. Equally, team performance was difficult to separate from organizational performance and was affected by extraneous factors.

The organizations which were ranked highest in terms of organizational performance improvements displayed quantified, written and corroborated evidence and respondents were unequivocal that management development had contributed to all prime measures of business efficiency. In such organizations, managers emphasized increased turnover and profit, sales and revenue growth, increased market share and competitiveness. Productivity, efficiency and quality gains were important factors, as was decreased unit costs. Other benefits reported were reductions in arrears and stock holding, shorter waiting times and queues, and reduced staff turnover.

In cases ranked lower than the best, evidence was provided of specific business benefits, which were largely attributable to management development activities. Where improvements in organizational performance were identified, the extent to which these were attributed to management development initiatives varied from the unequivocal cases where they would have been impossible without management development, to cases where the contribution of management development was implicit. Other cases showed how management development was the major, but not the only, contribution to success, or how management development was a necessary factor, in conjunction with other changes.

Problems of measurement of organizational performance were most serious in the weaker cases, and largely arose from the interaction of other factors affecting bottom line results. Difficulties of attribution were a consequence of being unable to produce counter-factual evidence as to what outcomes might have been expected in the absence of management development initiatives. In cases where improvements could not be attributed unambiguously to management development, few attempts had been made to measure its impact.

In the cases where written evidence and corroborated interviews showed how organizational strategy and management development were inter-related, the links between the two were pervasive and demonstrated in a variety of ways. Typically, management development was shown to be an intrinsic part of the business plan, and to support strategic priorities. Business objectives were shown to be linked to strategy through defined competences, strategic objectives were mapped onto performance standards, and personal development plans related to business plans. Roles and responsibilities for management development were devolved to individuals and their line managers, with only limited HR intervention, thereby embedding management development within OS.

Major changes provided both the opportunity and necessity of linking management development to organizational strategy, and management development initiatives responded to changes in the organization's environment. Extensive restructuring or business process re-engineering provided opportunities for linking management development to organizational strategy and focused attention on the competences required to achieve the organizational transformation. Throughout, the MCI Standards and NVQs were seen to provide a structure for the links.

Even where the links between management development and organizational strategy were less clear, there was some evidence of management development initiatives to support specific aspects of organizational strategy. In other cases, problems were identified in establishing the link; for example difficulty in identifying which competences would improve organizational performance. Also, management development was found invariably to lag organizational strategy where this was dynamic, and immediate priorities inevitably took precedence over longer-term strategic management development. An apparent paradox was also highlighted between devolving responsibility for management development and linking it to organizational strategy, since much management development is focused on the needs of the individual, not the organisation.

In four organizations, the Management Standards were comprehensively adopted in HRD systems and processes. In these organizations, all or most management development activities were competence-based. The Management Standards were central to appraisal, training and development, although they were used less extensively in job descriptions, recruitment and remuneration. Written evidence and corroborated interviews demonstrated the ways in which the Standards were adopted and the benefits of building management development initiatives around the MCI Framework.

The major benefit identified from adopting the Management Standards was the coherent structure that they provided for training, management development and personal development. Gaps in competence, for example, are more readily identified through appraisal, training and development needs are specified more precisely in relation to the competences required for individuals to meet the needs of the organisation, and there are clear criteria for human resource planning and career succession. In addition, management development is linked to a qualifications framework.

In three cases, the Management Standards had been partially adopted, and were used to a limited extent in some HRD systems and processes. The remaining nine organizations had either not attempted to adopt the Management Standards or had only made limited progress in this direction, so that they were regarded as non-users. The research identified some limitations to the adoption of the Management Standards both in the extent to which they had percolated through an organisation and in the range of HRD systems and processes involved. The main limitations were that the Standards were not extensively used in recruitment and selection, other than in relation to job profiles, and reward and remuneration systems were rarely linked to the achievement of competences defined in the Standards. Additional criteria were sometimes used alongside the Standards, especially in relation to specific technical competences, and familiarity with the Management Standards was less extensive outside the HR specialists.

Critical Analysis

The sixteen organizations provided very positive and highly significant results demonstrating performance improvements as a result of management development. Despite the difficulty of measuring performance, and especially team performance, the three measures of performance were significantly correlated. The overall coefficient of concordance between the rank orders of individual, team and organizational performance was significant at the 1 per cent level, showing that the rank position of an organisation in terms of one performance measure was similar to its rank position for another performance measure. Moreover, each pair of performance measures correlated at the 5 per cent level or better, especially in the case of individual and organizational performance. Of the three performance measures, organizational performance was the most problematic, but the significant rank correlation coefficients suggested that team performance could be 'captured' adequately by individual and organizational performance measures.

Significantly, the results of the rank correlation also provided support for the conditional hypothesis that management development was more likely to improve performance when linked with organizational strategy.

The Spearman rank correlation coefficients between organizational strategy and both individual and organizational performance were significant at the 1 per cent level. There was no significant correlation between organizational strategy and team performance, which may reflect the difficulties of measurement and attribution already noted. In the case of individual and organizational performance, these results offer unambiguous support for the importance of linking management development to organizational strategy in order to realise business benefits.

The rank correlation also provided support for the conditional hypothesis that management development was more likely to improve performance when HRD systems and processes were based on the competence statements in the MCI Standards. The Spearman rank correlation coefficients between HRD and both individual and organizational performance are significant at the 5 per cent level, although again there is no significant correlation between HRD and team performance. In the case of individual and organizational performance, these results again offer support for the importance of designing management development around the Management Standards in order to improve organizational performance.

The conclusions and learning points to be drawn from the research outlined above relate both to the substantive findings, which contribute to the debate on the role of HRD in improving performance, and the procedural aspects of the methodology developed to undertake the study.

In substantive terms, three policy implications follow from the above conclusions, relating to the performance measures that should be used to monitor the business benefits of management development, linking management development to organizational strategy, and adopting the Management Standards.

First, the most reliable performance measures for monitoring the business benefits of management development are individual and organizational performance, which correlate with, and therefore probably also incorporate, the less tangible organizational performance measures. The strength of the link between management development and both individual and team performance suggests that management development should be promoted with the message that developing people contributes to business success.

Second, performance benefits are more likely to arise from management development where this is strongly linked with organizational strategy. The link between management development and organizational strategy should be seen as complementary to the value of developing people since this is the mechanism through which the development of individuals contributes to business performance. In policy terms, these findings provide further support for the Investors in People approach, through which development is linked to organizational strategy.

Third, performance is improved additionally where organizations adopt the Management Standards as a framework for development within HRD systems and processes. The additionality is important and provides support for further promoting the MCI Standards, encouraging their adoption by organizations to provide coherence in management development and to support mobility within the managerial workforce.

The key learning points are procedural ones, relating to the development of an appropriate methodology to test the hypotheses established at the outset. A detailed case-study protocol was developed to cope with the complexity of identifying performance improvements at individual, team and organizational levels in a wide range of different settings. In process terms, the protocol was also designed to investigate the nature of links between management development and organizational strategy and the ways in which HRD systems and processes incorporated competence statements.

A complex protocol was inevitable given the need to reduce causal ambiguity and to relate performance improvements to specific developmental events. However, the complexity operated as a barrier to entry in many organizations, creating major difficulties in negotiating access. The protocol was stretched to the limit in being applied to organizations in such different sectors, but it proved possible, by using generic terms and analogous measures, to translate into all sector contexts. The different sizes of organizations, however, proved most challenging; the methodology was less well suited to the largest case studied and proved unworkable in a very small firm that was removed from the final case list.

A case-study approach was necessary in order to capture qualitative information, including such 'soft' measures as perceptions of individuals, as well as exploring the relevant development and performance processes within organizations at different levels. In adopting such a methodology, however, there was a risk of marginalizing the findings because policy makers invariably seek 'hard' measures, with quantitative data that can be subject more easily to statistical tests. The challenge, therefore, was to devise a methodology that could permit hard conclusions from soft data.

By using a team of consultants to make independent comparative evaluations of the case reports (i.e. ranking them against established criteria), it was possible to employ non-parametric techniques and arrive at concrete statistical conclusions. In other words, the study demonstrated the potential for combining the richness of case-study research and subjective evaluation by independent experts with robust statistical methods capable of offering a quantitative measure of the extent of correlation between the factors being investigated.

2

Building a More Ethical Business Environment

One of the most critical tasks facing human resource professionals in the 1990s and beyond will be identifying and developing aspiring top executives. The information presented will provide useful data, options, and recommendations for the development and implementation of such programs. This will not be an easy task. Imagine the following mythical fable.

Once upon a time there existed a land in which most of the people worked on the rich farmland at the foot of a range of semi-active volcanoes. While their lives were comfortable, many were attracted to the challenge of climbing the volcanic mountains in the hope of finding great riches and power at the top. It was a very difficult climb and only a small number ever reached the peaks.

Eager young climbers often studied the methods used by the older successful climbers in the hope that, by following proven paths and using proven techniques, they too might reach the summit. Unfortunately, these volcanic mounts were constantly changing; sometimes in subtle, almost imperceptible ways, sometimes violently and catastrophically. Relatively easy paths to the top became very difficult, almost vertical ascents, or led into impassable chasms. At the same time, new, previously unknown routes to the top were created.

The nature of the mountains was such that some whose specialized climbing techniques had proven unsuccessful on one peak found that the exact same methods worked extremely well in another location. It was a very long and difficult climb and many grew tired. About halfway up the mountains, some discovered a lush and apparently safe plateau. Here they often stopped to rest and many chose to stay. This was a dangerous decision, however. There occasionally occurred periods of increased volcanic activity during which the middle sections of the mountains were completely destroyed while the tops and bottoms were left relatively unscathed.

Because of the uncertain nature of these times, the older leaders became concerned. Perhaps those who reached the top would be foolhardy adventurers who just happened to have luck on their side. How could they train and counsel young climbers so that the most competent would reach the peaks?

The Current Business Environment

The environment in which today's business managers operate is even more volatile and unpredictable than the mythical situation described above. Twenty years ago, a young businessperson entered the world of work with the expectation that there were certain well defined rules that, if followed, would allow them to pursue a successful career. Today, the young manager or professional does not know what to expect. The young person, however, can probably deal with this uncertainty and adapt. They never thought that they knew what the rules were. The older, mid-career manager may be the true victim of change; his or her world is crumbling or, to return to the volcano analogy, is being blown apart.

In 1982, John Naisbitt correctly identified ten "Megatrends" that were transforming our society. We are still experiencing the effects of these force—and others. American businesses have been forced to try to adapt to powerful economic, technological, and societal changes. With the Reagan years we saw runaway inflation tamed and government regulations eased. However, these were two bogeymen behind which many American firms had been hiding. No longer could costs be easily passed on to the customer. Foreign competition has increased tremendously. We have lost our position as the leading industrial power in the world.

The Japanese have driven many industries out of existence and are now busy acquiring many of those that remain. Our own financial community has seen profits to be made in the weakened condition of many firms. The merger and acquisitions mania of the 1980s has caused many firms to restructure or be restructured. The power of corporate top management has been significantly weakened. Outside money managers have more influence over business strategy and structure. Economic uncertainties will continue to increase with the rise of the newly industrialized countries in Asia and Latin America. The European Community will be more of a threat after 1992 and opportunities for development will appear throughout Eastern Europe and China.

The major technological change of the 1980s was the development and application of powerful personal computers and work stations. That revolution has only just begun and will surely continue to change our lives and the way we do business into the twenty-first century. In addition, the 1990s will surely bring other major technological shifts. For example, it is likely that patterns of energy usage will be altered as applications of superconductivity and cold fusion are developed.

A significant demographic shift which will continue to change our society, our business practices, and surely the career paths within businesses is the aging of the baby boom generation. Within hierarchical organizations of all sorts, there will be a greater supply of candidates for middle and upper level positions. At the same time, because of the economic and technological changes discussed above, there will be fewer such positions in the organizations of the future. In addition, there will be fewer candidates for entry-level positions. This will result in major disruptions in the traditional, seniority-based promotion systems of many organizations. It will also open up opportunities for many classes of people who have been under-utilized in the past, such as women, minorities, and handicapped people.

There is growing documentation of this point. It is generally well accepted that successful firms adapt their strategy and structure to match the demands of the external environment. Thus as the external environment (economic, technological, and social) changes so must organizations modify, or in some cases revolutionize, their goals and their traditional means of doing business. These changes will mean that historically well established career paths will be disrupted and new ones created.

MANAGEMENT CAREERS

We believe that many career decisions are based on invalid information. For example, while some believe that every American has a chance to rise to the top of major business organizations, others contend that only those born with the proverbial "silver spoon" have a real shot at the top. Of course the truth lies somewhere in between.

Many people, including human resource managers, are not aware of the realities of career paths within large corporations. Vroom and MacCrimmon (1968) conducted a study of the promotion system in one large company. They were able to predict promotion chances based on career histories and determined that those in finance and marketing had significantly greater opportunities to move up than employees in manufacturing; and that those in personnel had very little chance for upward mobility. This information came as a shock to many in the company-especially to the senior personnel manager who had recently given a talk to lower level managers about the Horatio Alger-type opportunities that existed within the firm. Other studies indicate that lower and middle level managers typically overestimate their chances for promotion.

Many people are aware of the studies of top executives that identify the functional areas from which they came and conclude that most chief executives have backgrounds in marketing and finance or, more recently, that banking is the most common background of CEOs. These conclusions are widely cited and readily accepted, however, they are overgeneralizations. Our research indicates that it is not meaningful to lump together firms from different industries when examining career paths. Different industries have different needs for technical expertise at the top and the most common functional background found at the top varies quite a bit across industries. In addition, the distribution of functional backgrounds of chief executives has varied over the years as the need for critical technical skills has changed.

Women have been barred from the executive suites by a "glass ceiling" at the general management level and by the even more formidable "wall" behind which top management status lies. Our research shows that women have, in fact, made significant, albeit slow, progress in climbing the corporate ranks. Unfortunately, until recently their numbers have been very small in relation to the number of men in middle and upper management positions. Therefore, although the probability that they will be promoted may equal or exceed that for a man in the same position, it will still take a great deal of time before we see women in large numbers at the top of business organizations.

Many people still believe in the myth of the "mobile manager". That is, they think that one must make frequent changes in employers in order to reach higher levels in the business world. This has never been true and in fact numerous studies, including our research, show that in most industries the successful top executive may make a few moves early in his career but then settles down and spends most of his life working for the same firm.

Recent work by John Kotter has focused on the importance of developing general management skill (specifically, an intimate familiarity with the firm and the industry) among the leaders and future leaders of business firms. While we generally agree with this prescription, we have found evidence that many functionally specialized leaders are chosen to head major corporations. This is often in the best interest of the firm and we must recognize that there are actually numerous paths to the top in many industries.

Finally, the career management literature recommends that future top executives need a fast start. They need lots of early challenge and responsibility in order to experience a cycle of success. They must also receive early promotions or they will fall behind in the "tournament" which determines who will reach the top. Again we believe that this is an overgeneralization. We will review the existing research on this topic and show that different early experiences may be appropriate in different situations.

This is built around a series of studies that we have conducted over the past ten years. Our presentation of the various executive career studies and issues will follow a rough chronological sequence. In the second study, we analyzed almost 700 management promotions as announced. The data revealed two general paths to top management. The first is an insider, general management track with little inter-firm or inter-industry movement. The alternative path involves greater functional specialization but requires less firm or industry specialization.

There is greater opportunity to move among different firms and industries. We will discuss the need for change in how executives are identified and developed, and will show how organizational-level strategic planning techniques may be used to help individuals make career planning decisions in today's complex and unpredictable world. Although it may take 25 to 30 years for a person to reach the top of a major corporation, there is considerable evidence that the early years are a critical phase. Much like the launching of a satellite into orbit, unless the powerful booster works perfectly to overcome the force of gravity, the space vehicle will fall back to earth.

The nature of human development and maturation is such that we pass through various predictable stages. These stages are identifiable by the challenges that must be met in order to develop further. Behavioral scientists have mapped out these phases in childhood and in adulthood. Careers also seem to consist of regular stages during which certain tasks must be accomplished.

Douglas Hall has identified five career stages: entry, socialization, advancement, maintenance, and withdrawal. During the entry or exploration stage, the individual is still searching for the right occupation and organisation. Once a choice has been made, the socialization or establishment stage begins. This is a time of learning, testing, and evaluation for the individual and for the employer. Having learned the ropes of the new occupation and organisation and finding a positive evaluation of the match by both the new employee and the employer, attention usually turns to moving up in the organisation. This indicates movement into the advancement stage. For many people advancement starts to level off eventually. When a career plateau is reached the individual has entered the maintenance stage. At this point, career paths diverge. Some people continue to advance in their careers, some plateau, and others begin to decline. Finally, at the end of the career comes the withdrawal stage.

We will examine early career issues; that is, those occurring during the socialization and advancement stages. However, since we will be focusing on those who did not plateau, who instead reached the top, we will later introduce a new set of stages that seems to better describe the career of the top executive.

The early years of any career can be a critical period. Both the individual and the organisation are learning about each other. As is true with any new relationship, first impressions are very important. The individual may be overwhelmed with new information. Whether planned or unplanned the new employee will experience a period of socialization during which he or she will learn not only the official requirements of the job but also the unwritten expectations of their new role. The new employee will be evaluating this information in an attempt to determine whether or not the decision to join this particular organisation was the correct choice. Often the individual actually experiences a feeling of "reality shock" or "culture shock." The first sensation occurs primarily among those just entering the business world from school; the latter to those more experienced people moving to a radically new corporate culture.

The shock occurs because of the gap between expectations about the job and the world of work and the reality of the situation. The change between school and a work organisation brings with it many differences: differences in tasks, differences in schedules, differences in relationships with people, differences in time horizons, differences in evaluation criteria. However, the greatest problem encountered at this time is disappointment with the quality of the job. Many college graduates expect to be given jobs with more responsibility, more freedom, more interesting work, and more challenge, and also shorter and more convenient working hours than provided by the typical entry-level position.

The organisation is often disappointed with the new recruit, who they find to be overly ambitious and unrealistic in their personal expectations, too theoretical in their approach to work, and naive with respect to knowledge of how things really work in the business world. They often need to be "broken in."

While this phase may result in some dissatisfaction and often turnover among those who did not have a realistic preview of the job, it is also a time during which the individual is especially susceptible to major change in behaviour, attitudes, and even values. In fact, many organizations intentionally create an environment which causes the new recruit to question past behaviors, feelings, and beliefs. Consider the rigours of Marine Corps boot camp or the experiences of new members of certain religious cults. It has recently been noted that many business firms with strong corporate cultures do much of the same thing. Pascale describes a process in which "hazing" and "debasement," and working in the "trenches" is combined with exposure to strong role models, folklore, tradition, and corporate values to mold the new recruit into the corporate image.

What kinds of experiences should the business firm provide for the new employee so that his or her career within the organisation is not derailed before it begins? There is general consensus that the following human resource management practices will help to make the transition a successful one.

- Recruitment and selection programs that are based on an understanding of the personal characteristics required for successful performance in the entry-level position as well as on later jobs to which promotion is likely.
- Selection using valid measures of these personal characteristics.
- The use of realistic job previews to acquaint the prospective employee with the negative as well as the positive aspects of the job and the company.
- The design and use of effective orientation programs.
- If necessary, the use of effective training programs.
- The development and consistent use of appropriate socialization practices.

Since it has received less attention in the human resource literature than the other points listed above and because of its great importance in helping to launch young careers, we will discuss the meaning of "appropriate socialization practices." Organizational socialization may be defined as, "The process by which individuals are transformed from total outsiders of companies to participating, effective members of them". This process actually begins for many people before they enter the organisation. "Anticipatory socialization" refers to the fact that individuals may begin to change their habits and attitudes even before they start working. For example, business students often start to dress, talk, and perhaps even think like business people as a result of their educational programs and part-time and summer work experiences.

The second stage of socialization is referred to as "encounter" or "breaking in". This phase lasts three or four months and involves learning new tasks and organizational practices, and establishing new social relationships. The final stage is known as "change and acquisition" or "settling in". During this phase the "metamorphosis" of the individual is completed. This stage typically begins during the third or fourth month and ends by the sixth or seventh month, although in some situations it may well last longer. By this time the individual should have settled down, adjusted to the new situation, and be ready to make more meaningful contributions to the organisation.

The new person is now able to play a more active role—they have "learned the ropes" and been accepted by the organisation. This acceptance is often marked by some symbolic action that signifies passage through the probationary testing period. The newly initiated member may receive a change in job title, a transfer, a promotion, a raise, or a party; or the shift in status may be signalled more subtly by sharing more "secret" information with the new person. Successful socialization results in mutual acceptance. Not only does the organisation accept the individual but the junior member of the organisation agrees to a "psychological contract" in which he or she accepts the demands and expectations of the job and the organisation.

Organizational socialization should be a mutual influence process. A business organisation must not try to make every new recruit into an exact clone of their stereotype of the successful manager. Clearly, the new employee must fit in; however, too much conformity is harmful to the individual and to the organisation. Youthful enthusiasm and fresh ideas will soon be forgotten in an environment that discourages or punishes them. A capability that is critical for survival in today's business world is the ability to be innovative and to change and adapt to ever changing threats and opportunities. Organizations must nurture this natural talent of youth and try to re-awaken it in older employees.

Schein has noted that there exist two types of norms within organizations: pivotal and peripheral. Pivotal norms are essential for successful performance within the particular organisation. For example, a businessperson must not be opposed to the existence of the free market system. In a strong corporate culture he or she should accept a small number of core values. However, he or she need not accept the firm's short-term goals or current product line as the only way to achieve those goals within that system. The latter would be more peripheral norms. With respect to these norms, there are three individual responses to socialization: "rebellion" (the complete rejection of all organizational norms), "conformity" (the complete acceptance of all norms), and "creative individualism" (the acceptance of only the most pivotal norms).

Today more than ever creative individualism is the most desirable outcome for both the individual and the firm. The individual should not see the first year of employment as a period of "brainwashing" or as a "sink or swim" trial; rather, he or she should be made to feel that they are members of a fraternity/sorority pledge class; and that they have been selected because they are outstanding individuals and may have much to contribute to the group. First, however, they have to learn the values of the current sisters and brothers; decide whether they fit in and whether the benefits of membership are worth the costs; and prove their commitment to the group by suffering through a somewhat uncomfortable initiation process.

There are other social and psychological benefits of this process. Human decision processes are such that an uncomfortable feeling of "cognitive dissonance" occurs when we perceive discrepancies among our behaviors, feelings, and beliefs. Such a feeling is very likely to occur during group initiation or during organizational socialization. Having chosen to join a frat or a firm and then discovering that the initial experience is very dissatisfying creates an unsettling state of mind. The cognitive dissonance may be resolved by changing the decision (that is, leaving the situation). However, if one chooses to stay, then the decision is often justified by changing the perception of the worth of the group. We develop more positive feelings toward the group and are more likely to accept the beliefs and values of the group in order to justify our suffering through the initiation/socialization process.

In addition, new recruits are often put through the socialization process as a group. The more demanding the experience, the more likely that this group will become a tight knit, cohesive unit whose members trust one another, can openly communicate with one another, and can depend upon one another throughout their careers. In order to facilitate this group identification, the firm should provide adequate opportunities for the new recruits to communicate, commiserate, and coalesce as a unit.

While there are many similarities, the end of the socialization period may not be as clear in the business firm as it is in the sorority or fraternity. Schein has identified four continuing issues to which the junior businessperson must attend. First, there must continue to be improvement in performance on the job. Second, the employee typically must increase his or her technical competence in a specialized functional area (e.g., accounting, computers, marketing). Third, the new employee must be willing to still accept a relatively junior role in the organisation. Fourth, this is the time to re-evaluate the choice of profession and organisation. Incorrect career decisions are often made; however, the sooner they are altered the sooner the individual may begin making progress on a more satisfying and productive track.

The Importance of Early Movement

While often described as following the socialization or establishment stage, the advancement stage actually may begin sooner. "Fast tack" or "high potential" employees are expected to start proving their worth to the organisation immediately. Research within the former Bell System indicated that early job challenge could have a long-lasting, positive effect on an individual's career. Berlew and Hall studied management trainees over a four year period. Those who were given more demanding initial assignments were more successful than those who received less demanding jobs. Initial job challenge led to quicker promotion to higher management positions. Also, Bell System managers who experienced greater job challenge during their first eight years had reached higher levels in their companies after 20 years.

This phenomenon is generally explained as a socialization effect. The early challenge, which is successfully met, causes the new employee to internalize high standards of work behaviour. They experience a sense of psychological success which boosts their self-esteem and their feelings of competence and motivates them to seek even more challenge. This creates a self perpetuating "success cycle."

While individual ability and motivation are related to career success in large organizations, there are alternative explanations for the early job challenge results and there are other factors which strongly affect career attainment. Promotion decisions are not (and should not be) made solely on the basis of individual characteristics such as ability, personality, and motivation. Such information is extremely valuable for selection decisions and for identifying high "potential" employees.

However, potential and performance are two quite different things. In their very impressive 20 year study of managers in Bell System companies, Howard and Bray found that of those predicted to reach middle management (high potential managers) by the initial assessment centre evaluation, 60 percent had been successful. Of course, that means that 40 percent of those with potential did not actually perform as predicted.

In business organizations, most promotions are based on performance—primarily most recent performance, but also past performance. In fact there is evidence that one's entire career history (performance, promotions, transfers, etc.) has a significant impact on ultimate career success. The ability and motivation are not typically measured directly, instead they are inferred from "signals" in the candidate's track record—his or her career history. What signals are important, long-term predictors of upward mobility? We will look at research studies that have attempted to answer that question.

Movement in a hierarchical organisation may be described in a number of ways. An individual may move laterally: from job to job within the same functional area (for example, production management); across different functions; even across different divisions or businesses. Researchers may record the number of such moves, the frequency of moving, or the average time in each job. Of course, a member of the organisation may move upward. The velocity of upward movement may be determined by examining the rate of such movement over time.

We can also examine changes in the speed of vertical movement—does the movement accelerate or decelerate at different points in the career? There is also a third type of movement which is very important but not easily measured.

This is "radial" movement within a career cone. Using this model, one may move vertically—from the base of the cone toward the point, horizontally—changing position on the surface of the cone (at the same height between base and point), and radially—toward the inner core of the cone. Radial movement implies that greater trust is being placed in the member and that they will be given access to special privileges and more confidential information. This typically accompanies vertical movement but not always. Sometimes people are "kicked upstairs"—being promoted to a less critical, and probably dead-end activity. Unfortunately, access to this type of information is difficult to obtain and therefore there has been little empirical research on this kind of movement.

The research on early career issues includes the Bell System studies described above. In this research, the positive effects of early job challenge were explained as the result of improvement in the confidence and motivation of the new employees. However, an alternative explanation is that successful performance on these challenging jobs sent a positive signal to higher management about the ability of the new member, and that this signal influenced later promotion decisions. In fact, both effects were probably in action. Other research on the early career phase has focused on the signalling explanation.

The Tournament Mobility Model

The importance of early promotions was made clear by the research of Rosenbaum. He found that those who were promoted early rose to higher levels than those who were not. The first group remained in the "tournament," but those not promoted in the early rounds were effectively eliminated from later competition. If this model accurately describes promotion patterns in most business firms, the implications for individuals and for organizations are that success in the early years is critically important—without it the career is dead.

The ramifications may be appreciated by considering two earlier "ideal" sociological models of occupational mobility: contest and sponsored mobility. Our nation in general, and the business community in particular, values the norm of open opportunity. Everyone, regardless of origins or past positions, should have an equal opportunity to continue to compete for advancement. This is the contest mobility norm. In this system, decisions about who will move up are delayed as long as possible and individuals are allowed maximum freedom of career mobility. This model would create high levels of employee motivation since everyone—the mailboy as well as the Harvard MBA-has a shot at promotion. It provides continuing opportunity for "late bloomers," assures a large pool of candidates from which to choose when filling positions, and would result in better quality management selection decisions.

In a sponsored mobility system, decisions are made as early as possible. The advantage of this process comes from the efficiencies of specialized socialization, training, and development. Turner used the British educational system as an example of the application of this norm. Of course, the testing and separation of students into various tracks also occurs in this country. In addition, our business firms, especially those with the most sophisticated human resource management systems, such as AT&T and the Bell operating companies, have relied heavily on this model.

It is interesting to note that the purpose of the assessment centre is to create a more open contest—at least prior to the assessment. Consistent with their policy of promoting from within, AT&T needed a method to accurately predict management potential among craftsmen and technical personnel whose current jobs did not allow them opportunities to display supervisory or managerial skills. The assessment centre gives these employees a chance to demonstrate such abilities under controlled conditions with objective evaluation. Without this their talents might never be noticed.

However, following the assessment, the norms of sponsored mobility appear to hold. The employees who do well in the assessment centre will be provided with opportunities and experiences that are designed to develop their potential. While not officially out of the running, the others will not have comparable attention paid to their careers. In addition, the rating from the assessment sends a strong and clear signal to higher level decision makers about who should be promoted.

In the tournament system, a similar early decision is made. Here it is based on an evaluation of early performance as indicated by promotion to a higher level job. The model proposes that business firms initially allow all their members to compete in an open tournament. However, those who lose in the first round (by not being promoted) are eliminated from further competition. Furthermore, the remaining contestants must continue to win each successive contest or they too will be eliminated. Rosenbaum's research, which will be described in more detail below, strongly demonstrated the existence of such a system.

Another closely related issue addressed by Rosenbaum was whether "historical" or "ahistorical" models best describe career paths and chances for further mobility. Ahistorical models assume that an individual's chances of moving to a new position are a function of his or her current state or position; earlier, historical career information does not matter. Kelley, in a study of occupational attainment, found that status at various points in life depended mainly on occupational status in the preceding period. Earlier positions only indirectly affected current status: "past failures are forgiven, and past successes are forgotten". These are also known as "path independent" models because it does not matter how you reached your current position. The tournament model and the studies of early job challenge do stress the importance of early positions, and thus are historical or path dependent models.

Rosenbaum obtained data supporting the tournament concept from an "old, well established, autonomous, investor-owned firm, having offices in many cities and towns across a large geographic region". The firm employed between 10,000 and 15,000 persons during the period studied, 1962-75. The firm was not identified further.

Focusing on movement through the five lowest levels in the firm, Rosenbaum (1979) analyzed personnel data for 671 employees who entered the firm between 1960 and 1962 and who remained through 1975. The results indicated that those promoted in the first period (the first three years) were much more likely to receive further promotions and reach higher levels than those who were not promoted early. In fact, only those promoted in the earliest period were able to reach middle management within the 13 year span of the study.

In a later analysis of the same group, Rosenbaum (1984) used a different measure of career attainment. Job status (a measure that reflected the demands and requirements of each job) was predicted both by in dividual attributes and by early job status. In addition, job status in 1962 had an effect on status attained by 1975 that was independent of intermediate job status (in 1965). This supported the lasting effects of early position.

Signalling Theory

Rosenbaum (1984) suggested signalling theory as an explanation of the tournament pattern of mobility. This theory says that early movement is important as a criterion for later promotion because more objective standards are not available. Decision makers rely on the rate of upward mobility in relation to age or tenure as a signal of the individual's ability.

We agree with this explanation. Despite models prescribing how to improve the process, those who make decisions about promotions often work with very subjective information and operate under conditions of bounded rationality. Modern human resource information systems and skills inventories will never replace personal contacts as a key factor in decisions concerning selection or promotion. Decision makers often conduct a limited sequential search for acceptable candidates for a position. They will first consider familiar candidates and those who have had experience similar to that requited in the open position. A high level in the organisation and an impressive track record contribute to an employee's familiarity to decision makers, increase the individual's managerial experience, and promote an image of high potential. In her case study of mobility in one large corporation, Kanter discussed the importance of such visibility.

Another recent study has investigated the importance of early signals of employee ability and the generalizability of the tournament model. Also investigated were the effects of the "power" of the department in which the new employee started his or her career.

According to strategic contingency theory, the departments within an organisation may acquire differing amounts of power as a result of differences in their ability to deal with critical environmental exigencies. For example, in a consumer products company, the marketing department may have a great deal of power; while in a high tech company, the power may lie in the engineering or research and development department. Pfeffer has noted how the organisation will benefit by allowing power differences to influence the executive succession process—those who reach the top should be the ones who have the most critical skills. Sheridan et al. hypothesized that power differences would effect early career mobility as well. Those who start in powerful departments have the advantage of mentors who may intercede favourably on their behalf, assist them in gaining visibility to the top managers, and provide them with important information earlier than others. Increased visibility, networking, and resources will provide the new recruit with a lasting boost for his or her career.

Sheridan et al. studied all employees who started a management career with a large public utility during a ten year period from 1977 to 1987. The researchers believed that a strong signal about an employee's ability would be transmitted by entrance into their first management position through the company's management trainee programme. Management trainees were carefully screened college graduates who were introduced to the company's officers and department heads as the future leaders of the firm. They completed a two month orientation programme in which they rotated through various departments.

There were special dinners with officers of the company and group meetings with the vice president of human resources. Each trainee's progress was carefully watched and they were given feedback on job-related as well as personal issues. After the orientation, they worked as trainees in one department for 12 months; and then upon successful completion of the trainee year, they received their first management position.

Other managers were hired from outside without a training programme or were promoted into management from non-management jobs. These employees received none of the special attention described above.

Departmental power, defined as "the ability of a department to influence other departments to bring about its desired outcomes", was rated by 23 senior executives of the firm. Six departments were classified as having a high level of power in this firm; ten fell into the medium power category; and another six were low power departments. The high power functions were customer service, distribution, operations, engineering, marketing, and the executive offices. It was felt that the members of these departments dealt with the most critical organizational contingencies.

The trainees generally showed faster career mobility than the other groups; that is, they changed jobs more frequently. Salary increases were greater for those in the trainee programme, but this was mainly a catch up effect since they started lower than the other new managers. Department power affected career progress in a number of ways. Internal movements tended to be to new departments with the same level of power. Those who started in high power departments moved more quickly and experienced greater increases in salary than those who started in the low power functions.

This effect diminished as the employees changed jobs, however. The number of different jobs held was strongly related to salary in crement. This led the researchers to suggest that successful new managers in this firm may be those who "churn" through the largest number of jobs. It should be noted that the effects described in this study were not of large magnitude. The differences in job tenure that were attributed to career start or to department power were measured in months. Salary gaps and differences in job level were relatively small.

The tournament mobility concept received mixed support in this study. Tenure half-lives were determined for trainees, direct hires, and internal promotions. This is a measure of the point in time at which 50 percent of the managers have left a position. "Fast starters" were those who left their first job in less time than the half-life. Those who stayed longer than the half-life were classified as "slow starters." Fast starters continued to move more quickly. They had an average of 4.3 months less time in each job held after their first management position. However, 40 percent of the moves in this study were lateral transfers. The fast starters attained only slightly higher levels than the slow starters. Overall, the differences were not statistically significant.

The authors point out that the career management practices of this firm are consistent with their corporate strategy. This is a "steady state" firm which is committed to its current business. Such firms invest heavily in management development in order to help employees understand the entire business and to create a cohesive corporate culture through extensive socialization.

Japanese management development techniques are believed to be quite different from those found in most American firms. Ouchi compared the management styles in typical Japanese firms with those of typical American firms, and then described the Type Z American firm which exhibits many practices similar to the Japanese. One characteristic of the Japanese firm is "slow evaluation and promotion." Ouchi describes a fictitious young man—

Sagao, who enters a major bank after graduation from the University of Tokyo.

For ten years, Sagao will receive exactly the same increases in pay and exactly the same promotions as the 15 other young men who have entered with him. Only after ten years will anyone make a formal evaluation of Sagao and his peers; not until then will one person receive a larger promotion than another.

This system encourages cooperative behaviour oriented toward long-term results. It should also ensure that Sagao and his peers will continue to be highly motivated during this ten year period of evaluation and that the best promotion decisions will ultimately be made. This process is very close to the contest mobility norm described earlier—everyone is in the contest for as long as possible.

Recent research, however, indicates that even in Japan open contests may not be reality. Wakabayashi, Graen, and associates have followed a group of 71 Japanese managers through their first 13 years of job tenure with "one of the leading corporations in Japan." This group of male college graduates joined the company in 1972, having passed an assessment centre administered in 1971. The career paths of these young men appear to have been determined very early.

Measures of career attainment in 1985 such as bonus, salary, speed of promotion (from 1978 to 1985), and a promotability index were predicted by ratings obtained during the first three years of employment (1972-1974). The predictors were job performance, the 1974 promotability index, and a measure of the quality of "vertical exchange" over the first three years. This last variable was measured by having the new recruits respond to a questionnaire which assesses the leader-member relationship. A ranking of the prestige of their university predicted speed of promotion, promotability, and salary; while a measure of potential from the assessment centre also predicted speed of promotion.

It was hypothesized that later measures of performance and promotability would improve upon the prediction based on the early indicators. This was not the case. Evaluations during the seventh year did not predict thirteenth year performance any better than the third year measures.

Although the final outcomes seem to have been determined in three years, no one was actually promoted for seven years. All of the managers were promoted in the first round, although the promotions came at three different times over a one year period. About three years later a second round of promotions occurred, again at three different times. In another three years, promotions came again, but this time to only 32 of the 71 managers. The small differences in the timing of the earlier promotions proved to be significant. Of the 32 who received the final promotions, 28 had been promoted in the first group six years earlier, and were also in the first group for the second promotion. The other four had been in the second group for the first promotion but in the first group for the second round of promotions.

This study clearly contradicts our earlier beliefs about Japanese promotion systems. Rather than having a relatively open contest, this company at least used a strong tournament model with some features of the sponsored mobility approach. The timing of the first promotion (after seven years) strongly predicted the third promotion (after 13 years). However, the information available after seven years did not predict any better than that which had been gathered in the first three years. This is consistent with the findings of Rosenbaum. The winners are determined in the first three years of the competition. The fast tracks are partially set even before the contest begins, as evidenced by the impact of university ratings and assessment centre potential ratings.

The authors of the study believe that those young managers who developed high quality relations with their superiors became part of an "in group" who began to move upward and inward toward the core of the career cone as proposed by Schein. Those who were not able to do this found themselves on an "out group" track which leads laterally around the outside of the cone.

This very structured career system is administered by a highly respected management development that has tremendous power. Their recommendations were almost always followed—top management approval would be required to change a derision made by this group. In this company, it was felt that such critical, long-term management development issues should be handled by a specialized staff, not entirely by line management.

There is much to be accomplished during the first few years of a career. The new employee must learn his or her job; must learn to work with peers, superiors, and possibly subordinates; must learn all the written and unwritten rules of the game; and must learn all about the corporate culture in order to be able to function competently. In addition, studies cited here indicate that the new employees must also prove their ability to perform at a high level and start to move very early—at least by the third year of employment.

Let us briefly review the evidence. The Bell System studies showed that those who received challenging first year assignments were more successful later on. Rosenbaum found that only those who were promoted within the first three years of their career made it to middle management within 13 years. Sheridan et al. found that entering the firm through a trainee programme and starting in a powerful department enhanced one's career mobility. Finally, we saw that even in Japan career track decisions are made very early. The data reviewed so far seem to clearly describe sponsored and tournament models. You must prove yourself to be a winner very early or else you are out of the race.

What are the implications of such practices? We feel that there are generally negative consequences, both for the individual and for the organisation. The individual may be still adjusting to an intense socialization experience—still "learning the ropes." The fast starter is likely to be the person whose anticipatory socialization was particularly effective or whose personality and family and school background prepared them well for this particular firm. But what about the person who does not "hit the ground running"? What about the "late bloomer"? There is little or no opportunity for this person in many firms. Often they do not know how limited their chances for upward mobility are, and they continue to work hard for many years, always expecting that maybe the next time they will get that ever elusive promotion. When they do realise that they are out of the competition, it may be too late for a change. The firm and the society are left with many frustrated employees with very negative attitudes toward their work and their employer.

Why do business firms make such decisions so early? The organisation may feel that the development of top management skills takes many years and therefore early identification of management potential is necessary. But how accurate can such early evaluations be? We know that the necessary mix of technical, human, and conceptual skills changes as one rises in an organisation. Can performance on an entry-level job predict performance as a top executive 20 years later? Can the problem be solved by using well designed assessment centers?

The 20 year longitudinal study by Howard and Bray provides us with the best data on this question, both because of the length of the study and because the initial assessments were never used in making the later promotion decisions. There were statistically significant correlations between the level reached within the organisation and certain measures taken 20 years earlier. The best predictor was education—was the man a college graduate or not? Other predictors, such as personality and motivation, ability, and performance on managerial simulations (in basket, competitive group discussion, business game, and interview) were more effective in forecasting which of the non-college men would be successful than they were with the college group.

For the college men there were fewer significant predictors and the strength of the correlations was in the .20 to .30 range. This indicates that less than ten percent of the variance in career attainment can be explained by these factors. Predictions were made of those who would "succeed" (reach middle management or above). For the college group, almost 45 percent of those predicted to move up did reach level four or higher. Of those predicted to not be successful, slightly over 20 percent reached the same levels.

From an academic or scientific point of view, this is very impressive. However, let us consider the practical implications. If this information had been used, a strong signal would have been given to immediate supervisors and to higher level management that one group had potential and should be moved up, while the others could not and should not make it. Without this signal to help them, over 55 percent of the "high potential" group did not move up, while over 20 percent of those who might have been ruled out of further consideration for upward movement actually did make it.

The figures from the Howard and Bray research indicate the difficulty of predicting at the middle management level. Prediction at higher levels is much less accurate. Therefore, managed career system-sponsored or tournament mobility systems which create separate and usually irreversible tracks for employees based upon early assessment or early performance—are less efficient from the firm's point of view than are more open competitions. Management development is an expensive investment on the part of the firm. However, managed career systems often cause the firm to invest heavily in the wrong people and to miss many other attractive candidates for promotion. Therefore we recommend that business firms try to delay such decisions as long as possible—at least five to ten years, if not indefinitely. Create truly open contests in which everyone, at every point in their career, still has a shot at a step up. Employees will be more motivated and productive and the task of finding talented candidates for upper management positions will be made much easier since there will be so many more people to choose from.

We will see that early identification and development is only one of a number of options for career systems and that career systems should be related to corporate strategy. We win further discuss the advantages and disadvantages, both to the firm and to the individual, of the various alternatives.

Only two empirical studies have clearly demonstrated the existence of tournament mobility and only one of these was conducted in an American firm. One other study described found only mixed support for this model: "fast starters" did not reach higher levels in the firm but did have significantly shorter time in later jobs as compared to "slow starters." However, in this analysis, no distinction was made between promotions and lateral job movement. The fast starters did not necessarily move upward, they just moved sooner, and they continued to move more quickly; but many of the moves were just transfers. More moves did lead to greater salary increments. Career mobility was also enhanced by starting in the company's trainee programme and by starting in a powerful department.

Other investigators have noted similar problems in measuring career progression. Many "promotions" and interorganizational moves do not necessarily represent upward mobility for they may actually be lateral moves. Veiga (1983) found time spent in a first position within a firm to be strongly related to average time per position later in a career. This again seems to imply that early movement leads to later success. However, he also showed that a very rapid rate of movement was associated with lateral moves and transfers and that manager from different functional areas move at different rates. Managers on a "slow track" moved less frequently, but they reached the same level as those on the "fast track" by taking larger steps.

The motivational effects of the challenging first job have also been challenged. Taylor (1981) conducted a laboratory study in which subjects performed a variety of tasks, such as puzzles and memory exercises. The challenge of their first task assignment had less effect on performance standards, attitudes, and perceptions of competence than did the challenge of later tasks. A large survey by Williams and Van Sell (1985) sampled over 2,000 employees of hundreds of business, nonprofit, and educational organizations. In this study, good, challenging first jobs were negatively associated with self-reports of career advancement. Advancement was measured by numbers of promotions, jobs, functional areas, and organizations, all statistically controlled for numbers of years worked.

We believe that lateral mobility should not be confused with upward mobility but that it is probably a signal that higher level decision makers use when deciding who to promote. Kanter (1977) has described this as a factor which predicts chances of promotion in a large industrial firm. This may be because those who make such decisions see breadth of knowledge of different areas as a prerequisite for higher levels of responsibility; or it may be that having held multiple jobs merely increases an individual's visibility within the firm.

Another variable that may act as a signal affecting chances for promotion is the functional background of the employee. Several studies have noted that firms in certain industries tend to choose their chief executives from particular functional areas. Pfeffer (1981) developed a model of executive succession in which different functional areas gain power as a result of their abilities to deal with critical environmental issues.

At a lower level, Vardi and Hammer showed that the type of job technology—long-linked, mediating, or intensive—used by rank and file workers within a plant affected their chances for mobility. In a comparison of managers drawn from three similar major manufacturing firms, Veiga found that career patterns were related to functional area. The fast track managers, who moved frequently but often laterally, were likely to be from areas representing mediating technologies like marketing and personnel, and the slow track managers, who moved less frequently but more often vertically, were likely to be from intensive technologies like research and development and engineering.

The effect of business strategy on opportunities for promotion in different functions was studied by Slocum, Cron, Hansen, and Rawlings (1985). They found that in a defender firm, in which financial and production issues were more critical than growth and new products, there were more plateaued sales people than in an analyzer firm, which would be seeking new products and markets. The ability of different functions to contribute to the critical business issues seems to affect career paths.

The strict tournament model implies that employees place out of major organizational tournaments when they fail in very early contests, and consequently they have little or no chance to be as successful as those who win the early contests. No data will fit this ideal model perfectly. However, modified models of sports competition may better fit the organizational promotion process. I considered three different sets of rules, varying with respect to the effects of early success:

- Single elimination tournament—only those who win early contests are eligible to compete for the highest positions.
- Round robin tournament—an early record of winning counts, but the major predictor of success is later competition—one loss does not necessarily mean elimination.
- Horse race early success may give a candidate a head start, but there are no extra points for an early lead. Later position is the best predictor of success.

Three hypotheses corresponded to these rules:

Hypothesis 1: All those who reach the highest levels in a tournament will have won in the early contest.

Hypothesis 2: Recent position will best predict final attainment, but early position will add significantly to the variance accounted for.

Hypothesis 3: Later position will best predict final attainment and early position will not add to the variance accounted for.

The first of these three hypotheses concerning the effects of prior promotions states the theory of the tournament mobility model, the second proposes a less strict form of path dependence, and the third implies path independence in the employee's careers. In framing hypotheses concerning the two other types of signals that may affect decisions on promotions—functional area background and the number of jobs held—I paid close attention to the research setting, because the role and nature of the signals will vary with organizational characteristics. The data for this study were gathered from a firm in the oil and gas industry.

Any firm competing in this industry in the 1970s was very much dependent on its technical experts. Critical competitive issues included the highly uncertain activity of exploration for new resources as well as complex problems of production, transportation, and processing. In addition, on the assumption that oil prices would remain high, this firm and many others were experimenting in areas such as the production of synthetic fuels and engaging in much basic research and development.

Therefore, I hypothesized that a technical background would be valued by this firm and therefore related to greater career attainment during this period. Final level of career attainment will be positively related to having initially held a position within a technical area. I felt that the ideal candidate for promotion would have a technical background, but would also have experience in other functional areas. Final level of career attainment win be positively related to the number of different jobs held. Finally, I believed that each of these signals provides unique information. Therefore, early career attainment, initial technical function, and the number of different jobs held will each contribute significantly to the prediction of final career attainment.

RESEARCH METHODS

A large domestic oil company with personnel widely dispersed across the United States served as the research setting. The economic conditions within this industry and the financial position of this particular firm improved dramatically during the 1970s, the period of the study. During this period, the firm also underwent a major transition in business strategy. An earlier emphasis on the processing and regional marketing of petroleum products gave way to a new emphasis on producing, transporting, and distributing crude oil. The firm was also actively exploring alternative energy sources. The number of employees remained relatively constant—about 22,000—during this period, and there were no major changes in human resource management policies.

Data Collection and Population

The data were obtained from the firm's computerized records. Since the study focused on early upward movement into managerial positions, I conducted a search for all exempt, or salaried, employees still with the firm in 1981 who had been hired into entry-level, non-management positions in 1968, 1969, or 1970. Some typical entry-level jobs were accounting analyst, field auditor, sales trainee, junior engineer, junior chemist, programmer, and staff assistant. One hundred and eighty cases were found that met these criteria. Demographic data such as age, gender, and education were not available.

Measures

The company's detailed systems for job classification and salary grades were the primary data. Classification codes fell into three general categories, which I used to identify initial job functions: (1) technical/professional—engineers and scientists; (2) administrative—administrators, accountants, sales/marketing personnel, computer specialists; and (3) other—laboratory technicians, clerks, administrative assistants, customer representatives, draftsmen, and so forth.

Examination of the list of each employee's job codes provided the number of different jobs each had held. I counted only a change in functional area or level of responsibility as a different job. For example, moving from chemist to senior chemist was not counted as a job change, although it would result in a higher salary grade; moving from chemist to personnel specialist or to manager—chemical analysis was counted as a job change.

The actual salary grades served as one measure of career attainment. Company job analysts determined these grades, which were similar to Hay system grades and also similar to the measure of job status used in the Rosenbaum (1984) study. These grades reflected the worth of the employee's contribution to the company. As in many technically oriented firms, there were some technical specialists with high salary grades who did not manage large groups of people. However, their grades did reflect their status, salary, and career attainment. I measured career attainment yearly, using the highest grade attained during the calendar year.

Rosenbaum early report (1979) used only broad management level to measure career attainment. To facilitate comparisons with that study, I created a second measure, grouping the salary grades into five divisions corresponding to levels in the organisation. These ranged from nonmanagement to upper-middle management, immediately below the vice presidential level. Promotions were defined as movements from a lower level to a higher one.

Two other differences existed between the measures used in Rosenbaum's 1979 study and the present one. Data were available for every year in this study, not merely for three to four year intervals as in the earlier research. Also, Rosenbaum identified movements by calendar year. However, since his group included employees hired in 1960, 1961, and 1962, those promoted in a given calendar year—1965, for example-may have had from three to five years tenure with the firm. In this study, I identified movements according to how long each individual had been with the firm, not by calendar year.

Analysis by Level

Comparing this study's data on movement through the general levels of the organizational hierarchy and Rosenbaum's 1979 data required that competition periods be defined. Because such a division is somewhat arbitrary, I followed his choice of three to four year periods, which allowed the time span to be divided into three portions.

Examining the actual pattern of promotions confirmed that natural breakpoints occurred at three to four year intervals. Inspection of a career tree for the cohort indicated that the firm promoted seven employees one level (into lower management) within their first four years. No one received another promotion until year 5. Furthermore, in years 5, 6, and 7, six employees were promoted to the second level of management, then none were promoted farther until year 8. Therefore, I defined years 1 through 4 as the first competition period and years 5 through 7 as the second competition period.

Comparing the progress of the seven employees who won (i.e., were promoted) the earliest competition with those who lost (were not promoted) shows that the early move increased the chances for further movement. However, many of those who did not move in the first period also moved up later. Of the seven early winners, three were still in lower management at the end of the 11 year study, two were in lower-middle management, one was in middle management, and one had reached upper-middle management.

Slightly over one-quarter had reached lower management; however, 21 of these employees had been promoted to lower-middle management, eight to middle management, and three made it all the way to upper middle management.

Attainment by the end of the second competition was more strongly related to position at the end of the study; however, there was again evidence of later initial movement. Of the four employees who made upper-middle management, one had not yet received his first promotion at the end of the seventh year. Three of the nine who attained the next highest level, middle management, had received no promotions by the end of year seven. Therefore, the results did not support Hypothesis 1—the strict tournament model. It was not necessary to receive a promotion in the first competition or even in the second competition in order to move up later.

The relationship between advancement in the firm and initial job classification was examined. Those who entered the firm in technical positions were very highly represented in management by year 11 and constituted the highest proportions of managers at all levels. In fact, by year 11, 78 percent of the technical entrants were in management positions, in comparison to 41 percent of those who started in administrative positions and 21 percent of those from other entry points.

An interesting interaction was discovered between entry position and movement during the various competition periods. In the first competition period, six of the seven early promotions to lower management were from administrative positions. By the end of the second competition period, there was no significant relationship between entry position and level attained. However, by year 11 technical employees were way ahead. It seems that the timing of promotions was related to functional background and that initial functional area was more important than early promotion in determining who reached the higher levels.

More detailed analyses were possible by using salary grades instead of general management level. I looked at the intercorrelations, among salary grade level each year, type of entry position, and number of different jobs held. These statistics may be found in Forbes. Salary grades in the early years were related to grades in the later years but the correlations were relatively weak. The highest correlations were found between adjacent years. In addition, correlations among later years were consistently stronger than those among the earlier years, a pattern likely in any contest where all start in approximately the same position and spread out over time. Later grade levels clearly predicted final success in terms of salary grade much better than early grade levels.

The correlations also confirmed the interactions between type of entry position and time on the job. Having an administrative entry position was related to higher salary grade in years 1 through 5, but not in years 6 through 11. A technical entry position correlated positively with salary grade in years 1 and 2, not in years 3, 4, and 5, but again in years 6 through 11. This indicates that either of these entry points provided an initial advantage. Furthermore, administrative employees maintained their advantage through year 5 but then lost it. Technical employees temporarily lost their advantage following the second year but regained it again from year 6 on. This pattern again suggests that different career patterns exist for administrative versus technical managers.

The data described the careers of only those who stayed with the firm through the entire period studied. Different patterns of retention might also explain the advantage of a technical background. Perhaps superior technical personnel stayed with the firm while superior administrative personnel left. Such movement, which would contribute to different patterns of promotion for the two functions, could result from employees' awareness of differences between internal and external opportunities. However, the data were not available to test these possibilities.

Finally, the number of different jobs held did not make any difference in salary grade in the early years but was related to attainment in years 5 through 11. The number of jobs was not related to entry position.

Multivariate Analyses

We earlier decided that a strict single elimination tournament was not descriptive of the career patterns in this company. Many of those who were passed over the first time were later successful. In addition, later positions and salary grades were better predictors of final positions and salary grades than were the early standings. That is, are we looking at a round robin tournament—where losses count against you but do not eliminate you—or at a horse race—in which early position may have little or no effect on the final winner.

This statistical technique allows us to determine whether early progress in the promotion tournament actually adds anything to our ability to predict career attainment. Numerous combinations of early and later years were possible; however, to be consistent with the conventions adopted initially, I chose year 7, the end of the second competition period, as the later year and year 4, the end of the first competition period, as the early year. Year 4 did not add significantly to the variance accounted for. In fact, no earlier year added significantly to predictions based on attainment by year 7. The data were consistent with Hypothesis 3, which supports the ahistorical model of path independence. That means that past history is essentially forgotten and that later, more recent attainments are the best predictors of success.

Finally, I had hypothesized that early career attainment, early position, and the number of different jobs would all make independent contributions to the prediction of later success. Since year 7 was a better predictor of final career attainment than year 4, I decided to investigate whether entry in a technical function and job mobility would add significantly to the already appreciable relationship between years 7 and 11.

By year 7, the end of the second competition period, 38 employees had received at least one promotion, but none had yet moved above lower-middle management. After year 7, small numbers of managers started to reach the highest levels attained during the study. Therefore, year 7 appears to be the year before the final competition begins. I computed a forward stepwise regression, entering year 7 first and entering the two other variables in the order of their contributions to additional predictability. The statistics indicated that all three variables—past attainment, initial function, and number of different jobs-contributed uniquely to the prediction of final career attainment. Early promotions (by year 4) had little impact in comparison to later progress (year 7), functional background, and breadth of experience.

The results of this study offered only weak support for the tournament model of career mobility. Although early promotions were related to later attainment, strict tournament rules were not in force, because the losers—those passed over in the early periods—were later able to move up quickly. In addition, the data did not support the concept of path dependence in which the entire career path is critical. When attainment at the end of the second period of competition was used as the basis for the prediction of final career attainment, attainment after the first stage of competition added nothing to predictions. The results were more closely analogous to a horse race than to a tournament: position out of the gate had relatively little effect in comparison to position entering the home stretch.

Different mobility patterns for administrative and technical personnel may explain in part why the pattern of the early years did not always persist. Those who started in administrative positions began to move up early, but their progress seemed to level off quickly. A technical background meant a longer wait before upward movement; however, for some this was followed by rapid promotion.

The number of different jobs, which in this study meant different functional areas or different levels of managerial responsibility, also predicted higher career attainment. This was previously noted by Kanter and, since more jobs implies less time in any one position, this finding is also consistent with the research of Sheridan and his colleagues and Veiga. Three different types of information: past position, functional background, and the number of different jobs all seemed to act as signals to those making decisions about promotions. These signals were all strongly related to career attainment and together they accounted for 60 percent of the variance in level achieved after 11 years in the firm.

CORPORATE NEEDS

The research that has been reviewed here shows that more than one type of career pattern exists. Is there a way to explain the differences? It appears that there is. If we accept the premise that human resource management practices evolve in order to help the organisation accomplish its strategic goals, and that successful strategies are those that help the firm to deal with its specific environmental threats and opportunities, then there should be a relationship between human resource practices such as career paths and the organizational setting. Let us review the settings in which different career systems were found.

The AT&T studies showed the importance of successful performance on a challenging first job and the importance of successful performance in an assessment centre evaluation. This indicates that the Bell operating companies emphasized the early identification of management potential and that subsequent promotion opportunities were determined at a very early point in the career. This could be described as sponsored or tournament mobility. The setting was one in which there was a very stable and benevolent environment. At the time, the Bell operating companies were part of a regulated monopoly delivering a service that was based on well established technology. Success was a result of satisfying the customer and the state public utility commissions. Rather tall, centralized, bureaucratic organizations evolved in which everything was done according to Bell System standard operating procedures. Promotion within these firms was a carefully planned process.

The firm studied by Rosenbaum was described as an old, well established firm. Examination of the distribution of personnel across hierarchical levels shows that this firm had a rather tall organisation chart with narrow spans of control. There were seven levels of management and over 9,365 nonmanagement employees in 1975. Of course, in this firm there was the clearest evidence of the tournament model of mobility. Other factors also influenced career attainment in this most comprehensive study including education, college selectivity, gender, and race-indicating the possible sponsoring of certain groups.

The research recently reported by Sheridan et al. also seems to support a tournament model, although the findings are not that clear due to the fact that "mobility" includes both horizontal and vertical movements. However, the importance of entering the company trainee programme and having an early assignment within a powerful department are evidence of a sponsored mobility career system. This company was also a public utility and thus in a regulated, relatively stable environment.

The Japanese study indicated that although promotions are delayed in comparison to American firms, early decisions are made about who will be promoted. Here a relatively strong tournament appeared to be in effect. There were also indications of sponsored mobility, as evidenced by the effects of university ranking and assessment centre potential measures. This firm is described only as "one of the leading corporations in Japan." It is a firm in which a desirable starting position is a sales job in a large branch store. This firm was clearly concerned about stability, as shown by the fact that "executives repeatedly emphasized that the future competitive position of their corporation depended critically on their ability to reproduce themselves".

Finally, a clearly different career pattern was found in our study of a large natural resource company. Here there were delayed patterns of promotion; early movement was not terribly important. However, early assignment and experience in the technical area was influential, as was the number of different jobs held. The most obvious difference between this firm and all the others was change. This firm was undergoing a major change in business strategy and beginning to experience rapid growth in earnings toward the end of the period studied. As a result, the company was also beginning to recruit and hire more managers and technical personnel from the outside.

Internal promotions were not sufficient to satisfy the demand for talented personnel. In addition, it may not have been clear what type of personnel would be needed in the future—thus hindering long-term career planning and management. Highly structured, tournament-based career systems seem to evolve in the more stable or more regulated settings.

CORPORATE STRATEGY

A number of models exist which may help us to understand the relationship between corporate strategy and career systems. Slocum and Cron (1988) have focused on the two types of business strategies known as defenders and analyzers. Defenders protect their niche in relatively stable environments. They rely on internal efficiency to competitively price their existing products or services. They generally utilize formalized, centralized control systems. There is often functional organisation and managers are specialists who are promoted within their specialized areas. Because of the strategic orientation toward low cost, efficient production or operations, the powerful functions in such firms are the financial, accounting, and production areas.

Analyzers operate like defenders in some product markets but also are poised to move quickly to take advantage of new opportunities. There is a greater need for marketing expertise and scanning of the external environment. The firm must be organized to allow for flexibility as well as efficiency.

In the defender firm there is more stability and an emphasis on carefully developing those who are in the critical areas of production and accounting/finance. These firms use extensive on-the-job training and detailed succession planning programs. They typically hire into lower level positions and promote from within. They are likely to rely on early predictors of management potential. Although most managers move up within their functional areas, those who have been identified as high potential employees may have the opportunity to learn various functions.

Because the analyzers are looking for new opportunities as well as trying to protect established areas, the human resource practices and career patterns are different. Some individuals are brought in at entry level and trained within specific functions, but others are recruited from outside to provide immediate expertise. The areas of marketing, engineering, and production are all important. There is more of an emphasis on movement across functions and products as a means of learning about the various departments.

The opportunities for upward mobility varied in relation to strategy within a sample of seven mature industrial products manufacturers studied by Slocum and Cron. The career phenomenon of plateauing occurs when the probability of further promotion in a company becomes very low. By considering both the perceived likelihood of future promotion and the current level of performance, we may classify employees into four categories. "Stars" are employees who are doing well and who are expected to continue to move up in the organisation. "Comers" have been identified as having the potential to move up but are currently performing below their potential. "Solid citizens" are performing well but are unlikely to move any farther.

And finally, "deadwood" are employees who are performing below standard and have little chance of moving up. Both solid citizens and deadwood are considered plateaued employees. In the defender firms, 66 percent of the employees were plateaued as compared to 27 percent in the analyzer firms. Fifty percent of the employees in the analyzers were considered comers compared to 19 percent in the defender firms, and 23 percent were seen as stars in an analyzer situation in contrast to 15 percent in the defender scenario.

Despite the plateauing, defender employees were less likely to leave the firm but more willing to relocate for another job in the company. They were more concerned about immediate promotions than were the employees of the analyzer firms. Employees in the defender firms also reported less challenge and involvement with their work, less satisfaction, and less visibility and influence to senior managers. In analyzer firms, employees are generally more motivated both by the challenge of their work and by the greater opportunities for advancement.

In the studies that we have reviewed earlier, the firms in which sponsored or tournament mobility systems were the norm appear to be those with a defender strategy: the Bell System companies before deregulation, the established firm studied by Rosenbaum, and the public utility in the Sheridan study. The study in which a horse race was found to describe the promotion pattern was in an analyzer mode. This company's business was changing; it was looking for new opportunities to supplement its traditional strengths; it was looking outside for new managerial and professional talent. The very early identification and development of higher level management candidates was not consistent with the strategy being adapted at this point in time.

The nature of career opportunities can be thought of as part of the organization's reward system. The relationships among business strategy, reward systems, and corporate culture have been studied recently by Kerr and Slocum. This in-depth study of 14 companies focused on their corporate growth strategies. The authors used the steady state versus evolutionary dichotomy. Steady state firms are primarily internally focused. They may grow as the result of internally developed new products or through increased penetration of existing markets. On the other hand, evolutionary firms actively pursue new products and markets through mergers and acquisitions. Kerr and Slocum found that all but one firm with a steady state strategy had adapted what they called a hierarchy-based reward system. All of the firms with an evolutionary strategy used a performance-based reward system.

In a hierarchy-based reward system, performance evaluation is subtle and subjective. Performance is defined qualitatively as well as quantitatively. Superiors have a great deal of control over evaluation and, consequently, mobility within the firm. A close relationship with superiors and other mentors is essential in order to be successful. Parenthetically, this type of vertical exchange was found to be very important in the study of upward mobility in the Japanese firm discussed earlier. The reward system motivates more cooperative effort and long-term commitment. Managers are promoted from within and promotions are often given to an employee more for developmental reasons than for business reasons.

There are many lateral and diagonal moves designed to help the employee understand the whole company and build stronger internal relationships. The system performs the function of completely socializing the younger manager into a strong corporate culture. As Kerr and Slocum point out, this type of system has been described by Ouchi as a "clan culture." A clan culture fosters long-term loyalty and commitment through this lengthy, sometimes arbitrary, socialization process. The performance-based system is more objective. Rewards are based upon clearly defined expectations. The employee is much less dependent on the superior for evaluation or development.

In fact, there is generally little concern with employee development. Socialization is not a primary purpose of the performance-based reward system. Neither cooperation with others nor learning the whole system were emphasized. Promotions were not necessarily from within—many top managers were brought in from outside. Kerr and Slocum describe the situation as a "mutually exploitive relationship." This is consistent with a "market culture" in which relationships are clearly spelled out and there is little need for loyalty or long-term commitments. There is an emphasis on individual initiative and accomplishment, however.

Each reward system seems to fit the needs of the firms in which they were found. The steady state firms were mature capital-intensive operations such as aluminum, forest products, power generation, pharmaceuticals, and machine tools. It was felt that successful managers would have a long-term commitment to the firm and be able to function well in a highly integrated organisation. The hierarchy-based reward system develops such managers.

The firms with an evolutionary strategy were generally conglomerates whose success depends on the management of a portfolio of businesses. In this situation, commitment to a particular business is of less value (and some might argue is actually a liability).

Such firms are successful when the various businesses or divisions are given a high level of autonomy and are evaluated as objectively as possible. Loyalty and commitment are not a concern in a system where the possibility of divestment of businesses is a part of the corporate strategy. Again, the reward system promotes the type of behaviour that is most compatible with the corporate strategy. Returning again to our studies of career mobility, those firms with sponsored or tournament mobility appear to have been following a steady state strategy and therefore used these promotion systems to ensure an adequate supply of well trained, well socialized managers who understood the entire system and appreciated the subtleties of getting things done in a clan culture.

This was the case in the utilities, Rosenbaum's firm, and of course in the Japanese firm. A more open system of competition was found in the oil and gas firm, which in fact was attempting to diversify and acquire new products and markets through acquisition. Here there was a great deal of emphasis on individual entrepreneurial ability and relatively little concern for loyalty or cooperation. The firm was looking for the most capable managers and was not terribly concerned about their earlier socialization, their networks, or even their early record of promotions.

At this point, we will discuss one more system for classifying career systems. While similar to those described above, this model introduces additional categories and further refinements that may prove helpful for our understanding of managerial careers. This model of career systems, developed by Sonnenfeld and Peiperl (1988), is based on two dimensions: supply flow and assignment flow. Supply flow refers to the degree to which personnel may easily move into and out of the firm. An internal supply flow implies promotion from within. External supply means that the firm actively recruits managerial and professional personnel from external sources. Assignment flow describes the bases for making job assignment and promotion decisions.

These are seen within this model as being based primarily on either individual performance or on the degree of contribution to the group effort. Combining these two career properties results in four cells, some of which are very similar to the categories discussed previously. When an internal supply flow is combined with assignment based on contribution to the group, we have the career system that Sonnenfeld and Peiperl call the "club." Internal supply combined with assignment based on individual contribution is referred to as the "academy." External supply plus individual assignment criteria results in the "baseball team" and external supply with a group assignment basis is known as the "fortress."

The club recruits new employees primarily at the entry level and develops them slowly and carefully. The socialization of those selected into the trainee programme in the public utility described by Sheridan et al. would be typical of club practice. There is an emphasis on fair treatment of members and loyalty to the organisation is expected. Assignments and promotions are based on contribution to the group, not just individual performance. Members see their firm as providing important services—as having an important mission. An employee's perceived value (and consequently his opportunity for advancement) is influenced by status attainment prior to joining the firm. Those who have the right background or schooling may enjoy what we have called sponsored mobility.

Strategically, clubs are likely to be "defenders," trying to perform efficiently and effectively within a limited domain. They are often monopolies or in regulated industries. Examples given by Sonnenfeld and Peiperl include utilities, airlines, banks, surface common carriers, as well as the military and government agencies. Firms where internal supply flow is combined with assignment based on individual contribution are the "academies." Here the emphasis is on recruiting employees early in their career and developing them in house. There is more emphasis on differentiating among employees based on their individual contributions according to Sonnenfeld and Peiperl (1988). Large, well established firms such as IBM, Kodak, and Exxon are typical examples of academies. The authors note how sharply career paths differ across different types of firms:

At IBM, point of entry is restricted to early career positions. An employee entering any given management group has an 80 percent chance of staying with IBM through to retirement. At a major New York City bank that same individual would have an 80 percent chance of quitting by the end of his or her first decade of employment. Within the academy there are often sophisticated career development practices: assessment centers, management development programs, career tracking and sponsorship of high potential employees, and dual career ladders. The system is designed to develop and retain in-house talent. As a result, employees are oriented toward personal growth and career development.

Strategically, firms using the academy career system are likely to be analyzers. They are protecting established core businesses but are also constantly looking for new products and services. They try to combine stability and innovation. They need employees who are motivated to learn new things and take moderate risks while remaining loyal to the firm. Sonnenfeld and Peiperl state that the following types of firms use the academy system: office products, pharmaceuticals, electronics, automobiles, and consumer products. The concept of tournament mobility fits nicely in this type of setting. There is an orientation toward longterm development of talented personnel; however, advancement is a function of individual performance which is evaluated on a regular basis. There are, in fact, likely to be multiple tournaments ongoing in various functions and divisions.

A number of forces dictate against the adherence to a strict tournament in which only early winners succeed. These include the nature of the business—multiple existing products or services plus the constant search for new opportunities—and the nature of the career system—long-term commitment plus lots of lateral movement. Where more uncertainty exists early predictions are much tougher to make with any accuracy. Future needs are unknown. It is better to delay selection and develop many people and give them opportunities to prove themselves in many different settings.

The third type of career system described by Sonnenfeld and Peiperl is the "baseball team." As the name suggests, the orientation here is toward obtaining the best available talent in the labour market. These firms are looking for proven individual performers and are open to external labour markets at all levels. There is little concern with employee training and development. High turnover is expected and therefore there is no point in succession planning. The firm is often looking for high levels of creativity and innovation, and would be categorized as a "prospector." Successful employees are highly, motivated people who see themselves as minor celebrities. Examples here include broadcasting, advertising, law firms, consulting firms, investment banks, and software development. The competition is very open, with employers continually searching for new talent and at the same time discarding those who are no longer that useful.

The last category is the "fortress" or the "institution under siege." This organisation is struggling to survive and its needs take precedence over any individual concerns. They are hiring and firing in reaction to immediate market conditions. They may be in highly competitive businesses or in a crisis or turnaround scenario. The firm may be reacting to a change in the external business environment and/or may have changed its business strategy. Such "reactor" firms are often out of control as a result of poor management or due to the nature of their business. Examples given by Sonnenfeld and Peiperl are hotels, retailing, textiles, and natural resources. Unsuccessful baseball teams become fortresses very quickly. Here neither the firm nor the individual are concerned about career paths, immediate survival is the only issue.

As we have noted above, the career paths adapted by a firm seem to be a means for dealing with its particular business environment. The club, in a stable and often regulated environment, attempts to identify top management talent very early. Therefore, we see evidence of sponsored or strict tournament mobility. To get ahead, you need the appropriate background and education and/or you need to prove your ability very early through outstanding performance. As we saw, this pattern existed in the Bell operating companies as well as another public utility. It was also seen in a Japanese firm and was originally identified in the well established firm studied by Rosenbaum.

Which did not find strong tournaments in effect, was done in an oil and gas company undergoing a change in business strategy. The firm was becoming a major producer of crude oil, having previously been a regional refiner and marketer. It was moving from a defender strategy toward an analyzer strategy and also from a steady state position with respect to growth towards an evolutionary strategy. Developing and selecting people according to the rules of clubs or clans would no longer serve all of its needs.

During this transition period, the firm was operating in many respects like a baseball team—seeking new talent in the external labour market and sending some existing players down to the farm. There was also evidence of a market culture with respect to the treatment of the new stars who were brought aboard and with respect to decisions concerning acquisitions and divestments. However, within the core business of this firm there were strong traditions, and loyalty and acceptance of corporate values were rewarded. Strategically, acquisitions were considered only if related to the core business. The career system would best be described as an academy which had entered the external labour market in order to cope with change.

Other factors affecting career paths were also operating in this case. The delayed promotion patterns found in this firm were at least partially due to changes in the profitability and size of the company. During the early portion of this longitudinal study, the company invested heavily in a very risky joint venture. The venture proved to be very successful with the payoffs coming toward the end of the period studied. Therefore, more opportunities for upward mobility were created in the later years. Different career patterns were found for those entering into different functional areas. This can be explained by again considering the firm's ability to deal with its external environment. Particular functional areas gain in power, influence, and upward mobility if they possess the skills needed to deal with critical environmental demands. In this firm, technical expertise was certainly related to the most critical tasks: exploration, production, processing, distribution, and research and development. Nontechnical administrative skills seem to have been less important. This is similar to the finding of Slocum and his colleagues (1985). Sales personnel were more likely to be plateaued when they worked in a defender firm in which financial and production issues were more critical than were marketing issues such as growth and new products.

The pattern of slower promotion for technical personnel may apply beyond this firm and industry. Veiga (1985) data on managers in manufacturing firms showed slower rates of movement were associated with what he called intensive technology—activities like research and development and engineering. Perhaps it takes longer to evaluate the managerial potential of technical personnel, or perhaps their skills are too valuable to lose by early promotion into managerial positions. Our study spanned 11 years and we concluded that a strict tournament was not in effect because early promotions did not make that much difference. However, perhaps in this case the "early" contests take longer—possibly up to seven years. If this were the case, then a tournament may have been in effect, but employees, especially technical employees, were given longer to prove themselves.

The corporate strategy approach described above is useful in understanding how career patterns evolve or are developed in order to help the organisation achieve its objectives. This does not just happen as if by magic, although it may appear that way to many people within the firm as well as to the more distant observer. A firm's success depends on the availability of competent human resources. Without the correct career system in place, the firm will not be able to accomplish its strategic objectives. Therefore it is essential that top managers and human resource professionals be aware of the strong connection between strategic planning and human resource planning—especially with regard to the design of the entire career system.

A key issue here is the promotion decision—what criteria are being used to choose those who move up and into contention for top executive positions? Following Rosenbaum's lead, we believe that human decision makers often rely on a small number of simple cues or in this case "signals." Academicians may infer the existence of different career systems by identifying the signals used in making promotion decisions. Practitioners may change existing career systems or develop new ones by influencing the choice of these signals. For example, if derision makers, consciously or unconsciously, look for signals such as socioeconomic background or the right education, then sponsored mobility will occur. If they believe that early performance and promotion are important indicators of ability, then we will see tournament mobility.

Other signals that we have seen in the studies discussed here have included university status, assessment centre evaluation, entry into a special trainee programme, entry into a powerful department, early functional area, and a high level of lateral intrafirm mobility. Many of these signals serve a useful purpose in the organisation. However, often career paths become institutionalized. That is, the use of a signal that seemed to make sense in the past leads to many powerful decision makers with similar backgrounds. These high level managers assume that the firm needs more of the same type of person and therefore select people just like themselves for promotion. Of course in a changing environment this practice can be disastrous.

ADVANTAGES AND DISADVANTAGES

So far we have discussed different career paths primarily from the organization's point of view. We have seen that many firms use early upward mobility as a signal indicative of management potential. Other firms that do not seem to emphasize early upward movement, such as the oil and gas company that we studied, still prefer those employees who have held a larger number of different jobs when making promotion decisions. At this point we will take a closer look at the advantages and disadvantages of such fast tracks—both for the organisation and for the individual.

Advantages

In addition to being a step in an individual's career, job changes, both promotions and transfers, serve many other organizational purposes. Open positions are constantly being created in any organisation. They are created by normal attrition and by growth and change in the organizational structure. Of course, someone must be found to fill these positions and the most obvious choices are people dose to the open position—that is, those in the same function and at the same level or slightly below. Often, however, the firm will choose to move employees across functions or divisions. This strategy allows cross-fertilization. The person being moved has a chance to learn much more about the range of activities and opportunities within the organisation. This is, of course, valuable experience for the employee who aspires to further upward mobility. The practice also may enrich those who have the opportunity to interact with the person from a different area. They may learn to appreciate the problems and issues faced by other functions and divisions by communicating with outsiders.

Frequent movement may also be an organizational tactic that helps create and maintain a strong corporate culture. Those who make frequent geographic moves come to identify more with the organisation than with any particular community. Those who frequently change functional area will also identify more strongly with the company than with any specific professional groups. This is seen clearly in the military and in companies like IBM, where many employees believe the firm's initials stand for "I've been moved."

For the individual, job change is generally an opportunity for new learning and growth. Even lateral moves expose the employee to new challenges and allow them to develop new skills. Promotions are a natural progression as the employee gains experience and acceptance within the organisation. People expect that they will be given more authority and responsibility as they mature in the job. They also expect that their status and financial position in life will improve with time on the job. The firm that does not satisfy these expectations will lose valued employees.

Disadvantage

From the organization's perspective, moving employees is very costly. There are the obvious costs of physically relocating the employee plus the somewhat hidden costs of reduced productivity both before and after the move. There is also a domino effect in which the first move creates another vacancy that must be filled, which creates another, and so on, thus multiplying the costs. Training costs must also be considered, as well as the possibility that the employee will refuse the move and may even leave the company.

Because fast track employees realise that they will be moved within a year or two, and that short-term performance is essential for their career progress, they tend to focus on immediate results. They may abandon useful programs initiated by predecessors and replace them with their own inventions in order to gain more visibility and credibility. They may not support long-term efforts involving needed organizational change and development because they will not pay off quickly enough.

Frequent job change can be a frustrating and stressful experience for the individual. Feldman (1988) has listed the many costs to the individual. These include increased demands for high performance with little training. They are expected to "hit the floor running" with a minimum of assistance from anyone else. Sometimes employees are moved so rapidly that they never learn the job. Feldman (1988) reports that:

One employee in production management had been promoted from plant manager to director of national operations to vice president, international operations in 18 months. At first, such quick promotions leave managers feeling exhilarated. Later, though, these managers feel frightened and out of control as they realise they are responsible for products or services about which they know virtually nothing. The fast track manager may be learning to adapt strategies that will hurt both them and their companies in the long run. They may never be satisfied with any job because all they care about is the next position and getting to it as quickly as possible. They may never master the technical aspects of any function. They may ignore their families and never develop any interests outside of work. Finally, they may burn out at a relatively early age as a result of the stress of this type of career.

Geographical relocation brings with it additional problems. Many employees do not want to move but are afraid of the possible negative impact of refusing. Economic hardship may accompany a move. This may come about as the result of higher costs of living or the difficulty of the spouse finding employment in the new location. Social relationships, both at work and outside, tend to suffer. Finally, there is the disruption of the lives of the spouse and children, however, recent research indicates that most families adapt rather well to moving.

POLICY IMPLICATIONS

James Rosenbaum, who first proposed the concept of tournament mobility, has also been the most articulate critic of this system. They minimize the number of employees in whom the firm must invest and they maximize the amortization time for the investment.

This efficiency, however, assumes three preconditions according to Rosenbaum: "(1) they must use appropriate selection criteria, (2) they must increase amortization time, and (3) they must not reduce productivity by their selections". With regard to the first point, the tournament model makes selections based upon short-term performance. Employees who demonstrate successful short-term results, perhaps even at the cost of long-term performance, will be promoted. As we noted above, the employees within such systems quickly learn the rules of the game and attend only to outcomes that will help them in the short run.

The system seems to be well designed to catch and correct errors of inclusion. If an individual with little true managerial ability wins the early contest, this may be discovered in the next competition. Ideally this would be the case. However, we feel that given the emphasis on short-term performance evaluations and the strong signals sent by early promotion, the lack of ability may not be detected until late in the career. Errors of exclusion are virtually undetectable. There are no second chances. Those who are not selected early are out of the running. This is an even more serious problem in sponsored systems. In these programs, identification of talented people occurs before any real performance evaluation can occur.

Once the selection is made, many forces come into play to reinforce and validate the decision. Those selected receive special socialization and developmental experiences, often promotion opportunities are created for these "high potential" employees, and before too long, everyone, including the top management candidate, begins to believe in their ability. This may have worked effectively in many situations in the past and may still work well enough in stable regulated industries (which, in fact, were where we saw the strongest evidence of this practice); however, in the fiercely competitive world of the 1990s and beyond we should be trying harder to make the very best selections.

Rosenbaum's second criterion for efficient selection was that amortization time will be increased. It seems obvious that earlier decisions would allow this to occur. However, that assumes that everyone stays with the organisation. In fact, selection of an employee for a fast track management development programme may increase the chances that he or she will leave the firm. Younger people in general are more likely to change employers, and when they have been through some early managerial development their value in the external labour market increases. Investing in older employees may actually result in a greater return to the firm.

Lastly, Rosenbaum proposed that tournaments must not reduce productivity. On this point he argues persuasively that a tournament system is a major contributor to the mid-career crises experienced by many employees:

The career system may be instrumental in building up the skills, status, and expectations of high-potential people, and it may be powerful in its destructive force in lowering the skills, status, and expectations of employees who have been eliminated from further competition. It withholds further investments from them, it attributes low-ability status to them, and it creates the expectation that these individuals are not going any further in their careers.

In addition to contributing to mid-career crises, Rosenbaum expresses concern over the level of early career stress generated by the tournament system. The timing of this pressure is also unfortunate because it forces many young employees to choose between their careers and the high demands of a young family. This is particularly troublesome for women in the workplace and is often used as justification for discrimination against young women. Rosenbaum concludes that the "economic justifications of early selections require rethinking" and recommends that tournament mobility systems be replaced by more open systems that allow for delayed selections. This should result in more accurate selection decisions and eliminate many of the negative consequences of the tournament model. We agree and feel that changes in the business environment, in organizational structures, and in demographics are combining to make this a feasible and practical alternative.

3

Accounting Information for Operations Management Decisions

DEFINITION OF MANAGEMENT

Management in all business areas and organizational activities are the acts of getting people together to accomplish desired goals and objectives. Management comprises planning, organizing, staffing, leading or directing, and controlling an organization or effort for the purpose of accomplishing a goal. Resourcing encompasses the deployment and manipulation of human resources, financial resources, technological resources, and natural resources.

Because organizations can be viewed as systems, management can also be defined as human action, including design, to facilitate the production of useful outcomes from a system. This view opens the opportunity to 'manage' oneself, a pre-requisite to attempting to manage others

Management can also refer to the person or people who perform the act(s) of management.

The verb manage comes from the Italian maneggiare, which in turn derives from the Latin manus. The French word mesnagement influenced the development in meaning of the English word management in the 17th and 18th centuries.

Some definitions of management are:

- Organisation and coordination of the activities of an enterprise in accordance with certain policies and in achievement of clearly defined objectives. Management is often included as a factor of production along with machines, materials, and money.
- Directors and managers who have the power and responsibility to make decisions to manage an enterprise. As a discipline, management comprises the interlocking functions of formulating corporate policy and organizing, planning, controlling, and directing the firm's resources to achieve the policy's objectives. The size of management can range from one person in a small firm to hundreds or thousands of managers in multinational companies.

In large firms the board of directors formulates the policy which is implemented by the chief executive officer.

Mary Parker Follett, who wrote on the topic in the early twentieth century, defined management as "the art of getting things done through people". She also described management as philosophy. One can also think of management functionally, as the action of measuring a quantity on a regular basis and of adjusting some initial plan; or as the actions taken to reach one's intended goal. This applies even in situations where planning does not take place.

From this perspective, Frenchman Henri Fayol considers management to consist of seven functions:

- Planning
- Organizing
- Leading
- Coordinating
- Controlling
- Staffing
- Motivating

Some people, however, find this definition, while useful, far too narrow. The phrase "management is what managers do" occurs widely, suggesting the difficulty of defining management, the shifting nature of definitions, and the connection of managerial practices with the existence of a managerial cadre or class.

One habit of thought regards management as equivalent to "business administration" and thus excludes management in places outside commerce, as for example in charities and in the public sector. More realistically, however, every organization must manage its work, people, processes, technology, etc. in order to maximize its effectiveness. Nonetheless, many people refer to university departments which teach management as "business schools." Some institutions use that name while others employ the more inclusive term "management."

English speakers may also use the term"management" or"the management" as a collective word describing the managers of an organization, for example of a corporation. Historically this use of the term was often contrasted with the term"Labour" referring to those being managed.

In for-profit work, management has as its primary function the satisfaction of a range of stakeholders. This typically involves making a profit, creating valued products at a reasonable cost, and providing rewarding employment opportunities. In nonprofit management, add the importance of keeping the faith of donors. In most models of management/ governance, shareholders vote for the board of directors, and the board then hires senior management. Some organizations have experimented with other methods of selecting or reviewing managers; but this occurs only very rarely.

In the public sector of countries constituted as representative democracies, voters elect politicians to public office. Such politicians hire many managers and administrators, and in some countries like the United States political appointees lose their jobs on the election of a new president/governor/mayor. Difficulties arise in tracing the history of management.

Some see it as a late modern conceptualization. On those terms it cannot have a pre-modern history, only harbingers. Others, however, detect management-like-thought back to Sumerian traders and to the builders of the pyramids of ancient Egypt. Slave-owners through the centuries faced the problems of exploiting/motivating a dependent but sometimes unenthusiastic or recalcitrant workforce, but many pre-industrial enterprises, given their small scale, did not feel compelled to face the issues of management systematically.

However, innovations such as the spread of Arabic numerals and the codification of double-entry book-keeping provided tools for management assessment, planning and control.

Given the scale of most commercial operations and the lack of mechanized record-keeping and recording before the industrial revolution, it made sense for most owners of enterprises in those times to carry out management functions by and for themselves. But with growing size and complexity of organizations, the split between owners and day-to-day managers gradually became more common.

BASIC FUNCTIONS OF MANAGEMENT

We have already discussed that management is a process. It comprises different stages. These stages in the process are known as the functions of management. Each of these functions are described below:

PLANNING

Planning is deciding in advance what is to be done, when it is to be done, howit is to be done and why it is to be done. It emphasises the fact that if one knows where he is going, he is more likely to get there.

Planning involves:

- Problem-solving;
- Decision-making.
- Decision-making.

Whenever there is a problem, the manager should know what alternatives are there to solve it. Out of the alternative courses of action he has to choose the most suitable one. This process of making choice is known as decision making. Planning requires decisions to be made on what should be done, how it should be done, who will do it, where it will be done, and why it is to be done. The essential part of the planning consists of setting goals and programmes of activities.

ORGANISING

After plans have been drawn, the management has to organise the activities. Managers determine what activities are necessary to achieve the objectives and how these activities should be divided among the departments and employees. The performance of any activity requires different type of work.

Suppose the manager of a sugar mill decides to produce 100 tons of sugar. This is his objectives. Now to achieve this, he has to divide the activities and operations into certain departments. The production work is given to the production department; finance department is assigned the work of arranging funds; personnel department is to procure people with required skills and the sales department is to take care of sales. The organising function of management involves creating departments and defining the duties and responsibilities of people in different positions within each department.

STAFFING

Staffing is concerned with employing people for the various activities to be performed. The objectives of staffing is to ensure that right type of people have been recruited for different positions. It includes the function of recruitment, selection, and placement of employees.

DIRECTING

The directing function of management includes guiding the subordinates, supervising their performance, communicating information and motivating. A manager should be a good leader. He should be able to instruct and guide his subordinates in the work assigned to them.

He should keep a watch on the vperformance of his subordinates and help them out whenever they come across any difficulty. The communication system, i.e, exchange of information should take place in clearly understandable words and without delay.

Information should flow from managers to workers and from workers to managers at the right time. Managers should also understand the needs of subordinates and accordingly inspire them in their work.

CONTROLLING

This function of management consists of the steps taken to ensure that the performance of work is in accordance with the plans. Controlling means measuring the actual performance with the planned one. If differences are noticed, corrective steps are taken which may include revision of plans, improvement in the division of work and providing better guidance.

CO-ORDINATION

We have discussed each of the five vital functions of management separately. But it is important to note that all the activities should contribute to the achievement of the objectives of the business as a whole. The heads of different departments should not treat each other as competitors but should work as organs of one body.

As the proper functioning of every organ of a human body is important for a healthy body, the work of every department is important for the organisation as a whole. Managers should, therefore, see that everybody in the organisation understands its objectives and works in co-operation with others to achieve these objectives. This function of management is called co-ordination. It consists of harmonising group effort so as to achieve common objectives.

FORMATION OF THE BUSINESS POLICY

- The mission of the business is its most obvious purpose — which may be, for example, to make soap.
- The vision of the business reflects its aspirations and specifies its intended direction or future destination.
- The objectives of the business refers to the ends or activity at which a certain task is aimed.
- The business's policy is a guide that stipulates rules, regulations and objectives, and may be used in the managers' decision-making. It must be flexible and easily interpreted and understood by all employees.
- The business's strategy refers to the coordinated plan of action that it is going to take, as well as the resources that it will use, to realise its vision and long-term objectives. It is a guideline to managers, stipulating how they ought to allocate and utilize the factors of production to the business's advantage. Initially, it could help the managers decide on what type of business they want to form.

HOW TO IMPLEMENT POLICIES AND STRATEGIES

- All policies and strategies must be discussed with all managerial personnel and staff.
- Managers must understand where and how they can implement their policies and strategies.
- A plan of action must be devised for each department.

- Policies and strategies must be reviewed regularly.
- Contingency plans must be devised in case the environment changes.
- Assessments of progress ought to be carried out regularly by top-level managers.
- A good environment and team spirit is required within the business.
- The missions, objectives, strengths and weaknesses of each department must be analysed to determine their roles in achieving the business's mission.
- The forecasting method develops a reliable picture of the business's future environment.
- A planning unit must be created to ensure that all plans are consistent and that policies and strategies are aimed at achieving the same mission and objectives.

All policies must be discussed with all managerial personnel and staff that is required in the execution of any departmental policy.

- Organizational change is strategically achieved through the implementation of the eight-step plan of action established by John P. Kotter: Increase urgency, get the vision right, communicate the buy-in, empower action, create short-term wins, don't let up, and make change stick.

WHERE POLICIES AND STRATEGIES FIT INTO THE PLANNING PROCESS

- They give mid- and lower-level managers a good idea of the future plans for each department in an organization.
- A framework is created whereby plans and decisions are made.
- Mid- and lower-level management may add their own plans to the business's strategic ones.

MULTI-DIVISIONAL MANAGEMENT HIERARCHY

The management of a large organization may have about five levels:

- Senior management
- Middle management
- Low-level management, such as supervisors or team-leaders
- Foreman
- Rank and File

TOP-LEVEL MANAGEMENT

- Require an extensive knowledge of management roles and skills.

- They have to be very aware of external factors such as markets.
- Their decisions are generally of a long-term nature
- Their decisions are made using analytic, directive, conceptual and/or behavioural/participative processes
- They are responsible for strategic decisions.
- They have to chalk out the plan and see that plan may be effective in the future.
- They are executive in nature.

MIDDLE MANAGEMENT

- Mid-level managers have a specialized understanding of certain managerial tasks.
- They are responsible for carrying out the decisions made by top-level management.
- Finance, marketing etc are comes under middle level management

LOWER MANAGEMENT

- This level of management ensures that the decisions and plans taken by the other two are carried out.
- Lower-level managers' decisions are generally short-term ones.

CHARACTERISTICS OF MANAGEMENT

You have just read about the meaning of management.
Now let us discuss its characteristics:

- There is always a definite objective of management and managers help in achieving that objective successfully. Management, thus, is a goal directed activity.
- In a group activity, the manager alone cannot achieve the objectives. He has to take the help of others. He has to see that different employees perform their activities in such a manner that there is no conflict, that work is performed in an orderly manner and completed at the right time. Besides, different activities should support each other. This is called co-ordination. It shows that management is concerned with arranging group activity in a co-ordinated manner.
- Managers have to make a number of decisions to manage the activities properly. Suppose a factory manager aims at increasing the profits through increased production and sales. Then he will first have to take steps to increase the level of production and then try to sell the goods produced. To increase production there may be a few alternatives, e.g. increase in working hours, installing another machine, hiring more workers, improvement in the methods of work

and so on. He has to choose the most suitable alternative to achieve his objective. This is known as decision making. Managers are involved in decision making, that is, choosing between alternative courses of action at all stages of management.

- Management aims at securing maximum results with minimum of effort and cost. Managers use various methods to reduce wastes and increase the efficiency of work. Management, in this sense, is an economic-activity.
- Managers have to get work done in different types of situations with the help of people having different types of skills. Managers have, therefore, to think of different ways of getting things done. In this sense management is a creative activity.

IMPORTANCE OF MANAGEMENT

- *It helps in Achieving Group Goals*: It arranges the factors of production, assembles and organizes the resources, integrates the resources in effective manner to achieve goals. It directs group efforts towards achievement of pre-determined goals. By defining objective of organization clearly there would be no wastage of time, money and effort. Management converts disorganized resources of men, machines, money etc. into useful enterprise. These resources are coordinated, directed and controlled in such a manner that enterprise work towards attainment of goals.
- *Optimum Utilization of Resources*: Management utilizes all the physical and human resources productively. This leads to efficacy in management. Management provides maximum utilization of scarce resources by selecting its best possible alternate use in industry from out of various uses. It makes use of experts, professional and these services leads to use of their skills, knowledge, and proper utilization and avoids wastage. If employees and machines are producing its maximum there is no under employment of any resources.
- *Reduces Costs*: It gets maximum results through minimum input by proper planning and by using minimum input and getting maximum output. Management uses physical, human and financial resources in such a manner which results in best combination. This helps in cost reduction.
- *Establishes Sound Organization*: No overlapping of efforts. To establish sound organizational structure is one of the objective of management which is in tune with objective of organization and for fulfillment of this, it establishes effective authority and responsibility relationship i.e. who is accountable to whom, who can give instructions to whom, who are superiors and who are subordinates. Management fills up various positions with right

persons, having right skills, training and qualification. All jobs should be cleared to everyone.

- *Establishes Equilibrium*: It enables the organization to survive in changing environment. It keeps in touch with the changing environment. With the change is external environment, the initial co-ordination of organization must be changed. So it adapts organization to changing demand of market/changing needs of societies. It is responsible for growth and survival of organization.
- *Essentials for Prosperity of Society*: Efficient management leads to better economical production which helps in turn to increase the welfare of people. Good management makes a difficult task easier by avoiding wastage of scarce resource. It improves standard of living. It increases the profit which is beneficial to business and society will get maximum output at minimum cost by creating employment opportunities which generate income in hands. Organization comes with new products and researches beneficial for society.

MANAGEMENT AS A PROCESS

As a process, management refers to a series of inter – related functions. It is the process by which management creates, operates and directs purposive organization through systematic, coordinated and co-operated human efforts, George R. Terry, "Management is a distinct process consisting of planning, organizing, actuating and controlling, performed to determine and accomplish stated objective by the use of human beings and other resources".

As a process, management consists of three aspects:

- Management is a social process – Since human factor is most important among the other factors, therefore management is concerned with developing relationship among people. It is the duty of management to make interaction between people – productive and useful for obtaining organizational goals.
- Management is an integrating process – Management undertakes the job of bringing together human physical and financial resources so as to achieve organizational purpose. Therefore, is an important function to bring harmony between various factors.
- Management is a continuous process – It is a never ending process. It is concerned with constantly identifying the problem and solving them by taking adequate steps. It is an on-going process.

MANAGEMENT AS AN ACTIVITY

Like various other activities performed by human beings such as writing, playing, eating, cooking etc, management is also an activity because a manager is one who accomplishes the objectives by directing the efforts of others. Koontz, *"Management is what a manager does"*.

Management as an activity includes:

- *Informational activities*: In the functioning of business enterprise, the manager constantly has to receive and give information orally or in written. A communication link has to be maintained with subordinates as well as superiors for effective functioning of an enterprise.
- *Decisional activities*: Practically all types of managerial activities are based on one or the other types of decisions. Therefore, managers are continuously involved in decisions of different kinds since the decision made by one manager becomes the basis of action to be taken by other managers..
- *Inter-personal activities*: Management involves achieving goals through people. Therefore, managers have to interact with superiors as well as the sub-ordinates. They must maintain good relations with them. The inter-personal activities include with the sub-ordinates and taking care of the problem.

MANAGEMENT AS A DISCIPLINE

Management as a discipline refers to that branch of knowledge which is connected to study of principles and practices of basic administration.

It specifies certain code of conduct to be followed by the manager and also various methods for managing resources efficiently. Management as a discipline specifies certain code of conduct for managers and indicates various methods of managing an enterprise. Management is a course of study which is now formally being taught in the institutes and universities after completing a prescribed course or by obtaining degree or diploma in management, a person can get employment as a manager.

Any branch of knowledge that fulfils following two requirements is known as discipline:

- There must be scholars and thinkers who communicate relevant knowledge through research and publications.
- The knowledge should be formally imparted by education and training programmes.

Since management satisfies both these problems, therefore it qualifies to be a discipline. Though it is comparatively a new discipline but it is growing at a faster pace.

FEATURES OF MANAGEMENT

Management is an activity concerned with guiding human and physical resources such that organizational goals can be achieved.

Nature of management can be highlighted as:

- *Management is Goal-Oriented*: The success of any management activity is accessed by its achievement of the predetermined goals or objective. Management is a purposeful activity. It is a tool which helps use of human and physical resources to fulfill the predetermined goals. For example, the goal of an enterprise is maximum consumer satisfaction by producing quality goods and at reasonable prices. This can be achieved by employing efficient persons and making better use of scarce resources.

- *Management integrates Human, Physical and Financial Resources*: In an organization, human beings work with non-human resources like machines. Materials, financial assets, buildings etc. Management integrates human efforts to those resources. It brings harmony among the human, physical and financial resources.
- *Management is Continuous*: Management is an ongoing process. It involves continuous handling of problems and issues. It is concerned with identifying the problem and taking appropriate steps to solve it. E.g. the target of a company is maximum production. For achieving this target various policies have to be framed but this is not the end. Marketing and Advertising is also to be done. For this policies have to be again framed. Hence this is an ongoing process.
- *Management is all Pervasive*: Management is required in all types of organizations whether it is political, social, cultural or business because it helps and directs various efforts towards a definite purpose. Thus clubs, hospitals, political parties, colleges, hospitals, business firms all require management. When ever more than one person is engaged in working for a common goal, management is necessary. Whether it is a small business firm which may be engaged in trading or a large firm like Tata Iron and Steel, management is required everywhere irrespective of size or type of activity.
- *Management is a Group Activity*: Management is very much less concerned with individual's efforts. It is more concerned with groups. It involves the use of group effort to achieve predetermined goal of management of ABC and Co. is good refers to a group of persons managing the enterprise.

PRINCIPLES OF MANAGEMENT

A principle refers to a fundamental truth. It establishes cause and effect relationship between two or more variables under given situation. They serve as a guide to thought and actions. Therefore, management principles are the statements of fundamental truth based on logic which provides guidelines for managerial decision making and actions.

These principles are derived:

- On the basis of observation and analysis i.e. practical experience of managers.
- By conducting experimental studies.

There are 14 Principles of Management described by Henri Fayol.

- *Division of Labour*:
  - Henry Fayol has stressed on the specialization of jobs.
  - He recommended that work of all kinds must be divided and subdivided and allotted to various persons according to their expertise in a particular area.
  - Subdivision of work makes it simpler and results in efficiency.
  - It also helps the individual in acquiring speed, accuracy in his performance.
  - Specialization leads to efficiency and economy in spheres of business.
- *Party of Authority and Responsibility*:
  - Authority and responsibility are co-existing.
  - If authority is given to a person, he should also be made responsible.
  - In a same way, if anyone is made responsible for any job, he should also have concerned authority.
  - Authority refers to the right of superiors to get exactness from their sub-ordinates whereas responsibility means obligation for the performance of the job assigned.
  - There should be a balance between the two i.e. they must go hand in hand.
  - Authority without responsibility leads to irresponsible Behaviour whereas responsi-bility without authority makes the person ineffective.
- *Principle of One Boss*:
  - A sub-ordinate should receive orders and be accountable to one and only one boss at a time.
  - In other words, a sub-ordinate should not receive instructions from more than one person because
    a. It undermines authority
    b. Weakens discipline
    c. Divides loyalty
    d. Creates confusion
    e. Delays and chaos
    f. Escaping responsibilities
    g. Duplication of work
    h. Overlapping of efforts

- Therefore, dual sub-ordination should be avoided unless and until it is absolutely essential.
- Unity of command provides the enterprise a disciplined, stable and orderly existence.
- It creates harmonious relationship between superiors and sub-ordinates.

• **Unity of Direction**:
- Fayol advocates one head one plan which means that there should be one plan for a group of activities having similar objectives.
- Related activities should be grouped together. There should be one plan of action for them and they should be under the charge of a particular manager.
- This principle efforts of all the members of the organization should be directed towards common goal.
- Without unity of direction, unity of action cannot be achieved.
- In fact, unity of command is not possible without unity of direction.

Basis	Unity of command	Unity of direction
Meaning	It implies that a sub-ordinate should receive orders & instructions from only one boss.	It means one head, one plan for a group of activities having similar objectives.
Nature	It is related to the functioning of personnel's.	It is related to the functioning of departments, or organization as a whole.
Necessity	It is necessary for fixing responsibility of each subordinates.	It is necessary for sound organization.
Advantage	It avoids conflicts, confusion & chaos.	It avoids duplication of efforts and wastage of resources.
Result	It leads to better superior sub-ordinate relationship.	It leads to smooth running of the enterprise.

Therefore it is obvious that they are different from each other but they are dependent on each other i.e. unity of direction is a pre-requisite for unity of command. But it does not automatically comes from the unity of direction.

• *Equity*:
- Equity means combination of fairness, kindness and justice.
- The employees should be treated with kindness and equity if devotion is expected of them.
- It implies that managers should be fair and impartial while dealing with the subordinates.
- They should give similar treatment to people of similar position.
- They should not discriminate with respect to age, caste, sex, religion, relation etc.
- Equity is essential to create and maintain cordial relations between the managers and sub-ordinate.

- But equity does not mean total absence of harshness.
- Fayol was of opinion that, "at times force and harshness might become necessary for the sake of equity".

- *Order*:
  - This principle is concerned with proper and systematic arrangement of things and people.
  - Arrangement of things is called material order and placement of people is called social order.
  - Material order- There should be safe, appropriate and specific place for every article and every place to be effectively used for specific activity and commodity.
  - Social order- Selection and appointment of most suitable person on the suitable job. There should be a specific place for every one and everyone should have a specific place so that they can easily be contacted whenever need arises.
- *Discipline*:
  - Fayol, "Discipline means sincerity, obedience, respect of authority and observance of rules and regulations of the enterprise".
  - This principle applies that subordinate should respect their superiors and obey their order.
  - It is an important requisite for smooth running of the enterprise.
  - Discipline is not only required on path of subordinates but also on the part of management.
  - Discipline can be enforced if –
    a. There are good superiors at all levels.
    b. There are clear and fair agreements with workers.
    c. Sanctions are judiciously applied.
- *Initiative*:
  - Workers should be encouraged to take initiative in the work assigned to them.
  - It means eagerness to initiate actions without being asked to do so.
  - Fayol advised that management should provide opportunity to its employees to suggest ideas, experiencesand new method of work.
  - It helps in developing an atmosphere of trust and understanding.
  - People then enjoy working in the organization because it adds to their zeal and energy.

- To suggest improvement in formulation and implementation of place.
- They can be encouraged with the help of monetary and non-monetary incentives.

- *Fair Remuneration*:
  - The quantum and method of remuneration to be paid to the workers should be fair, reasonable, satisfactory and rewarding of the efforts.
  - As far as possible it should accord satisfaction to both employer and the employees.
  - Wages should be determined on the basis of cost of living, work assigned, financial position of the business, wage rate prevailing etc.
  - Logical and appropriate wage rates and methods of their payment reduce tension and differences between workers and management creates harmonious relationship and pleasing atmosphere of work.
  - Fayol also recommended provision of other benefits such as free education, medical and residential facilities to workers.
- *Stability of Tenure*:
  - Fayol emphasized that employees should not be moved frequently from one job position to another i.e. the period of service in a job should be fixed.
  - Therefore employees should be appointed after keeping in view principles of recruitment and selection but once they are appointed their services should be served.
  - Fayol. "Time is required for an employee to get used to a new work and succeed to doing it well but if he is removed before that he will not be able to render worthwhile services".
  - As a result, the time, effort and money spent on training the worker will go waste.
  - Stability of job creates team spirit and a sense of belongingness among workers which ultimately increase the quality as well as quantity of work.
- *Scalar Chain*:
  - Fayol defines scalar chain as 'The chain of superiors ranging from the ultimate authority to the lowest".
  - Every orders, instructions, messages, requests, explanation etc. has to pass through Scalar chain.
  - But, for the sake of convenience and urgency, this path can be cut shirt and this short cut is known as Gang Plank.

– A Gang Plank is a temporary arrangement between two different points to facilitate quick and easy communication as explained below:

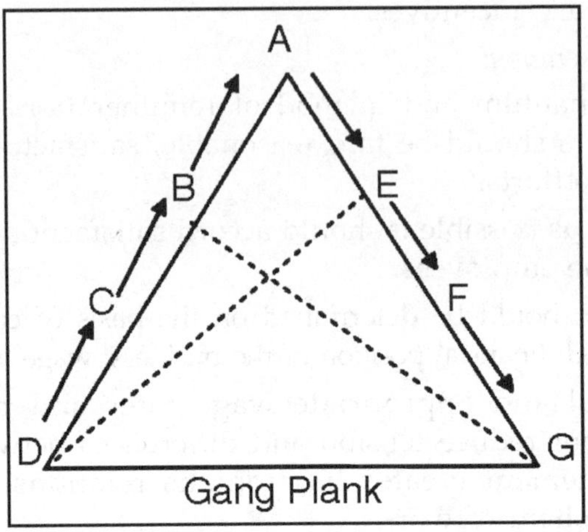

If D has to communicate with G he will first send the communication upwards with the help of C, B to A and then downwards with the help of E and F to G which will take quite some time and by that time, it may not be worth therefore a gang plank has been developed between the two.

– Gang Plank clarifies that management principles are not rigid rather they are very flexible. They can be moulded and modified as per the requirements of situations

- *Sub-Ordination of Individual Interest to General Interest*:
  – An organization is much bigger than the individual it constitutes therefore interest of the undertaking should prevail in all circumstances.
  – As far as possible, reconciliation should be achieved between individual and group interests.
  – But in case of conflict, individual must sacrifice for bigger interests.
  – In order to achieve this attitude, it is essential that.
    a. Employees should be honest and sincere.
    b. Proper and regular supervision of work.
    c. Reconciliation of mutual differences and clashes by mutual agreement. For example, for change of location of plant, for change of profit sharing ratio, etc.
- *Espirit De' Corps*:
  – It refers to team spirit i.e. harmony in the work groups and mutual understanding among the members.

- Spirit De' Corps inspires workers to work harder.
- Fayol cautioned the managers against dividing the employees into competing groups because it might damage the moral of the workers and interest of the undertaking in the long run.
- To inculcate Espirit De' Corps following steps should be undertaken
  a. There should be proper co-ordination of work at all levels
  b. Subordinates should be encouraged to develop informal relations among themselves.
  c. Efforts should be made to create enthusiasm and keenness among subordinates so that they can work to the maximum ability.
  d. Efficient employees should be rewarded and those who are not up to the mark should be given a chance to improve their performance.
  e. Subordinates should be made conscious of that whatever they are doing is of great importance to the business and society.
- He also cautioned against the more use of Britain communication to the subordinates i.e. face to face communication should be developed. The managers should infuse team spirit and belongingness. There should be no place for misunderstanding. People then enjoy working in the organization and offer their best towards the organization.

- *Centralization and De-Centralization*:
  - Centralization means concentration of authority at the top level. In other words, centralization is a situation in which top management retains most of the decision making authority.
  - Decentralization means disposal of decision making authority to all the levels of the organization. In other words, sharing authority downwards is decentralization.
  - Fayol, "Degree of centralization or decentrali-zation depends on no. of factors like size of business, experience of superiors, dependa-bility and ability of subordinates etc.
  - Anything which increases the role of subordinate is decentralization and anything which decreases it is centralization.
  - Fayol suggested that absolute centralization or decentralization is not feasible. An organization should strike to achieve a lot between the two.

DEFINITION OF ACCOUNTING

Accounting is the language of business. It is a standard set of rules for measuring a firm's financial performance.

Assessing a company's financial performance is important for many groups, including:

- The firm's officers
- Investors
- Lenders
- General public

Standard financial statements serve as a yardstick of communicating financial performance to the general public.

For example, monthly sales volumes released by McDonald's Corp. provide both its managers and the general public with an opportunity to assess the company's financial performance across major geographic segments

IMPORTANCE OF ACCOUNTING

MAKING CORPORATE DECISIONS

Suppose a telecom company is looking to acquire a regional company to boost its presence in that region. There are several potential targets that fit the bill.

How does this company determine which of these targets, if any, would make a good acquisition candidate?

MAKING INVESTMENT DECISIONS

A mutual fund is looking to invest in several diverse technology companies— Microsoft, Oracle, and Intel. How does this mutual fund determine in which of these targets it should make an investment?

ACCOUNTING FACILITATES CORPORATE AND INVESTMENT DECISIONS

Accounting, the standard language by which such financial information can be assessed and compared, is fundamental to making these decisions.

USES OF ACCOUNTING

Accounting is used by a variety of organizations, from the federal government to nonprofit organizations to small businesses to corporations. As suggested, be discussing accounting rules as they pertain to publicly traded companies.

Accounting attempts to standardize financial information, and like any language, follows rules and regulations. What are these accounting rules, how are they established, and by whom?

Exhibit | Who Uses Aoccounting?

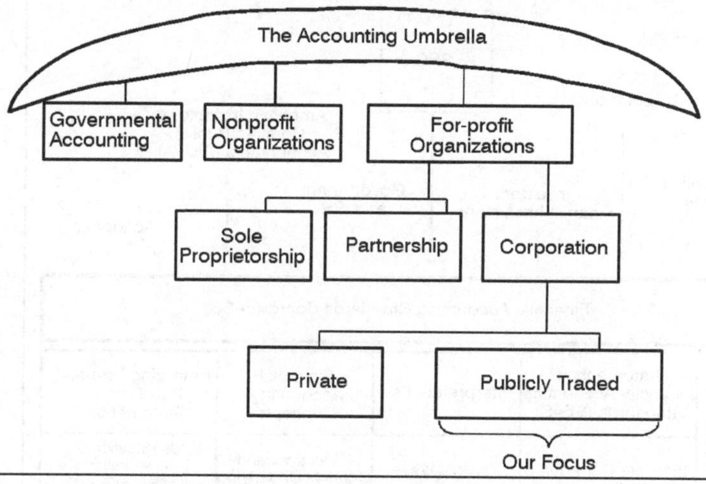

U.S. ACCOUNTING REGULATIONS

GENERALLY ACCEPTED ACCOUNTING PRINCIPLES

In the United States, a governmental agency called the Securities and Exchange Commission authorizes the Financial Accounting Standards Board to determine U.S. accounting rules. FASB communicates these rules through the issuance of Statements of Financial Accounting Standards. These statements make up the body of U.S. accounting rules known as the Generally Accepted Accounting Principles. These rules have been developed to provide guidelines for financial accounting in order to ensure that businesses present their financial information on a fair, consistent, and straightforward basis. Financial statements of U.S. companies must be prepared according to U.S. GAAP.

INTERNATIONAL ACCOUNTING REGULATIONS

Up to now, we have discussed accounting regulations and the bodies that oversee them in the United States. But what about companies that must answer to the accounting regulations of other countries? Fortunately, there has been unprecedented convergence between the accounting standards for the United States and other countries over the last 30 years. Here is a brief recap of the history of this convergence.

In 1973, the International Accounting Standards Committee was founded by accountancy bodies in Australia, Canada, France, Germany, Ireland, Japan, Mexico, the Netherlands, the United Kingdom, and the United States, with the goal of developing global accounting standards.

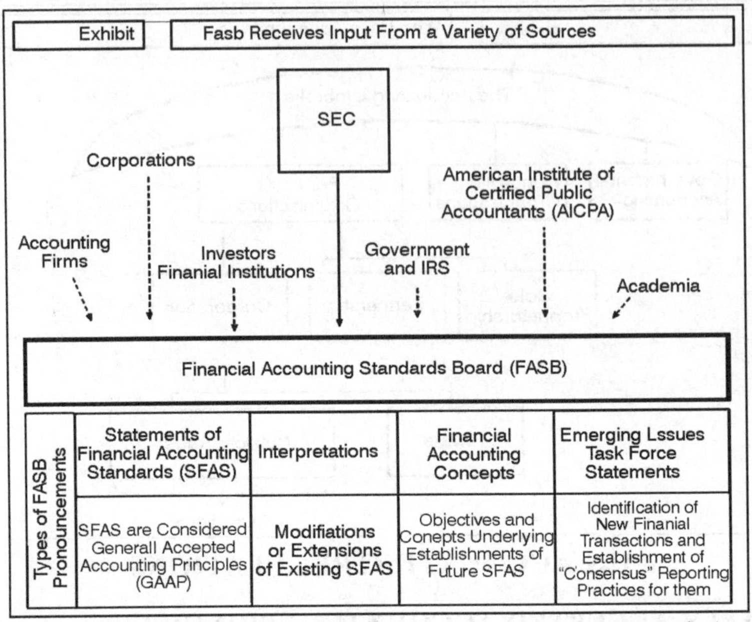

In 2001, the IASC was replaced by the International Accounting Standards Board, an independent entity based in London, in order to oversee the continued convergence of global accounting standards. IASB comprises 14 board members appointed by the Trustees of the IASC Foundation, a parent organization. IASB has the sole responsibility of developing International Financial Reporting Standards.

In 2005, all EU countries adopted IFRS. In addition, accounting standards for many countries outside of Europe, including Japan, are largely equivalent to IFRS.

4

Short-Run Planning and Control: Responsible Data Management in Research

Short-run management decisions differ in a number of respects from long-run decisions. Long-run decisions generally involve selection of courses of action that extend over perhaps many years, such as introducing a new product line. Those courses of action, once selected, require controlled implementa-tion. The latter constitutes management's concern in the short run.

Short-run management objectives are therefore typically derived from the implementation requirements of long-run programs, projects, and product lines that management has selected.

Short-run management decisions are constrained by all of the factors that limit long-run courses of action. In addition, further limitations are imposed on short-run decisions by the specific long-run courses of action that have been selected. For instance, current production volume is limited not only by the available supply of labor (a largely externally imposed constraint) but also by factory capacity, the result of past capital-budgeting decisions.

THE SHORT-RUN MANAGEMENT DECISION CYCLE

Short-run management decisions have two important distinguishing features:

- They are usually oriented toward a period of activity, and
- A distinct pattern of decisions is usually repeated each period (along with decisions necessitated by previously unanticipated developments).

Periodicity of Short-run Decisions

The periodicity of short-run decisions is a result of their relationship to long-run courses of action that have been decided upon. Since the long-run programs and product lines of an enterprise may be quite divergent in nature, time of origination, and life expectancy, there is a need for some unifying scheme to coordinate their implementation and execution. One way of achieving this is to manage all projects and programs on a one-period-at-a-time basis repetitively over the same calendar interval, such as a month, a quarter, or a year. Another reason for periodicity in short-run implementation and execution of long-run courses of action is the need for continuous evaluation and adaptation. Long-run courses of action are adopted in a state of uncertainty based on expectations of achievable results. As long-run programs are implemented and executed, periodic surveillance is necessary to detect results that are significantly different from the expectations on which initial adoption of the programs was based. Furthermore, if needed alterations in a programme are to be made on a timely basis, experience indicates that the surveillance activity should not be left to chance. Therefore surveillance and evaluation of programs is generally formalized as part of a periodic cycle of short-run management decisions.

The Short-run Cycle

The preceding paragraph not only explains the periodicity of short-run management decisions, it also implies that there usually is a pattern of short-run decisions that is repeated with each new period. The pattern may be thought of as a cycle composed of two major phases-an *operations planning* phase and a *control* phase.

Operations Planning:

Operations planning consists of all of the activities engaged in by management to initiate a programme of productive activity for a period, in accordance with established long-run enterprise objectives.

Control

Control consists of those activities engaged in by management to ensure that

- The programme of activities for a period is accomplished to the fullest, and
- Performance deficiencies are detected, their causes are determined, and remedial action is taken.

The cyclical aspect of short-run decisions results from the interrelationship of planning and control activities. Performance evaluation implied in the control phase of the short-run decision cycle is dependent on having a recognized plan with which to compare the results of actual activities. On the other hand, as one period's actual results are materializing and being evaluated, plans are made for the coming period's operations.

To be as realistic as possible, all new plans must incorporate the experience gained from current control activities. Thus there is a sequencing of activities with one period's control efforts based on the prior planning phase and leading into the next planning phase. Similarly, every period's plan is based on prior control experience and provides the basis of evaluation in the coming control phase.

OPERATIONS PLANNING AIDED BY ACCOUNTING INFORMATION

Many kinds of activities are involved in both the operations planning and the control phases of the overall short-run management decision cycle. Both of these phases, however, can best be described as sequences of steps necessary to accomplish the purpose of each phase. Accounting makes significant contributions to both phases. We first describe the planning phase step by step, including descriptions and illustrations of accounting's contributions.

The major steps in the planning phase of the short-run decision cycle that receive detailed attention are the following:

- Goals are assigned to responsibility centers.
- Plans are developed for responsibility centre operations.
- Production plans of responsibility centers are translated into budgets.
- Responsibility centre budgets are combined and coordinated: the master budget.
- Review of the master budget and replanning are undertaken.

Goals Are Assigned to Responsibility Centers

Within the planning phase all requirements of long-run programs, projects, and product lines are first interpreted and then broken down into specific descriptions of output goals or activity requirements corresponding to responsibility centers within the enterprise.

Responsibility centre:

A responsibility centre is any identified organizational unit, within the enterprise, that

- Consists of one or more individuals,
- Is given responsibility for accomplishing a specific enterprise objective, and
- Is given authority (within limits) to accomplish that objective.

As overall output goals for the whole organization are decomposed into contributing goals to be assigned to various major responsibility centers, care is taken to allow for interactions between such centers. For instance, in a typical manufacturing situation, a realistic sales objective must usually be worked out with the sales staff first.

This is followed by an evaluation of inventory requirements to determine whether finished goods on hand should be increased or decreased over the period to correspond to expected increases or decreases in sales.

Only after inventory requirements are known can demands be worked out which must be made on the production department. Production schedules, in turn, are used to derive demands for labor to be scheduled by the personnel department, along with demands for materials and supplies required for production (or for various inventory stocks) to be acquired by the purchasing department. After goals are assigned to the large responsibility centers that perform major functions in the organization, each major responsibility centre further divides and subdivides its goal. The total sales goal is divided by territories and then again by salesmen within territories.

Similarly, the production goal is divided by factories, and then again by departments within the various factories. To illustrate this and other steps in the planning phase of the short-run decision cycle, we introduce a simple but comprehensive example.

Example: National Marketing Corporation (NMC) is a small publicly owned manufacturer of an adult game called Block. Block resembles Monopoly in format but is based on the rules of professional football.

The company entered the field a number of years ago with a capital investment in plant and equipment capacity to produce 120,000 sets of Block per year.

So far Block is NMC's only product. The company's research programme is expected to produce several new games in the next few years.

Like other adult games, Block is expected to have several years of growing sales followed by many years of steady but modest sales. Sales projections in units for the next five years are as follows:

Year	1	2	3	4	5
Block sales	100,000	120,000	90,000	50,000	50,000

All Block sales over the foreseeable future are expected to be at $10 per set. Last year's sales were only 50,000 units. But production was greater than sales by 10,000 units, building inventory up to 20,000-in partial anticipation of the coming year's increase in sales.

The company has followed a policy of ending each year with an inventory of finished goods equal to 20 percent of the next year's sales estimate.

Based on this policy and the sales forecasts of the coming year and the following year, the production schedule for the coming year can be worked out.

National Marketing Corporation Block Production Schedule

Sales (coming year)	100,000 units
Sales (following year)	120,000
Inventory requirements @ 20 per cent of	

following year sales	24,000
Total sales and inventory requirements	124,000
Less present inventory level	20,000
Production requirement (coming year)	104,000 units.

The production of every Block game requires the fabrication of sets of wooden pieces. They are the responsibility of the fabrication department. Each game also requires assembly of a play board and the wooden pieces, along with a set of instructions, into colorful boxes that the company uses to package the game. This is the responsibility of the assembly department. Since the company's operations are not too complicated, it is a simple matter to pass along the same production schedule of 104,000 units to both the fabrication and the assembly department. Both departments consist of only one foreman and a crew of hourly laborers. Hence there is no further subdivision of the production goal. Assuming that production methods, level of labor skill, and quality of materials are all predetermined, the assignment of production goals will determine the materials and labor acquisition requirements placed on the purchasing and personnel departments, respectively.

Plans Are Developed for Responsibility Centre Operations

When goals have been divided and subdivided until the smallest responsibility centers (sometimes individual employees) have been assigned their goals for the coming period, the "top-to-bottom" direction of the planning process stops. The first step in working back toward a total plan for the organization is devising the "best" (least cost) plan of operations for accomplishing the goals assigned to each of the smallest individual responsibility centers. At the lowest responsibility centre levels within an organization, where a goal may be to perform just one or two operations on each product produced, success usually hinges on minimization of costs. Thus the accountant's skill in bringing together cost data and engineering or production data often facilitates the selection of the "best" plan of operations at that level.

Example: Suppose that the management of NMC has not been entirely satisfied with the level of costs incurred in the fabricating department. The primary problem is in the production of the wooden pieces. The fabricating department uses direct material in the form of soft white pine, which machine operators cut into sets of pieces. Besides direct materials and labor, whose use varies proportionately with the number of sets of pieces produced, the process requires certain indirect inputs called overhead items, such as machine time, lubricants, gloves for the workers, heat, light, and power. Some of these items vary proportionately with the numbers of labor hours of activity, averaging $1.50 per hour worked (under good conditions). Other overhead inputs are fixed, amounting to approximately $20,000 *per year* (under good conditions) for the whole fabricating operation, regardless of activity. Presently, the production of one set of pieces requires two feet of 1" by 10" pine board and 35 hours of labor. The engineers feel that there are two basic ways of altering the process for better or worse:

- Change the quality of wood used, or
- Increase or decrease the level of skill of the machine operators (presently all are about medium in skill). Management has rejected lower-quality wood because it might affect sales of the game. But it wishes to consider various combinations of labor skill and either pine (now in use) or birch (a better-quality wood).

Table: Production Possibilities Block Wood Pieces

	Wood Used		*Labor Skill*			*Amount Required per Set*	
Combination	*Pine*	*Birch*	*Low*	*Medium*	*High*	*Wood(ft.)*	*Labor (hrs.)*
1	x		x			2.5	.40
2	x			x		2.0	.35
3	x				x	2.0	.25
4		x	x			2.0	.35
5		x		x		1.5	.30
6		x			x	1.5	.25

But management cannot choose on the basis of physical production estimates alone. Here the accountant serves in a coordinating role by integrating production data with price data to arrive at relevant financial or money flows. In this case, the accountant has sought out the prices of the various quality inputs with the cooperation of purchasing and personnel managers.

One foot of 1" by 10" pine of proper quality can be purchased for $.30, whereas a one-foot length of birch costs $.50. *Including variable overhead* of $1.50 per hour, one hour of low-, medium-, and high-skilled labor costs $4.00, $5.00, and $6.00, respectively. Combining this cost data with the last two columns of the production data from, the accountant arrives at per-unit costs for each production combination.

Table: Costs of Alternate Production Possibilities Block Wood Pieces

Combination	*Input Requirements*	*Input Cost*	*Cost per Set of pieces*		*Wood (ft.)*
Labor (hrs.)	*Wood*		*Labor*		
1	2.5	.40	$.30	$4.00	$2.35
2	2.0	.35	.30	5.00	2.35
3	2.0	.25	.30	6.00	2.10
4	2.0	.35	.50	4.00	2.40
5	1.5	.30	.50	5.00	2.25
6	1.5	.25	.50	6.00	2.25

The best (lowest-cost) combination is combination 3, which requires the use of the same pine wood but higher-skill labor. The engineers had already indicated that a switch in labor force could be made almost immediately by rescheduling employees around the factory plus a small amount of on-the-job training, causing a minimum of layoffs and rehiring. Management adopts the new production plan.

Production Plans Are Translated into Budgets

After the best feasible production plan is determined for each responsibility centre, a financial representation of that plan, called a *budget*, is formulated. Accountants assist operating personnel at all levels in formulating budgets. The process consists of combining

- Individual unit resource requirements, based on a selected plan, with
- The assigned production activity goal. The budget process relies heavily on prediction of cost behaviour patterns.

Example: Based on the "least-cost" production combination selected for the fabrication department the budget for production of 104,000 sets of pieces for Block games for the coming year.

National Marketing Corporation Fabricating Department Budget for 19XX

Expected production level:	104,000 units
Expected costs:	
Direct material:	
2' of 1" by 10" pine @ $.30 per ft.,	
or $.60 X 104,000	$ 62,400
Direct labor:	
.25 hours X 104,000,	
or 26,000 hrs. @ $4.50	117,000
Variable overhead items:	
26,000 direct labor hours @ $1.50	39,000
Total variable costs	$218,400
Fixed overhead costs	20,000
Total expected costs	$238,400

Responsibility Centre Budgets Are Combined and Coordinated: The Master Budget

After a budget or financial plan has been formulated for all of the lowest-level responsibility centers, there follows a process of combining the budgets of those units into budgets for the higher-level responsibility centers of which they are a part.

Example: At NMC, the fabricating department, along with the assembly, purchasing, and personnel departments, all come under the authority of the responsibility centre labeled "manufacturing." To get the total budget for manufacturing, we have to combine the budgets of all of the responsibility centers subordinate to it. The manufacturing budget for NMC for the coming year. Notice that total budgeted costs for the whole manufacturing activity are greater than the sum of the budgeted costs for separate subunits of responsibility within it. This is a common phenomenon in budgeting. The reason, of course, is that some costs incurred at the higher level (like the salary, secretarial help, and supplies for the factory superintendent) are not the responsibility of lower-level managers and, therefore, are not included in their individual budgets.

After the budgets of the various responsibility centers have been combined at successively higher levels, they are finally put together into a coordinated whole called the *master budget*.

Master Budget

A master budget consists of a coordinated set of financial estimates for the budget period, including a balance sheet, an income statement, and whatever other statements are considered useful.

The master budget differs from the budgets of such high-level responsibility areas as sales and manufacturing in that it is not a "summing up" of lower-level budgets. Instead, it allows for the financial consequences of divergent volumes of such major activities as production and sales.

Example: The income statement included in the master budget for NMC for the coming year might look something like the statement. Notice particularly that the statement is an income statement and therefore oriented toward sales activity rather than production activity. Thus total cost of units manufactured is adjusted to get the total *cost of units sold*.

Review of Master Budget and Replanning

Since the master budget integrates the plans for all activities of the enterprise in financial terms, it provides a check on all of the individual plans. The master budget does not pinpoint potential production bottlenecks and other technical planning defects. But it is useful in other ways. For instance, if several areas of responsibility have been careless in seeking optimal plans of operation, the lack of rigor may not be discernible in their individual budgets. But when all budgets are combined in the master budget, the result will be a less-than-satisfactory estimated income figure.

If the master budget produces unsatisfactory results, some form of adaptation is desirable before operations start. The exact form of the adaptation depends on the cause of the disappointing outcome. If it is felt that the cause is lack of rigorous planning on the part of the various responsibility centers or selection of overambitious goals on the part of management, the entire planning process must be reiterated. In the former case, more attention must be devoted to selecting the best (least-cost) plans for each subunit. In the latter case, more realistic goals must be assigned throughout. On the other hand, if the cause of the disappointment is beyond the control of management in the short run, that is, if it is due to some identifiable internal or external constraint, the problem becomes a matter for the long-run consideration of management; the initial plan of operation, though disappointing, is not necessarily abandoned—unless adaptation could lead to a better plan *under the circumstances*.

Control of Operations Through Accounting Information

Once management has arrived at a satisfactory set of operating plans for a period, control activity takes over. The scope of control activities encompasses virtually every effort made by management to ensure that accepted plans are executed to the fullest. Because most control activity is preventive it goes on more continuously than short-run planning, which is distinctly cyclical.

Control of operations includes all of the following types of activities to some degree:

- Organizational control
- Standard conditions and procedures for operations and related cost standards
- Selecting, training, informing, and motivating employees
- Performance measurement, evaluation, and remedial action

Although accountants become heavily involved as information specialists only in the second and the fourth activity, all of the activities tend to blend together. They interact in achieving the purpose of control. We therefore comment below on each kind of activity in turn. Special attention is given to points of substantial accounting contributions.

Organizational Control

The organizational aspects of control are simple in principle but often difficult to apply. Essentially, organizational control means creating recognized lines of authority and responsibility throughout the business enterprise. If plans are to be carried out properly, it is imperative that some individual within the organization be responsible for every activity included in the plans. It is equally imperative that the individual responsible for a particular activity have sufficient authority to accomplish his or her goal. But organizational control is also a matter of balance and coordination. Obviously, no single segment of the enterprise should pursue success in its own activities in such a way as to restrict other segments from accomplishing their goals according to plan.

Two important techniques of organizational control are

- Built-in redundancy, and
- Separation of duties in certain areas susceptible to serious malfunction. Redundancy means that more than one individual is able to perform key functions. Even though only one individual may be given responsibility for a specific function at any given time, the other qualified individual is available if an emergency arises.

He or she may also notice impending difficulties that escape the attention of the person with primary responsibility.

Separation of duties is another label for building in "checks and balances." In a business enterprise, separation of duties takes such forms as assigning one individual the responsibility of recording all cash receipts from customers (to reduce respective account balances), while another individual counts the customers' checks and makes the bank deposits. Neither individual is given control of both the records and the cash. This tends to ensure accuracy, and in the absence of a conspiracy of at least two employees, protects against misappropriations of enterprise resources.

Standard Conditions and Procedures for Operations and Related Cost Standards

Although the input requirements (and their costs) of any given plan of operations largely determine its desirability, many more factors determine whether a given plan can be successfully implemented and executed. Two things that embody these "other factors" are

- Well-conceived sets of standard conditions and procedures for combining input resources to achieve the desired output at the lowest cost, and
- Sets of standard input costs which characterize the level of resource sacrifice achievable through use of standard operating conditions and procedures. The former serve as guides to action for employees; the latter serve both as goals to be striven for and as a basis for evaluating actual employee performance.

To see the importance of a set of standard or recommended conditions and procedures to the success of an operation, think of the features that make up a good recipe in cooking. A list of ingredients and quantities, by itself, is usually inadequate. Without instructions on how to combine the ingredients, and in what order, the outcome of any given attempt at preparation is likely to be disastrous. The same is true of most productive activity, particularly manufacturing activity calling for specific product outputs while utilizing limited resource inputs.

To ensure success of any plan of operations, appropriate methods must be worked out in advance. As weaknesses become apparent, these methods should be corrected. Over time, the effect will be to continually move each operation in the enterprise toward its simplest, safest, lowest cost, and most easily learned form. This means that not only will the goal of low cost be achieved over the long run, but in any given period the likelihood is minimal that planned activities will go seriously awry.

Earlier we noted that the selection of a best plan of operations is usually based on the *expected* costs of production, employing that plan. But the expected costs of production under a particular plan may not be the same as the *standard costs* of production under the same plan.

Standard Cost

Standard cost is the dollar amount of sacrifice associated with consumption of input resources when standard operating conditions and procedures are followed completely. Estimated costs will differ from (usually exceed) standard costs whenever management expects that standard conditions and methods will not be achieved at all times. But, although management may not expect its employees to perform consistently according to standard procedures in a given planning period, standard cost is relevant for control purposes. If standard procedures are attainable by reasonably competent and conscientious employees, then the standard cost level of efficiency ought to be held out as a goal that employees should strive for and against which their performance may be fairly compared.

EXAMPLE: The important distinction between estimated and standard costs for an operation, reconsider the National Marketing Corporation case. Recall that in planning the activity of the fabricating department for the coming budget period, one of six possible combinations of material and labor skill was chosen on the grounds that it had the lowest expected cost. The combination selected was *expected* to consume two feet of pine board at $.30 per foot and.25 hours of highly skilled labor at $6.00 per hour ($4.50 labor; $1.50 variable overhead) for a variable cost per unit of output of $2.10.

Now, it is likely that if all the standard procedures in the fabrication operation were followed to the letter, a lower level of cost per unit could be achieved with the combination of material and labor skill selected. We can realistically assume, for instance, that if everything goes according to standard engineering design of the operation, only 1.9 feet of wood and.24 hours of labor would be required to complete each unit. Thus, standard cost for each unit of output is (1.9 × $.30) + (.24 × $6.00) = $2.01. Provided the standard engineering design of the operation is actually achievable by reasonably motivated and industrious employees, this standard cost, not the estimated cost of $2.10, ought to be the goal for which employees should be striving. In addition, actual employee productivity should be measured relative to the achievable standard, not the expected, costs of production. Otherwise some real potential for improved performance may be overlooked.

If standard costs are the proper target and basis for evaluation of employees performing an operation, then why bother with expected costs of production in the first place? The answer is, of course, that a realistic estimate of resource consumption for each responsibility centre is necessary to coordinate planning of the various functions within the enterprise.

Example: In order for the fabricating department of NMC to produce 104,000 sets of Block pieces in the coming period, the purchasing department must acquire the proper amount of materials. If the standard materials quantity per set were used as the basis for the purchasing plans, 197,600 board feet (104,000 × 1.9') of pine lumber would be purchased. But it is realistically expected that actual usage will be 2.0 feet per set, or 208,000 feet in total. A purchasing plan based on standard performance would, therefore, result in a shortage of materials. At expected input levels and with standard materials purchased, actual production might be restricted to 98,800 finished units (197,600 ÷ 2.0), or 5,200 units short of the output goal of the fabricating department.

Thus both estimated costs and standard costs are relevant to short-run management decisions. Estimated costs form the basis for planning. Standard costs are held out as models for employee performance and are established as a basis for performance evaluation-provided the standards are considered reasonably achievable by competent and conscientious employees.

Before leaving the topic of standard procedures and standard costs, an important qualification should be made. Standardization of procedures and costs in and of itself can be harmful as well as beneficial for an organization. If standard procedures and costs become outdated, they may no longer be useful. If standard procedures are too rigid-if they do not allow for variations among employees in physical characteristics, disposition, or tolerance of fatigue-they may not necessarily produce the desired result and may even damage employee morale. In turn this may lead to costly employee turnover. A wise management will not deny latitude or flexibility in operating procedures if the variations adopted by employees result in achievement of output goals at reachable standard costs.

Selecting, Training, Informing and Motivating Employees

Selecting and training employees, and informing them about what is expected of them, are all important aspects of control of operations. Part of the standard or recommended conditions for successful performance of any task within the enterprise is possession of certain qualifications on the part of an employee. To assign a task to an unqualified employee reduces the likelihood of successful performance. It may jeopardize the morale of the employee or perhaps even his physical safety. If an employee is to be qualified to perform a given task, his selection should be based on possession of any innate qualities required for the task. Then the person must become thoroughly acquainted with the demands of the task, and, through training, innate ability should be refined into specific competence for the job. The more successful the enterprise is with respect to selecting and preparing employees, the greater the probability that they will successfully carry out planned operations. Presumably every employee's goal in working for an enterprise is to contribute the most to the satisfaction of personal wants and needs. The purpose of the enterprise in employing a person is to use the person's resources to the fullest in satisfying enterprise goals. The best results for both parties are obtained when there is a maximum of *goal congruence* between the two.

Goal Congruence

Goal congruence is said to exist between an employee and the enterprise (management) if by working in the manner most satisfying to himself or herself, the employee is at the same time most likely to produce desired results for the enterprise.

Clearly it is essential to the success of any plan of operations that the goals of the employees who perform the operations be as congruent as possible with successful performance from the enterprise's point of view. At one time during the development of business management it was assumed that man was a purely economic being, motivated wholly by wealth. Hence it was further assumed that an employee could be induced to perform in any manner desired by management, within his or her physical and mental capability, if a sufficiently high wage or salary was offered. Experience, however, has been largely inconsistent with that theory. It is now widely recognized that human motivation is a much more complex phenomenon. Therefore, *employee motivation* is another aspect of control activity.

Employee Motivation

Employee motivation consists of actions by management taken to provide the conditions, rewards, or other incentives necessary for employees to adopt personal goals that are congruent with enterprise goals (and to conduct themselves accordingly).

To be sure, in most cases *some* employee motivations fall within the realm of economic incentives that are tied directly to a desired level of productivity.

Example Job Shop Machine Company hires machinists on a purely incentive system. The company performs several kinds of machining operations on various metal parts sent to it by its customers. Since Job Shop has a limited number of machines, its profitability depends on its full use of the capacities of the available machines. Rather than pay its machinists on an hourly basis, it pays them a fixed amount for each satisfactory piece of work completed. To maximize their own wages, therefore, the machinists simply produce as many satisfactorily completed pieces per hour as possible, thus maximizing the output (and the revenues) from the machines they operate.

Assuming that all machinists working for Job Shop are primarily interested in maximizing their wages, this sort of "piece-rate" incentive system might work quite effectively in inducing them to maximize output from the machines.

But evidently many factors other than wage incentives are also important in motivating employees. Actually, the possible factors are so numerous that space limitations do not permit exhaustive coverage. We can only list several kinds that seem to influence employee motivation:

- Employees seem to relate to small, informal groups of fellow employees and to be influenced by the values of those groups, as well as by the policies and incentives offered by management.

- Some employees seem to thrive in very authoritarian environments, while others seem to chafe under an authoritarian management.
- Some employees are challenged to excel by very high performance standards, while others may become frustrated or despondent because of the seeming impossibility of ever succeeding when such high standards are set.
- Many employees respond more favorably to standard methods and costs if they have participated in devising the methods and therefore accept the standard cost levels as "achievable" (fair) standards for measuring their performance.

The list could go on and on. And the reader can no doubt add to the list as well by imagining what things he or she would respond to favorably or unfavorably in various types of job situations.

Not only is our list incomplete, but knowledge about human motivation is still so inadequate that it is difficult to predict how various individuals will respond to the many different incentives that management may offer. It is for this reason that both practicing and academic accountants are turning more and more to behavioural sciences for relevant insights.

Performance Measurement, Evaluation, and Remedial Action

For ensuring the success of any plan of operations, the old adage "An ounce of prevention is worth a pound of cure" is very appropriate. But management cannot anticipate every problem in advance of implementing the plans for a given budget period. Periodic surveillance and adjustment of operations are also necessary and important parts of management's control activities. They are control activities to which accounting contributes significantly. Because control activities are costly in the sense that they consume scarce management resources and perhaps employee time that would otherwise be devoted to production, the concept of *management by exception* has evolved.

Management by Exception

Management by exception is the process of detecting and devoting remedial attention to only those facilities, employees, and operations that are not performing according to plan. The great advantage of management by exception is that time and efforts are not wasted on operations that are performing satisfactorily. But management by exception implies that management can locate trouble spots without detailed on-the-spot review of every responsibility center's activities. To do this, management typically relies on two sources. The first source and, indeed, the first line of defence and correction, is the employee. A well-selected, well-trained, and well-motivated employee who understands the standard conditions and procedures for his operation will detect and correct many problems directly. Furthermore, he will seek help in correcting problems that are seemingly beyond his immediate control, thus bringing them to the attention of management. Management's second source for detecting performance problems lies in performance reporting systems.

Performance Reporting Systems

Performance reporting systems are formal information systems for periodically gathering data on actual production activities, comparing actual data with standard performance, and thereby highlighting problem areas for management attention. Formal performance reporting is conducted on either a physical-data or a cost-data basis. The advantage of physical data, like quantities of material and labor consumed, is that they are stated in terms of the things that employees manipulate directly during operations. But a possibly greater comparative advantage of cost data is that they pinpoint problems in various operations in uniform (money) terms. This may have relatively greater economic significance to both management and employees.

Example: An employee working with expensive material has not been following standard procedures for his task. The result is that he has been *using 5 percent less of his time* per unit of output while he has been *using 5 percent more materials* than standard. The trade-off may seem reasonable to him when stated in percentages of physical inputs. But he may be shocked at the results on a cost basis if, for instance, standard material costs per unit of output are $100 while standard labor input is one hour at $5 per hour. What seems to be a one-for-one trade-off in input percentage utilization is really a twenty-to-one cost trade-off. Formal performance reporting based on cost data usually falls within the special area of expertise of the accountant. As with other contributions of accounting for management decisions, performance reporting on a cost (or money) basis involves association of costs (and revenues) with various kinds of real economic activities, such as the consumption of resources in production. Cost behaviour patterns are therefore applicable to performance reporting, just as they are applicable to other major managerial accounting contributions. One reason that cost behaviour patterns are a valuable tool for performance reporting is that it is useful to divide performance reporting into two major measures of performance called *effectiveness* and *efficiency*.

Effectiveness

Effectiveness is the degree to which a particular output or activity goal has been achieved.

Efficiency

Efficiency refers to the inputs consumed (measured in quantities or costs) *for a given level of output*.

Example: Suppose that the fabricating department actually completed 100,000 sets of pieces. It would be judged efficient if it incurred costs *less than or equal to* the standard input costs for 100,000 units; inefficient if it incurred more than standard costs *for that level of output*. Whereas effectiveness is measured against a goal that is set in advance, efficiency is measured with respect to actual output, which is not known until a particular performance period is over. Thus accounting performance reporting, which is mainly oriented toward measuring efficiency, must be flexible. The source of that flexibility is the use of cost behaviour patterns. Relying on cost behaviour patterns that have been determined in advance, accountants can construct standard cost levels for *actual* levels of output immediately after those levels are known. Accounting performance reporting usually follows these steps:

- As operations progress during a reporting period, quantities and costs of resources used in production are recorded for each responsibility centre.
- At the end of the reporting period, a performance report is prepared for each responsibility centre on which actual costs of production are compared with standard costs *for the achieved level of output*, and variances are noted.
- Variances are analyzed to highlight the nature of inefficiencies.
- Significant variances are investigated to determine the cause and appropriate action.

Table: National Marketing Corporation Fabricating Department Performance Report

Planned output: 104,000 units			
Actual output: 100,000 units			
Level of effectiveness: approximately 96%			
Cost Categories	**Standard Cost**	**Actual Costs**	**Variances**
Materials at standard	$ 57,000	$ 62,000	$ 5,000 (U)
$30 × 1.9' × 100,000 sets			
Labor at standard	108,000	119,600	11,600 (U)
$4.50/hr. × .24 hrs. × 100,000 sets			
Variable overhead (standard)	36,000	38,000	2,000 (U)
$1.50/hr. × .24 hrs. × 100,000 sets			
Fixed overhead	28,000	26,000	2,000(F)
Totals	$229,000	$245,600	$16,600 (U)
	======	======	=======

Before management investigates the causes of certain of the variances that require attention, further insights can usually be gained from analysis of the nature of variable cost variances.

The level of *actual variable* costs is usually a function of two influences, the *quantity* of the variable input used and the average *price* paid per unit used.

Thus, variable cost variances can be due to either:

- Differences between standard and actual prices or rates paid (called price, rate, or spending variances) or
- Differences between standard and actual quantities used to achieve the actual level of output (called usage or efficiency variances).

Example: Suppose that we have the additional information (besides total actual cost of materials used) that the fabricating department used an average of 2.0 feet of wood or 200,000 board feet in total to produce its output of 100,000 sets of pieces. Now we can separate the total unfavorable material cost variance of $5,000 into two parts. We recall that the total cost of 100,000 units at standard input quantity and standard price is $57,000.

By multiplying the actual materials usage of 200,000 board feet by the standard price of $.30 per foot, we find that if all wood actually used in production were purchased at standard prices, actual cost would have been $60,000.

This means that the variance due only to excess usage of wood is $3,000(U) or ($60,000 - $57,000). Now, since the $60,000 figure represents the actual quantity of wood used, times the standard price, it differs from actual cost of wood used only insofar as actual prices paid differed from standard prices. Subtracting the $60,000 from the actual cost of $62,000 gives a price variance of $2,000(U). These calculations are summarized below:

Standard cost of material	$3,000(U)
1.9' × 100,000 units × $30 = $57,000	Usage variance
Standard cost of actual material used	$2,000(U)
200,000 feet × $30 = $60,000	price variance
Actual cost of materials used	
(from supplier invoices) = $62,000	

The same reasoning as that used in the above example is applicable to other variable inputs besides material. The analysis of variable cost variances helps to focus management's attention on possible causes responsible for nonstandard performance even before costly investigations are begun.

Once a significant performance variance is noted and it is determined that it should be investigated, management first consults with the individual who is responsible for the activity that is not measuring up to standard.

Frequently it will be found that the cause for the off-standard performance has already been discovered and eliminated. If it has not, the investigation will start with those most familiar with and most responsible for the troublesome activity. In any case, performance reporting's role will have ended.

The solution to problems highlighted by the performance report will come from one of the other three types of control activities outlined above or from revising plans and standards for the next period. Those problems that do not have satisfactory short-run solutions become inputs to long-run decision activities of management. In this fashion, management can strive continually for an improvement of overall enterprise performance.

5

Role of Marketing Research

AN OVERVIEW

Managers need information in order to introduce products and services that create value in the mind of the customer. But the perception of value is a subjective one, and what customers value this year may be quite different from what they value next year. As such, the attributes that create value cannot simply be deduced from common knowledge. Rather, data must be collected and analyzed. The goal of marketing research is to provide the facts and direction that managers need to make their more important marketing decisions.

To maximize the benefit of marketing research, those who use it need to understand the research process and its limitations.

MARKETING RESEARCH VS. MARKET RESEARCH

These terms often are used interchangeably, but technically there is a difference. *Market research* deals specifically with the gathering of information about a market's size and trends. *Marketing research* covers a wider range of activities. While it may involve market research, marketing research is a more general systematic process that can be applied to a variety of marketing problems.

VALUE OF INFORMATION

Information can be useful, but what determines its real value to the organization?

In general, the value of information is determined by:

- The ability and willingness to act on the information.
- The accuracy of the information.
- The level of indecisiveness that would exist without the information.
- The amount of variation in the possible results.
- The level of risk aversion.
- The reaction of competitors to any decision improved by the information.
- The cost of the information in terms of time and money.

MARKETING RESEARCH PROCESS

Once the need for marketing research has been established, most marketing research projects involve these steps:

1. Define the problem
2. Determine research design
3. Identify data types and sources
4. Design data collection forms and questionnaires
5. Determine sample plan and size
6. Collect the data
7. Analyze and interpret the data
8. Prepare the research report

PROBLEM DEFINITION

The decision problem faced by management must be translated into a market research problem in the form of questions that define the information that is required to make the decision and how this information can be obtained. Thus, the decision problem is translated into a research problem. For example, a decision problem may be whether to launch a new product. The corresponding research problem might be to assess whether the market would accept the new product. The objective of the research should be defined clearly. To ensure that the true decision problem is addressed, it is useful for the researcher to outline possible scenarios of the research results and then for the decision maker to formulate plans of action under each scenario. The use of such scenarios can ensure that the purpose of the research is agreed upon before it commences.

RESEARCH DESIGN

Marketing research can classified in one of three categories:

- Exploratory research
- Descriptive research
- Causal research

These classifications are made according to the objective of the research. In some cases the research will fall into one of these categories, but in other cases different phases of the same research project will fall into different categories.

- *Exploratory research* has the goal of formulating problems more precisely, clarifying concepts, gathering explanations, gaining insight, eliminating impractical ideas, and forming hypotheses. Exploratory research can be performed using a literature search, surveying certain people about their experiences, focus groups, and case studies. When surveying people, exploratory research studies would not try to acquire a representative sample, but rather, seek to interview those who are knowledgeable and who might be able to provide insight concerning the relationship among variables. Case studies can include contrasting situations or benchmarking against an organization known for its excellence. Exploratory research may develop hypotheses, but it does not seek to test them. Exploratory research is characterized by its flexibility.

- *Descriptive research* is more rigid than exploratory research and seeks to describe users of a product, determine the proportion of the population that uses a product, or predict future demand for a product. As opposed to exploratory research, descriptive research should define questions, people surveyed, and the method of analysis prior to beginning data collection. In other words, the who, what, where, when, why, and how aspects of the research should be defined. Such preparation allows one the opportunity to make any required changes before the costly process of data collection has begun.

  There are two basic types of descriptive research: longitudinal studies and cross-sectional studies. Longitudinal studies are time series analyses that make repeated measurements of the same individuals, thus allowing one to monitor behavior such as brand-switching. However, longitudinal studies are not necessarily representative since many people may refuse to participate because of the commitment required. Cross-sectional studies sample the population to make measurements at a specific point in time. A special type of cross-sectional analysis is a cohort analysis, which tracks an aggregate of individuals who experience the same event within the same time interval over time. Cohort analyses are useful for long-term forecasting of product demand.
- *Causal research* seeks to find cause and effect relationships between variables. It accomplishes this goal through laboratory and field experiments.

DATA TYPES AND SOURCES

Secondary Data

Before going through the time and expense of collecting primary data, one should check for secondary data that previously may have been collected for other purposes but that can be used in the immediate study. Secondary data may be internal to the firm, such as sales invoices and warranty cards, or may be external to the firm such as published data or commercially available data. The government census is a valuable source of secondary data. Secondary data has the advantage of saving time and reducing data gathering costs. The disadvantages are that the data may not fit the problem perfectly and that the accuracy may be more difficult to verify for secondary data than for primary data. Some secondary data is republished by organizations other than the original source. Because errors can occur and important explanations may be missing in republished data, one should obtain secondary data directly from its source. One also should consider who the source is and whether the results may be biased.

There are several criteria that one should use to evaluate secondary data:

- Whether the data is useful in the research study.
- How current the data is and whether it applies to time period of interest.
- Errors and accuracy - whether the data is dependable and can be verified.
- Presence of bias in the data.
- Specifications and methodologies used, including data collection method, response rate, quality and analysis of the data, sample size and sampling technique, and questionnaire design.
- Objective of the original data collection.
- Nature of the data, including definition of variables, units of measure, categories used, and relationships examined.

Primary Data

Often, secondary data must be supplemented by primary data originated specifically for the study at hand.

Some common types of primary data are:

- Demographic and socioeconomic characteristics
- Psychological and lifestyle characteristics
- Attitudes and opinions
- *Awareness and knowledge*: For example, brand awareness
- *Intentions*: For example, purchase intentions. While useful, intentions are not a reliable indication of actual future behavior.
- *Motivation*: A person's motives are more stable than his/her behavior, so motive is a better predictor of future behavior than is past behavior.
- Behavior

Primary data can be obtained by communication or by observation. Communication involves questioning respondents either verbally or in writing. This method is versatile, since one needs only to ask for the information; however, the response may not be accurate. Communication usually is quicker and cheaper than observation. Observation involves the recording of actions and is performed by either a person or some mechanical or electronic device. Observation is less versatile than communication since some attributes of a person may not be readily observable, such as attitudes, awareness, knowledge, intentions, and motivation. Observation also might take longer since observers may have to wait for appropriate events to occur, though observation using scanner data might be quicker and more cost effective. Observation typically is more accurate than communication. Personal interviews have an interviewer bias that mail-in questionnaires do not have. For example, in a personal interview the respondent's perception of the interviewer may affect the responses.

QUESTIONNAIRE DESIGN

The questionnaire is an important tool for gathering primary data. Poorly constructed questions can result in large errors and invalidate the research data, so significant effort should be put into the questionnaire design. The questionnaire should be tested thoroughly prior to conducting the survey.\

MEASUREMENT SCALES

Attributes can be measured on nominal, ordinal, interval, and ratio scales:

- Nominal numbers are simply identifiers, with the only permissible mathematical use being for counting. Example: social security numbers.
- Ordinal scales are used for ranking. The interval between the numbers conveys no meaning. Median and mode calculations can be performed on ordinal numbers. Example: class ranking
- Interval scales maintain an equal interval between numbers. These scales can be used for ranking and for measuring the interval between two numbers. Since the zero point is arbitrary, ratios cannot be taken between numbers on an interval scale; however, mean, median, and mode are all valid. Example: temperature scale
- Ratio scales are referenced to an absolute zero values, so ratios between numbers on the scale are meaningful. In addition to mean, median, and mode, geometric averages also are valid. Example: weight

VALIDITY AND RELIABILITY

The validity of a test is the extent to which differences in scores reflect differences in the measured characteristic. Predictive validity is a measure of the usefulness of a measuring instrument as a predictor. Proof of predictive validity is determined by the correlation between results and actual behavior. Construct validity is the extent to which a measuring instrument measures what it intends to measure.

Reliability is the extent to which a measurement is repeatable with the same results. A measurement may be reliable and not valid. However, if a measurement is valid, then it also is reliable and if it is not reliable, then it cannot be valid. One way to show reliability is to show stability by repeating the test with the same results.

ATTITUDE MEASUREMENT

Many of the questions in a marketing research survey are designed to measure attitudes. Attitudes are a person's general evaluation of something.

Customer attitude is an important factor for the following reasons:

- Attitude helps to explain how ready one is to do something.
- Attitudes do not change much over time.
- Attitudes produce consistency in behavior.
- Attitudes can be related to preferences.

Attitudes can be measured using the following procedures:

- *Self-reporting*: Subjects are asked directly about their attitudes. Self-reporting is the most common technique used to measure attitude.
- *Observation of behavior*: Assuming that one's behavior is a result of one's attitudes, attitudes can be inferred by observing behavior. For example, one's attitude about an issue can be inferred by whether he/she signs a petition related to it.
- *Indirect techniques*: Use unstructured stimuli such as word association tests.
- *Performance of objective tasks*: Assumes that one's performance depends on attitude. For example, the subject can be asked to memorize the arguments of both sides of an issue. He/she is more likely to do a better job on the arguments that favor his/her stance.
- *Physiological reactions*: Subject's response to a stimuli is measured using electronic or mechanical means. While the intensity can be measured, it is difficult to know if the attitude is positive or negative.
- *Multiple measures*: A mixture of techniques can be used to validate the findings, especially worthwhile when self-reporting is used.

There are several types of attitude rating scales:

- *Equal-appearing interval scaling*: A set of statements are assembled. These statements are selected according to their position on an interval scale of favorableness. Statements are chosen that has a small degree of dispersion. Respondents then are asked to indicate with which statements they agree.
- *Likert method of summated ratings*: A statement is made and the respondents indicate their degree of agreement or disagreement on a five point scale.
- *Semantic differential scale*: A scale is constructed using phrases describing attributes of the product to anchor each end. For example, the left end may state, "Hours are inconvenient" and the right end may state, "Hours are convenient". The respondent then marks one of the seven blanks between the statements to indicate his/her opinion about the attribute.

- *Stapel Scale*: Similar to the semantic differential scale except that
  - Points on the scale are identified by numbers,
  - Only one statement is used and if the respondent disagrees a negative number should marked, and
  - There are 10 positions instead of seven. This scale does not require that bipolar adjectives be developed and it can be administered by telephone.
- *Q-sort technique*: The respondent if forced to construct a normal distribution by placing a specified number of cards in one of 11 stacks according to how desirable he/she finds the characteristics written on the cards.

SAMPLING PLAN

The sampling frame is the pool from which the interviewees are chosen. The telephone book often is used as a sampling frame, but have some shortcomings. Telephone books exclude those households that do not have telephones and those households with unlisted numbers. Since a certain percentage of the numbers listed in a phone book are out of service, there are many people who have just moved who are not sampled. Such sampling biases can be overcome by using random digit dialing. Mall intercepts represent another sampling frame, though there are many people who do not shop at malls and those who shop more often will be over-represented unless their answers are weighted in inverse proportion to their frequency of mall shopping.

In designing the research study, one should consider the potential errors. Two sources of errors are random sampling error and non-sampling error. Sampling errors are those due to the fact that there is a non-zero confidence interval of the results because of the sample size being less than the population being studied. Non-sampling errors are those caused by faulty coding, untruthful responses, respondent fatigue, etc.

There is a tradeoff between sample size and cost. The larger the sample size, the smaller the sampling error but the higher the cost. After a certain point the smaller sampling error cannot be justified by the additional cost.

While a larger sample size may reduce sampling error, it actually may increase the total error. There are two reasons for this effect. First, a larger sample size may reduce the ability to follow up on non-responses. Second, even if there is a sufficient number of interviewers for follow-ups, a larger number of interviewers may result in a less uniform interview process.

DATA COLLECTION

In addition to the intrinsic sampling error, the actual data collection process will introduce additional errors. These errors are called non-sampling errors. Some non-sampling errors may be intentional on the part of the interviewer, who may introduce a bias by leading the respondent to provide a certain response. The interviewer also may introduce unintentional errors, for example, due to not having a clear understanding of the interview process or due to fatigue.

Respondents also may introduce errors. A respondent may introduce intentional errors by lying or simply by not responding to a question. A respondent may introduce unintentional errors by not understanding the question, guessing, not paying close attention, and being fatigued or distracted. Such non-sampling errors can be reduced through quality control techniques.

DATA ANALYSIS - PRELIMINARY STEPS

Before analysis can be performed, raw data must be transformed into the right format. First, it must be edited so that errors can be corrected or omitted. The data must then be coded; this procedure converts the edited raw data into numbers or symbols. A codebook is created to document how the data was coded. Finally, the data is tabulated to count the number of samples falling into various categories. *Simple tabulations* count the occurrences of each variable independently of the other variables. *Cross tabulations,* also known as contingency tables or cross tabs, treats two or more variables simultaneously. However, since the variables are in a two-dimensional table, cross tabbing more than two variables is difficult to visualize since more than two dimensions would be required. Cross tabulation can be performed for nominal and ordinal variables. Cross tabulation is the most commonly utilized data analysis method in marketing research. Many studies take the analysis no further than cross tabulation. This technique divides the sample into sub-groups to show how the dependent variable varies from one subgroup to another. A third variable can be introduced to uncover a relationship that initially was not evident.

CONJOINT ANALYSIS

The conjoint analysis is a powerful technique for determining consumer preferences for product attributes.

HYPOTHESIS TESTING

A basic fact about testing hypotheses is that a hypothesis may be rejected but that the hypothesis never can be unconditionally accepted until all possible evidence is evaluated. In the case of sampled data, the information set cannot be complete. So if a test using such data does not reject a hypothesis, the cease is not necessarily that the hypothesis should be accepted.

The null hypothesis in an experiment is the hypothesis that the independent variable has no effect on the dependent variable. The null hypothesis is expressed as H0. This hypothesis is assumed to be true unless proven otherwise. The alternative to the null hypothesis is the hypothesis that the independent variable does have an effect on the dependent variable. This hypothesis is known as the alternative, research, or experimental hypothesis and is expressed as H1. This alternative hypothesis states that the relationship observed between the variables cannot be explained by chance alone.

There are two types of errors in evaluating a hypotheses:

- *Type I error*: occurs when one rejects the null hypothesis and accepts the alternative, when in fact the null hypothesis is true.
- *Type II error*: occurs when one accepts the null hypothesis when in fact the null hypothesis is false.

Because their names are not very descriptive, these types of errors sometimes are confused. Some people jokingly define a Type III error to occur when one confuses Type I and Type II. To emphasize the difference, it is useful to consider a trial by jury in which the null hypothesis is that the defendant is innocent. If the jury convicts a truly innocent defendant, a Type I error has occurred. If, on the other hand, the jury declares a truly guilty defendant to be innocent, a Type II error has occurred.

Hypothesis testing involves the following steps:

- Formulate the null and alternative hypotheses.
- Choose the appropriate test.
- Choose a level of significance - determine the rejection region.
- Gather the data and calculate the test statistic.
- Determine the probability of the observed value of the test statistic under the null hypothesis given the sampling distribution that applies to the chosen test.
- Compare the value of the test statistic to the rejection threshold.
- Based on the comparison, reject or do not reject the null hypothesis.
- Make the marketing research cease.

In order to analyze whether research results are statistically significant or simply by chance, a test of statistical significance can be run.

TESTS OF STATISTICAL SIGNIFICANCE

The chi-square goodness-of-fit test is used to determine whether a set of proportions have specified numerical values. It often is used to analyze bivariate cross-tabulated data.

Some examples of situations that are well-suited for this test are:

- A manufacturer of packaged products test markets a new product and wants to know if sales of the new product will be in the same relative proportion of package sizes as sales of existing products.
- A company's sales revenue comes from Product A (50%), Product B (30%), and Product C (20%). The firm wants to know whether

recent fluctuations in these proportions are random or whether they represent a real shift in sales.

To use the output of the chi-square function, one uses a chi-square table. To do so, one needs to know the number of degrees of freedom (df). For chi-square applied to cross-tabulated data, the number of degrees of freedom is equal to

(number of columns - 1) (number of rows - 1)

This is equal to the number of categories minus one. The conventional critical level of 0.05 normally is used. If the calculated output value from the function is greater than the chi-square look-up table value, the null hypothesis is rejected.

ANOVA

Another test of significance is the Analysis of Variance (ANOVA) test. The primary purpose of ANOVA is to test for differences between multiple means. Whereas the t-test can be used to compare two means, ANOVA is needed to compare three or more means. If multiple t-tests were applied, the probability of a TYPE I error increases as the number of comparisons increases. One-way ANOVA examines whether multiple means differ. The test is called an F-test. ANOVA calculates the ratio of the variation between groups to the variation within groups . While ANOVA was designed for comparing several means, it also can be used to compare two means. Two-way ANOVA allows for a second independent variable and addresses interaction.

To run a one-way ANOVA, use the following steps:

- Identify the independent and dependent variables.
- Describe the variation by breaking it into three parts - the total variation, the portion that is within groups, and the portion that is between groups . The total variation is the sum of the squares of the differences between each value and the grand mean of all the values in all the groups. The in-group variation is the sum of the squares of the differences in each element's value and the group mean. The variation between group means is the total variation minus the in-group variation.
- Measure the difference between each group's mean and the grand mean.
- Perform a significance test on the differences.
- Interpret the results.

This F-test assumes that the group variances are approximately equal and that the observations are independent. It also assumes normally distributed data; however, since this is a test on means the Central Limit Theorem holds as long as the sample size is not too small. ANOVA is efficient for analyzing data using relatively few observations and can be used with categorical variables. Note that regression can perform a similar analysis to that of ANOVA.

DISCRIMINANT ANALYSIS

Analysis of the difference in means between groups provides information about individual variables, it is not useful for determine their individual impacts when the variables are used in combination. Since some variables will not be independent from one another, one needs a test that can consider them simultaneously in order to take into account their interrelationship. One such test is to construct a linear combination, essentially a weighted sum of the variables. To determine which variables discriminate between two or more naturally occurring groups, discriminant analysis is used. Discriminant analysis can determine which variables are the best predictors of group membership. It determines which groups differ with respect to the mean of a variable, and then uses that variable to predict new cases of group membership. Essentially, the discriminant function problem is a one-way ANOVA problem in that one can determine whether multiple groups are significantly different from one another with respect to the mean of a particular variable.

A discriminant analysis consists of the following steps:

- Formulate the problem.
- Determine the discriminant function coefficients that result in the highest ratio of between-group variation to within-group variation.
- Test the significance of the discriminant function.
- Interpret the results.
- Determine the validity of the analysis.

Discriminant analysis analyzes the dependency relationship, whereas factor analysis and cluster analysis address the interdependency among variables.

FACTOR ANALYSIS

Factor analysis is a very popular technique to analyze interdependence. Factor analysis studies the entire set of interrelationships without defining variables to be dependent or independent. Factor analysis combines variables to create a smaller set of factors. Mathematically, a factor is a linear combination of variables. A factor is not directly observable; it is inferred from the variables. The technique identifies underlying structure among the variables, reducing the number of variables to a more manageable set. Factor analysis groups variables according to their correlation. The *factor loading* can be defined as the correlations between the factors and their underlying variables. A factor loading matrix is a key output of the factor analysis.

	Factor 1	Factor 2	Factor 3
Variable 1			
Variable 2			
Variable 3			
Column's Sum of Squares:			

Each cell in the matrix represents correlation between the variable and the factor associated with that cell. The square of this correlation represents the proportion of the variation in the variable explained by the factor. The sum of the squares of the factor loadings in each column is called an eigenvalue. An eigenvalue represents the amount of variance in the original variables that is associated with that factor. The *communality* is the amount of the variable variance explained by common factors. A rule of thumb for deciding on the number of factors is that each included factor must explain at least as much variance as does an average variable. In other words, only factors for which the eigenvalue is greater than one are used. Other criteria for determining the number of factors include the Scree plot criteria and the percentage of variance criteria. To facilitate interpretation, the axis can be rotated. Rotation of the axis is equivalent to forming linear combinations of the factors. A commonly used rotation strategy is the *varimax* rotation. Varimax attempts to force the column entries to be either close to zero or one.

CLUSTER ANALYSIS

Market segmentation usually is based not on one factor but on multiple factors. Initially, each variable represents its own cluster. The challenge is to find a way to combine variables so that relatively homogenous clusters can be formed. Such clusters should be internally homogenous and externally heterogeneous. Cluster analysis is one way to accomplish this goal. Rather than being a statistical test, it is more of a collection of algorithms for grouping objects, or in the case of marketing research, grouping people. Cluster analysis is useful in the exploratory phase of research when there are no a-priori hypotheses.

Cluster analysis steps:

- Formulate the problem, collecting data and choosing the variables to analyze.
- Choose a distance measure. The most common is the Euclidean distance. Other possibilities include the squared Euclidean distance, city-block distance, Chebychev distance, power distance, and percent disagreement.
- Choose a clustering procedure .
- Determine the number of clusters. They should be well separated and ideally they should be distinct enough to give them descriptive names such as professionals, buffs, etc.
- Profile the clusters.
- Assess the validity of the clustering.

MARKETING RESEARCH REPORT

The format of the marketing research report varies with the needs of the organization.

The report often contains the following sections:

- Authorization letter for the research
- Table of Contents
- List of illustrations
- Executive summary
- Research objectives
- Methodology
- Results
- Limitations
- Ceases and recommendations
- Appendices containing copies of the questionnaires, etc.

CONCLUDING THOUGHTS

Marketing research by itself does not arrive at marketing decisions, nor does it guarantee that the organization will be successful in marketing its products. However, when conducted in a systematic, analytical, and objective manner, marketing research can reduce the uncertainty in the decision-making process and increase the probability and magnitude of success.

ROLE AND LIMITATIONS OF MARKETING RESEARCH

"Marketing research does not make decisions and it does not guarantee success". Marketing managers may seek advice from marketing research specialists, and indeed it is important that research reports should specify alternative courses of action and the probability of success, where possible, of these alternatives. However, it is marketing managers who make the final marketing decision and not the researcher. The second observation, that marketing research does not guarantee success, is simply a recognition of the environment within which marketing takes place. In the fields of science and engineering researchers are often working with deterministic models of the world where $y = f(x)$. That is, x is a necessary and sufficient condition for y to occur. For instance, an increase in pressure is usually necessary and sufficient to bring about a rise in air temperature.

In the social sciences, and this includes marketing and marketing research, the phenomenon under investigation rarely, if ever, lends itself to deterministic modelling. Consider the marketing problem of determining how much to spend on promotion in order to achieve a given market share. The link between promotional expenditure and sales is not so direct as that between pressure and temperature. There are a great many more intervening variables, including: the media used, the effectiveness of the promotional message, the length and frequency of the campaign, not to mention the many dimensions of the product, price and distribution.

Marketing researchers work with probabilistic models of the form:

$$y = f(x_1)..(fx_2)...f(x_n)...$$

This reflects the fact that in order for a target market share to be reached some promotion is *necessary* but will not be *sufficient*, on its own, to achieve the target. Y is a function of a number of variables and the interactions between them. The model is further complicated by the fact that these interactions are themselves often not understood. It is for these reasons that marketing researchers cannot guarantee that decisions based on their information will always prove 'successful'. Rather the best that a competent researcher and a well designed study will be able to offer is a reduction in the amount of uncertainty surrounding the decision.

CHARACTERISTICS OF MARKETING RESEARCH

First, marketing *research is systematic*. Thus systematic planning is required at all the stages of the marketing research process. The procedures followed at each stage are methodologically sound, well documented, and, as much as possible, planned in advance. Marketing research uses the scientific method in that data are collected and analyzed to test prior notions or hypotheses.

Marketing research is *objective*. It attempts to provide accurate information that reflects a true state of affairs. It should be conducted impartially. While research is always influenced by the researcher's research philosophy, it should be free from the personal or political biases of the researcher or the management. Research which is motivated by personal or political gain involves a breach of professional standards. Such research is deliberately biased so as to result in predetermined findings. The motto of every researcher should be, "Find it and tell it like it is." The objective nature of marketing research underscores the importance of ethical considerations.

Marketing research involves the *identification*, collection, analysis, *and dissemination of information*. Each phase of this process is important. We identify or define the marketing research problem or opportunity and then determine what information is needed to investigate it., and inferences are drawn. Finally, the findings, implications and recommendations are provided in a format that allows the information to be used for management decision making and to be acted upon directly. It should be emphasized that marketing research is conducted to assist management in decision making and is not: a means or an end in itself.

COMPARISON WITH OTHER FORMS OF BUSINESS RESEARCH

Other forms of business research include:

- Market research is broader in scope and examines all aspects of a business environment. It asks questions about competitors, market structure, government regulations, economic trends, technological advances, and numerous other factors that make up the business environment. Sometimes the term refers more particularly to the financial analysis of companies, industries, or sectors. In this case, financial analysts usually carry out the research and provide the results to investment advisors and potential investors.

- *Product research*: This looks at what products can be produced with available technology, and what new product innovations near-future technology can develop.
- *Advertising research*: Is a specialized form of marketing research conducted to improve the efficacy of advertising. Copy testing, also known as "pre-testing," is a form of customized research that predicts in-market performance of an ad before it airs, by analyzing audience levels of attention, brand linkage, motivation, entertainment, and communication, as well as breaking down the ad's flow of attention and flow of emotion. Pre-testing is also used on ads still in rough form.

CLASSIFICATION OF MARKETING RESEARCH

Organizations engage in marketing research for two reasons:

1. To identify; and
2. Solve marketing problems.

This distinction serves as a basis for classifying marketing research into problem identification research and problem solving research. Problem identification research is undertaken to help identify problems which are, perhaps, not apparent on the surface and yet exist or are likely to arise in the future. Examples of problem identification research include market potential, market share, brand or company image, market characteristics, sales analysis, short-range forecasting, long range forecasting, and business trends research. Research of this type provides information about the marketing environment and helps diagnose a problem. For example, The findings of problem solving research are used in making decisions which will solve specific marketing problems.

The Stanford Research Institute, on the other hand, conducts an annual survey of consumers that is used to classify persons into homogeneous groups for segmentation purposes. The National Purchase Diary panel maintains the largest diary panel in the United States.

Standardized services are research studies conducted for different client firms but in a standard way. For example, procedures for measuring advertising effectiveness have been standardized so that the results can be compared across studies and evaluative norms can be established. The Starch Readership Survey is the most widely used service for evaluating print advertisements; another well-known service is the Gallup and Robinson Magazine Impact Studies.

These services are also sold on a syndicated basis:

- Customized services offer a wide variety of marketing research services customized to suit a client's specific needs. Each marketing research project is treated uniquely.
- Limited-service suppliers specialize in one or a few phases of the marketing research project. Services offered by such suppliers are classified as field services, coding and data entry, data analysis, analytical services, and branded products. Field services collect data through mail, personal, or telephone interviewing, and firms that specialize in interviewing are called field service organizations. These organizations may range from small proprietary organizations which operate locally to large multinational organizations with WATS line interviewing facilities. Some organizations maintain extensive interviewing facilities across the country for interviewing shoppers in malls.
- Coding and data entry services include editing completed questionnaires, developing a coding plan, and transcribing the data on to diskettes or magnetic tapes for input into the computer. NRC Data Systems provides such services.
- Analytical services include designing and pretesting questionnaires, determining the best means of collecting data, designing sampling plans, and other aspects of the research design. Some complex marketing research projects require knowledge of sophisticated procedures, including specialized experimental designs, and analytical techniques such as conjoint analysis and multidimensional scaling. This kind of expertise can be obtained from firms and consultants specializing in analytical services.
- Data analysis services are offered by firms, also known as tab houses, that specialize in computer analysis of quantitative data such as those obtained in large surveys. Initially most data analysis firms supplied only tabulations and cross tabulations . With the proliferation of software, many firms now have the capability to analyze their own data, but, data analysis firms are still in demand.
- Branded marketing research products and services are specialized data collection and analysis procedures developed to address specific types of marketing research problems. These procedures are patented, given brand names, and marketed like any other branded product.

MARKETING RESEARCH METHODS

Methodologically, marketing research uses the following types of research designs:

- *Based on questioning*: Qualitative marketing research - generally used for exploratory purposes - small number of respondents - not generalizable to the whole population - statistical significance and confidence not calculated - examples include focus groups, in-depth interviews, and projective techniques. Quantitative marketing research - generally used to draw ceases - tests a specific hypothesis - uses random sampling techniques so as to infer from the sample to the population - involves a large number of respondents - examples include surveys and questionnaires. Techniques include choice modelling, maximum difference preference scaling, and covariance analysis.

- *Based on observations*: Ethnographic studies -, by nature qualitative, the researcher observes social phenomena in their natural setting - observations can occur cross-sectionally or longitudinally - examples include product-use analysis and computer cookie traces. Experimental techniques -, by nature quantitative, the researcher creates a quasi-artificial environment to try to control spurious factors, then manipulates at least one of the variables - examples include purchase laboratories and test markets

Researchers often use more than one research design. They may start with secondary research to get background information, then conduct a focus group to explore the issues. Finally they might do a full nation-wide survey in order to devise specific recommendations for the client.

BUSINESS TO BUSINESS MARKET RESEARCH

Business to business (B2B) research is inevitably more complicated than consumer research. The researchers need to know what type of multi-faceted approach will answer the objectives, since seldom is it possible to find the answers using just one method. Finding the right respondents is crucial in B2B research since they are often busy, and may not want to participate. Encouraging them to "open up" is yet another skill required of the B2B researcher. Last, but not least, most business research leads to strategic decisions and this means that the business researcher must have expertise in developing strategies that are strongly rooted in the research findings and acceptable to the client.

There are four key factors that make B2B market research special and different to consumer markets:

- The decision making unit is far more complex in B2B markets than in consumer markets
- B2B products and their applications are more complex than consumer products
- B2B marketers address a much smaller number of customers who are very much larger in their consumption of products than is the case in consumer markets
- Personal relationships are of critical importance in B2B markets.

MARKETING RESEARCH IN SMALL BUSINESSES AND NONPROFIT ORGANIZATIONS

Marketing research does not only occur in huge corporations with many employees and a large budget. Marketing information can be derived by observing the environment of their location and the competitions location. Small scale surveys and focus groups are low cost ways to gather information from potential and existing customers. Most secondary data is available to the public in libraries or on the internet and can be easily accessed by a small business owner.

Here some steps that could do by SME to analyze the market :

- Provide secondary and or primary data ;
- Analyze Macro & Micro Economic data ;
- Implement the marketing mix concept, which is consist of: Place, Price, Product,Promotion, People, Process, Physical Evidence and also Political & social situation to analyze global market situation);
- Analyze market trends, growth, market size, market share, market competition ,etc.;
- Determine market segment, market target, market forecast and market position;
- Formulating market strategy & also investigating the possibility of partnership/ collaboration
- Combine those analysis with the SME's business plan/ business model analysis .

Note as important : Overall analysis is should be based on 6W+1H question.

INTERNATIONAL MARKETING RESEARCH

International Marketing Research follows the same path as domestic research, but there are a few more problems that may arise. Customers in international markets may have very different customs, cultures, and expectations from the same company.

In this case, secondary information must be collected from each separate country and then combined, or compared. This is time consuming and can be confusing. International Marketing Research relies more on primary data rather than secondary information. Gathering the primary data can be hindered by language, literacy and access to technology.

COMMONLY USED MARKETING RESEARCH TERMS

Market research techniques resemble those used in political polling and social science research. Meta-analysis refers to a statistical method of combining data from multiple studies or from several types of studies. Conceptualization means the process of converting vague mental images into definable concepts. Operationalization is the process of converting concepts into specific observable behaviors that a researcher can measure. Precision refers to the exactness of any given measure.

Reliability refers to the likelihood that a given operationalized construct will yield the same results if re-measured. Validity refers to the extent to which a measure provides data that captures the meaning of the operationalized construct as defined in the study. It asks, "Are we measuring what we intended to measure?"

- Applied research sets out to prove a specific hypothesis of value to the clients paying for the research. For example, a cigarette company might commission research that attempts to show that cigarettes are good for one's health. Many researchers have ethical misgivings about doing applied research.
- Sugging forms a sales technique in which sales people pretend to conduct marketing research, but with the real purpose of obtaining buyer motivation and buyer decision-making information to be used in a subsequent sales call.
- Frugging comprises the practice of soliciting funds under the pretense of being a research organization.

CAREERS IN MARKETING RESEARCH

Some of the positions available in marketing research include vice president of marketing research, research director, assistant director of research, project manager, field work director, statistician/data processing specialist, senior analyst, analyst, junior analyst and operational supervisor.

The most common entry-level position in marketing research for people with bachelor's degrees is as operational supervisor. These people are responsible for supervising a well-defined set of operations, including field work, data editing, and coding, and may be involved in programming and data analysis.

Another entry-level position for BBAs is assistant project manager. An assistant project manager will learn and assist in questionnaire design, review field instructions, and monitor timing and costs of studies. In the marketing research industry, however, there is a growing preference for people with master's degrees. Those with MBA or equivalent degrees are likely to be employed as project managers.

A small number of business schools also offer a more specialized Master of Marketing Research degree. An MMR typically prepares students for a wide range of research methodologies and focuses on learning both in the classroom and the field.

The typical entry-level position in a business firm would be junior research analyst or research analyst. The junior analyst and the research analyst learn about the particular industry and receive training from a senior staff member, usually the marketing research manager. The junior analyst position includes a training program to prepare individuals for the responsibilities of a research analyst, including coordinating with the marketing department and sales force to develop goals for product exposure.

The research analyst responsibilities include checking all data for accuracy, comparing and contrasting new research with established norms, and analyzing primary and secondary data for the purpose of market forecasting.

As these job titles indicate, people with a variety of backgrounds and skills are needed in marketing research.

Technical specialists such as statisticians obviously need strong backgrounds in statistics and data analysis. Other positions, such as research director, call for managing the work of others and require more general skills.

To prepare for a career in marketing research, students usually:

- Take all the marketing courses.
- Take courses in statistics and quantitative methods.
- Acquire computer skills.
- Take courses in psychology and consumer behavior.
- Acquire effective written and verbal communication skills.
- Think creatively.

Career ladder in marketing research:

1. *Vice-President of Marketing Research*: This is the senior position in marketing research. The VP is responsible for the entire marketing research operation of the company and serves on the top management team. Sets the objectives and goals of the marketing, research department.
2. *Research Director*: Also a senior position, the director has the overall responsibility for the development and execution of all the marketing research projects.
3. *Assistant Director of Research*: Serves as an administrative assistant to the director and supervises some of the other marketing research staff members.
4. *Project Manager*: Has overall responsibility for design, implementation, and management of research projects.
5. *Statistician/Data Processing Specialist*: Serves as an expert on theory and application of statistical techniques. Responsibilities include experimental design, data processing, and analysis.
6. *Senior Analyst*: Participates in the development of projects and directs the operational execution of the assigned projects. Works closely with the analyst, junior analyst, and other personnel in developing

the research design and data collection. Prepares the final report. The primary responsibility for meeting time and cost constraints rests with the senior analyst.

7. *Analyst*: Handles the details involved in executing the project. Designs and pretests the questionnaires and conducts a preliminary analysis of the data.
8. *Junior Analyst*: Handles routine assignments such as secondary data analysis, editing and coding of questionnaires, and simple statistical analysis.
9. *Field Work Director*: Responsible for the selection, training, supervision, and evaluation of interviewers and other field workers.

6

Role of Advertising Research

The rise of scanner data with its ability to measure the short-term effects of promotions, the growing American corporate interest in profits this quarter , and the rapidly increasing media alternatives to the traditional "big three" are all working in concert to diminish the perceived value of traditional advertising in the packaged goods categories. The companies with a longer-term perspective, however, will win the marketing wars through the effective use of advertising in the major media. This is not to say that other media cannot play an important supporting or supplemental role, for they certainly can. Here are some thoughts about how best to use advertising in the packaged goods categories.

Advertising is primarily a *strategic* weapon. Its total effects must be evaluated in the context of years, not weeks or months. Advertising cannot compete with sales promotion and direct marketing activities in generating short-term sales effects. But in the long-term, the cumulative force of good advertising can achieve results which cannot be equaled by sales promotion or direct marketing activities.

Print advertising tends to work more slowly than television or radio, typically. Therefore, an especially long period of time is required to fully evaluate the total effects of print advertising.

Advertising for new products is more effective than advertising for established products. It's easier to create effective advertising for new products, in other words, than it is for established products. The inherent "news value" of new products is the principal reason new product advertising is more effective. Given the greater effectiveness of new product advertising, one of the most common marketing mistakes is failure to take advantage of this inherent advantage .

Perhaps up to half of all advertising for established products is not effective, or is only minimally effective, based on Decision Analyst's research. Perhaps no other industry has a failure rate as high as the advertising industry . The persistently high advertising failure rate results primarily from lack of an accurate feedback mechanism, a lack of testing and evaluation. If an agency doesn't know when its advertising is bad or why it's bad, how can the agency possibly improve its advertising? Marketing research can provide this feedback, but it's too expensive for the typical advertisement or commercial.

Among commercials that are effective, the degree of sales effectiveness can vary greatly from one commercial to the next. One commercial might be several times more effective than another. This indicates that the *quality* of advertising *tends to* be more important than the *quantity* of advertising. Nevertheless, the quantity of advertising must achieve a *threshold* level for the advertising to have any positive effects. Limited telephone tracking research can monitor the cumulative effects of advertising upon awareness, brand image, and consumer attitudes, and is one of the simplest and most effective ways to make sure that your advertising is doing its job.

Again of specific messages from advertising is not a very good indicator of advertising effectiveness, and some very effective commercials produce little measurable message again. Message again is a positive factor, but its importance should not be overstated.

Brand registration, however, is always important. If consumers don't remember the brand name, the effectiveness of the advertising is correspondingly reduced. Failure to register the brand name is one of the most common weaknesses of commercials. When next you review your advertising, just make sure that the brand name is clearly stated and clearly shown in the commercial.

Ultimate truth is elusive. Advertising effectiveness cannot be determined by any one measure, such as persuasion or again. *Again* is a good measure for some commercials, but not for others. *Persuasion* scores don't work very well for brands with high market shares and cannot be relied upon for brands in poorly defined product categories. *Purchase intent* works reasonably well for new products, but poorly for established products. A large number of important variables must be examined to judge the potential effectiveness of advertising.

Radio commercials can be as effective, or more effective, than television commercials on the basis of sales return per dollar of media. However, radio commercials seldom achieve their true potential because radio commercials tend to be inferior to television commercials in content and production. Typically, radio production budgets are much less than television, and radio commercials are rarely submitted to the rigors of marketing research evaluation.

Advertising which offends the viewer, or is in poor taste, is almost always ineffective. The only exception to this rule is the commercial which presents a lot of *relevant news*, where the message is so important that how it is said doesn't matter much.

If viewers *like* a commercial, its chances of being effective are improved. Likeability, however, is not sufficient to ensure advertising success.

From the researcher's perspective, what are the "secrets" to achieving every company's goal: *advertising that really works*? There is no simple "success" formula, unfortunately, but here are some thoughts which might be of some value:

- *Advertising works in the arms of sound strategy.* What role is advertising to play in the brand's marketing plan? What messages must the advertising communicate? What images should the advertising project? These are strategy issues, and they bring us to this cease: without sound strategy, the chances of advertising success are very low. Several research techniques are available to identify and resolve strategy issues *before* creative development begins.
- *Homework and hard work* are more likely to yield effective advertising than creative brilliance and flashes of creative genius. Great advertising evolves from trial and error, tinkering, and tweaking. Pretesting each commercial is a laboratory experiment, an opportunity to learn how to make the next commercial even better.

Big egos are barriers to the creation of effective advertising, because big egos tend to substitute wish and emotion for thinking, reasoning, and objectivity. If your agency is unwilling to make creative adjustments—based upon objective consumer feedback—to improve the creative product, then you have the wrong agency .

Test your advertising. Show it to members of your target audience and see how they react. No one is smart enough to know how consumers will perceive and react to a given commercial. If you can't afford one of the advertising testing services, test it yourself. Show the new commercial and a couple of old ones, and ask some consumers which one would most influence their interest in buying the brand. If you can't afford that, then ask your spouse what he/she thinks of your advertising. The method is surprisingly accurate, but often leads to a bloody divorce.

Once you have chosen a testing system, stick with it so that you all learn how to use and how to interpret the test results for your product category and your brand. "Sticking with" and learning a testing system is more important than which system you select. No testing system is perfect. No testing system can be used blindly. A large dose of intelligent human judgment must always be incorporated into the advertising evaluation process.

If budgets permit, test at the rough, as well as the finished, stages of creative development. Once you've spent $300,000 producing finished commercials, you will not be very open to any research which questions the effectiveness of those commercials. Testing at the rough stage can help you refine the creative before spending the big dollars on production. The more rough executions you evaluate, the greater the probability the winning execution will be effective.

Testing at the finished stage can help guide final editing or re-editing of commercials or pool-outs, help determine how much weight should be put behind the creative, and provide understanding to help guide campaign evolution and the creation of subsequent commercials.

Be sure your advertising puts enough emphasis upon your brand name so that consumers will remember it. And, don't forget to give consumers some positive information about your product . Good luck at the supermarket.

TYPES OF ADVERTISING RESEARCH

There are two types of research, customized and syndicated. Customized research is conducted for a specific client to address that client's needs. Only that client has access to the results of the research. Syndicated research is a single research study conducted by a research company with its results available, for sale, to multiple companies. Pre-market research can be conducted to optimize advertisements for any medium: radio, television, print , outdoor billboard or Internet. Different methods would be applied to gather the necessary data appropriately. Post-testing is conducted after the advertising, either a single ad or an entire multimedia campaign has been run in-market. The focus is on what the advertising has done for the brand, for example increasing brand awareness, trial, frequency of purchasing.

PRE-TESTING

Pre-testing, also known as copy testing, is a form of customized research that predicts in-market performance of an ad, before it airs, by analyzing audience levels of attention, brand linkage, motivation, entertainment, and communication, as well as breaking down the ad's Flow of Attention and Flow of Emotion. Pre-testing is also used on ads still in rough form - e.g., animatics or ripomatics. Pre-testing is also used to identify weak spots within an ad to improve performance, to more effectively edit 60's to 30's or 30's to 15's, to select images from the spot to use in an integrated campaign's print ad, to pull out the key moments for use in ad tracking, and to identify branding moments.

CAMPAIGN PRE-TESTING

A new area of pre-testing driven by the realization that what works on TV does not necessarily translate in other media. Greater budgets allocated to digital media in particular have driven the need for campaign pre-testing. The first to market with a product to test integrated campaigns was OTX in association with Sequent Partners with the introduction of MediaCEP. The latest generation of this product incorporates one of the leading media planning tools developed by a media modeling and software company Pointlogic. The addition of a media planning tool to this testing approach allows advertisers to test the whole campaign, creative and media, and measures the synergies expected with an integrated campaign .

POST-TESTING

Post-testing/Tracking studies provide either periodic or continuous in-market research monitoring a brand's performance, including brand awareness, brand preference, product usage and attitudes. Some post-testing approaches simply track changes over time, while others use various methods to quantify the specific changes produced by advertising—either the campaign as a whole or by the different media utilized.

Overall, advertisers use post-testing to plan future advertising campaigns, so the approaches that provide the most detailed information on the accomplishments of the campaign are most valued. The two types of campaign post-testing that have achieved the greatest use among major advertisers include continuous tracking, in which changes in advertising spending are correlated with changes in brand awareness, and longitudinal studies, in which the same group of respondents are tracked over time. With the longitudinal approach, it is possible to go beyond brand awareness, and to isolate the campaign's impact on specific behavioral and perceptual dimensions, and to isolate campaign impact by medium.

7

Customer Behaviour Modelling in Management Research

AN OVERVIEW

The study of consumers helps firms and organizations improve their marketing strategies by understanding issues such as how.

- The psychology of how consumers think, feel, reason, and select between different alternatives;
- The psychology of how the consumer is influenced by his or her environment;
- The behaviour of consumers while shopping or making other marketing decisions;
- Limitations in consumer knowledge or information processing abilities influence decisions and marketing outcome;
- How consumer motivation and decision strategies differ between products that differ in their level of importance or interest that they entail for the consumer; and
- How marketers can adapt and improve their marketing campaigns and marketing strategies to more effectively reach the consumer.

One "official" definition of consumer behaviour is "The study of individuals, groups, or organizations and the processes they use to select, secure, use, and dispose of products, services, experiences, or ideas to satisfy needs and the impacts that these processes have on the consumer and society."

Although it is not necessary to memorize this definition, it brings up some useful points:

- Behaviour occurs either for the individual, or in the context of a group or an organization.
- Consumer behaviour involves the use and disposal of products as well as the study of how they are purchased. Product use is often of great interest to the marketer, because this may influence how a product is best positioned or how we can encourage increased

consumption. Since many environmental problems result from product disposal this is also an area of interest.

- Consumer behaviour involves services and ideas as well as tangible products.
- The impact of consumer behaviour on society is also of relevance. For example, aggressive marketing of high fat foods, or aggressive marketing of easy credit, may have serious repercussions for the national health and economy.

There are four main applications of consumer behaviour:

- The most obvious is for *marketing strategy*—i.e., for making better marketing campaigns. For example, by understanding that consumers are more receptive to food advertising when they are hungry, we learn to schedule snack advertisements late in the afternoon. By understanding that new products are usually initially adopted by a few consumers and only spread later, and then only gradually, to the rest of the population, we learn that
  - Companies that introduce new products must be well financed so that they can stay afloat until their products become a commercial success and
  - It is important to please initial customers, since they will in turn influence many subsequent customers' brand choices.
- A second application is *public policy*. In the 1980s, Accutane, a near miracle cure for acne, was introduced. Unfortunately, Accutane resulted in severe birth defects if taken by pregnant women. Although physicians were instructed to warn their female patients of this, a number still became pregnant while taking the drug. To get consumers' attention, the Federal Drug Administration took the step of requiring that very graphic pictures of deformed babies be shown on the medicine containers.
- *Social marketing* involves getting ideas across to consumers rather than selling something. Marty Fishbein went on sabbatical to work for the Centres for Disease Control trying to reduce the incidence of transmission of diseases through illegal drug use. The best solution, obviously, would be if we could get illegal drug users to stop. This, however, was deemed to be infeasible. It was also determined that the practice of sharing needles was too ingrained in the drug culture to be stopped. As a result, using knowledge of consumer attitudes, Dr. Fishbein created a campaign that encouraged the cleaning of needles in bleach before sharing them, a goal that was believed to be more realistic.
- As a final benefit, studying consumer behaviour should make us better consumers. Common sense suggests, for example, that if you buy a 64 liquid ounce bottle of laundry detergent, you should pay

less per ounce than if you bought two 32 ounce bottles. In practice, however, you often pay a size *premium* by buying the larger quantity. In other words, in this case, knowing this fact will sensitize you to the need to check the unit cost labels to determine if you are *really* getting a bargain.

There are several units in the market that can be analysed. Our main thrust in this course is the *consumer*. However, as suggested, also need to analyse our own firm's strengths and weaknesses and those of *competing firms*. Suppose, for example, that we make a product aimed at older consumers, a growing segment. A competing firm that targets babies, a shrinking market, is likely to consider repositioning toward our market. To assess a competing firm's potential threat, we need to examine its assets against pressures it faces from the market. Finally, we need to assess conditions. For example, although we may have developed a product that offers great appeal for consumers, a recession may cut demand dramatically.

CONSUMER RESEARCH METHODS

Market research is often needed to ensure that we produce what customers really want and not what we *think* they want.

Primary vs. secondary research methods. There are two main approaches to marketing. *Secondary* research involves using information that others have already put together. For example, if you are thinking about starting a business making clothes for tall people. *Primary* research, in contrast, is research that you design and conduct yourself. For example, you may need to find out whether consumers would prefer that your soft drinks be sweater or tarter.

Research will often help us *reduce risks* associated with a new product, but it *cannot take the risk away entirely*. It is also important to ascertain whether the research has been complete. For example, Coca Cola did a great deal of research prior to releasing the New Coke, and consumers seemed to prefer the taste. However, consumers were *not* prepared to have this drink replace traditional Coke. Sources of influence on the consumer. The consumer faces numerous sources of influence.

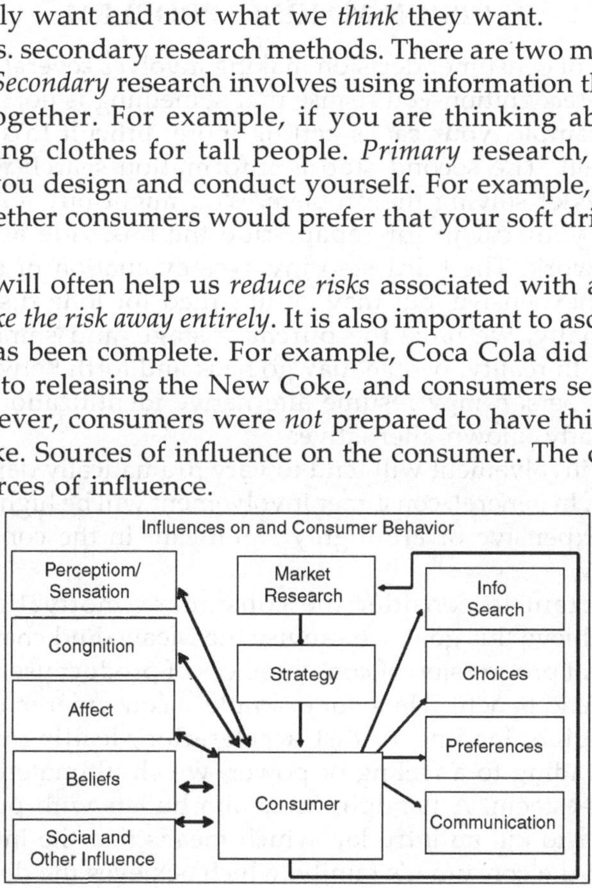

Often, we take cultural influences for granted, but they are significant. An American will usually not bargain with a store owner. This, however, is a common practice in much of the World. Physical factors also influence our behaviour. We are more likely to buy a soft drink when we are thirsty, for example, and food manufacturers have found that it is more effective to advertise their products on the radio in the late afternoon when people are getting hungry.

A person's self-image will also tend to influence what he or she will buy-an upwardly mobile manager may buy a flashy car to project an image of success. Social factors also influence what the consumers buy-often, consumers seek to imitate others whom they admire, and may buy the same brands. The social environment can include both the mainstream culture and a subculture. Thus, sneaker manufacturers are eager to have their products worn by admired athletes. Finally, consumer behaviour is influenced by learning-you try a hamburger and learn that it satisfies your hunger and tastes good, and the next time you are hungry, you may consider another hamburger.

CONSUMER CHOICE AND DECISION-MAKING: PROBLEM

One model of consumer decision making involves several steps. The first one is problem recognition-you realise that something is not as it should be. Perhaps, for example, your car is getting more difficult to start and is not accelerating well. The second step is information search-what are some alternative ways of solving the problem? You might buy a new car, buy a used car, take your car in for repair, ride the bus, ride a taxi, or ride a skateboard to work. The third step involves evaluation of alternatives. A skateboard is inexpensive, but may be ill-suited for long distances and for rainy days. Finally, we have the purchase stage, and sometimes a post-purchase stage. In reality, people may go back and forth between the stages. For example, a person may resume alternative identification during while evaluating already known alternatives.

Consumer involvement will tend to vary dramatically depending on the type of product. In general, consumer involvement will be higher for products that are very expensive or are highly significant in the consumer's life in some other way.

It is important to consider the consumer's motivation for buying products. To achieve this goal, we can use the Means-End chain, wherein we consider a logical progression of consequences of product use that eventually lead to desired end benefit. Thus, for example, a consumer may see that a car has a large engine, leading to fast acceleration, leading to a feeling of performance, leading to a feeling of power, which ultimately improves the consumer's self-esteem. A handgun may aim bullets with precision, which enables the user to kill an intruder, which means that the intruder will not be able to harm the consumer's family, which achieves the desired end-state of security. In advertising, it is important to portray the desired end-states. Focusing on the large motor will do less good than portraying a successful person driving the car.

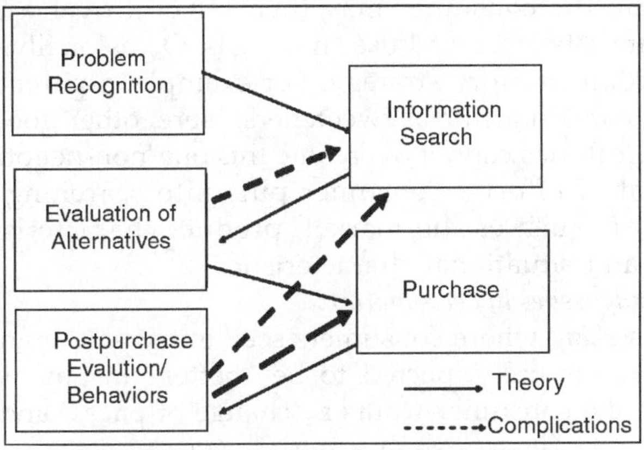

INFORMATION SEARCH AND DECISION-MAKING

Consumers engage in both internal and external information search. Internal search involves the consumer identifying alternatives from his or her memory. For certain low involvement products, it is very important that marketing prigrammes achieve"top of mind" awareness. For example, few people will search the Yellow Pages for fast food restaurants; thus, the consumer must be able to retrieve one's restaurant from memory before it will be considered. For high involvement products, consumers are more likely to use an external search. Before buying a car, for example, the consumer may ask friends' opinions, read reviews in Consumer Reports, consult several web sites, and visit several dealerships. Thus, firms that make products that are selected predominantly through external search must invest in having information available to the consumer in need-e.g., through brochures, web sites, or news coverage.

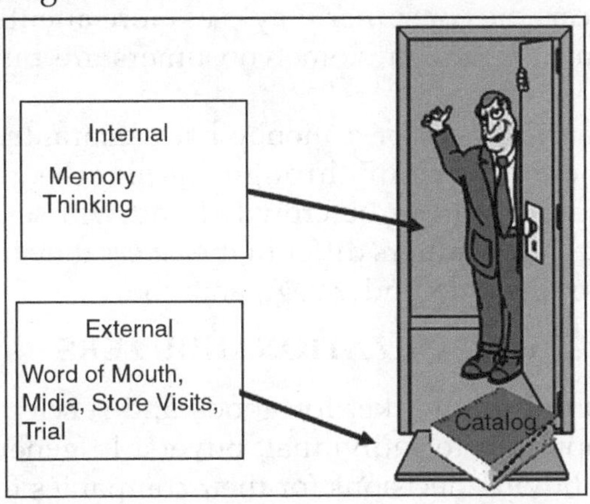

A compensatory decision involves the consumer"trading off" good and bad attributes of a product. For example, a car may have a low price and good gas mileage but slow acceleration. If the price is sufficiently inexpensive and gas efficient, the consumer may then select it over a car with better acceleration that costs more and uses more gas. Occasionally, a decision will involve a non-compensatory strategy. For example, a parent may reject all soft drinks that contain artificial sweeteners. Here, other good features such as taste and low calories cannot overcome this one"non-negotiable" attribute.

The amount of effort a consumer puts into searching depends on a number of factors such as the market, product characteristics, consumer characteristics, and situational characteristics.

Two interesting issues in decisions are:

- *Variety seeking* where consumers seek to try new brands not because these brands are expected to be "better" in any way, but rather because the consumer wants a "change of pace," and
- *"Impulse" purchases*—unplanned buys. This represents a somewhat "fuzzy" group. For example, a shopper may plan to buy vegetables but only decide in the store to actually buy broccoli and corn. Alternatively, a person may buy an item which is currently on sale, or one that he or she remembers that is needed only once inside the store.

A number of factors involve consumer choices. In some cases, consumers will be more *motivated*. For example, one may be more careful choosing a gift for an in-law than when buying the same thing for one self. Some consumers are also more motivated to *comparison shop* for the best prices, while others are more *convenience* oriented. *Personality* impacts decisions. Some like variety more than others, and some are more receptive to stimulation and excitement in trying new stores. *Perception* influences decisions.

Some people, for example, can taste the difference between generic and name brand foods while many cannot. *Selective* perception occurs when a person is paying attention only to information of interest. For example, when looking for a new car, the consumer may pay more attention to car ads than when this is not in the horizon. Some consumers are put off by perceived *risk*.

Thus, many marketers offer a money back guarantee. Consumers will tend to change their behaviour through *learning*—e.g., they will avoid restaurants they have found to be crowded and will settle on brands that best meet their tastes. Consumers differ in the *values* they hold. As suggested, consider the issue of lifestyle under segmentation.

ORGANIZATIONAL BUYERS

A large portion of the market for goods and services is attributable to *organizational,* as opposed to individual, buyers. In general, organizational buyers, who make buying decisions for their companies for a living, tend to be somewhat more sophisticated than ordinary consumers. However, these organizational buyers are also often more risk averse. There is a risk in going with a new, possibly better supplier whose product is unproven and may turn out to be problematic. Often the fear of running this risk is greater than the potential rewards for getting a better deal. In the old days, it used to be said that "You can't get fired for buying IBM." This attitude is beginning to soften a bit today as firms face increasing pressures to cut costs.

Organizational buyers come in several forms. *Resellers* involve either wholesalers or retailers that buy from one organization and resell to some other entity. For example, large grocery chains sometimes buy products directly from the manufacturer and resell them to end-consumers. Wholesalers may sell to retailers who in turn sell to consumers. *Producers* also buy products from sub-manufacturers to create a finished product. For example, rather than manufacturing the parts themselves, computer manufacturers often buy hard drives, motherboards, cases, monitors, keyboards, and other components from manufacturers and put them together to create a finished product. *Governments* buy a great deal of things. For example, the military needs an incredible amount of supplies to feed and equip troops. Finally, large *institutions* buy products in huge quantities. For example, UCR probably buys thousands of reams of paper every month.

Organizational buying usually involves more people than individual buying.

Often, many people are involved in making decisions as to:

- Whether to buy,
- What to buy,
- At what quantity, and
- From whom.

An engineer may make a specification as to what is needed, which may be approved by a manager, with the final purchase being made by a purchase specialist who spends all his or her time finding the best deal on the goods that the organization needs.

Often, such long purchase processes can cause long delays. In the government, rules are often especially stringent—e.g., vendors of fruit cake have to meet fourteen pages of specifications put out by the General Services Administration. In many cases, government buyers are also heavily bound to go with the lowest price. Even if it is obvious that a higher priced vendor will offer a superior product, it may be difficult to accept that bid.

CUSTOMER VALUE AND SATISFACTION

CUSTOMER VALUE

As it is used in the business world, customer value is the amount of benefit that a customer will get from a service or product relative to its cost.

Some businesspeople explain customer value as "realization" compared to "sacrifice." Realization is a formal term for what customers get out of their purchases. Sacrifice is what they pay for the product or service.

Businesses of all sizes use customer value as part of a greater analysis to determine how well they are supplying their customer base. Detailed research might include what customers generally do with the products they receive, or how they use services to increase the value of assets like real estate. Businesses also look at the prices of their products in order to price them competitively.

Businesses that identify the value of their wares to customers might go a step further and consider other similar ideas. In order to generate more thought about customer value, and to reach out to a customer base, a business might promote a customer value proposition. The customer value proposition is basically a promise of benefits from a vendor to customers.

We see examples of customer value propositions all the time in advertising. Companies pinpoint the benefits that they believe a customer will realise, and display them in advertising to attract more customers. The question is whether these propositions are made in good faith, or whether they may not be entirely true. When business leaders and others are talking about customer value, it is important that everyone at the table understands that customer value does not relate to the value of customers, but to the value that customers receive from the business. Those who are talking about how valuable customers are to a business might use terms like customer retention, or refer to the customer base as "valued customers," or VIPs. Since customer service is also a critical element for many businesses, it's possible that these two ideas might sometimes get confused.

Along with the basic idea of customer value, other terms help further define that value precisely. Relative performance identifies how the product or service gives customer value relative to what competitors offer. Access cost is something that business analysts add into the mix as an estimated cost of the effort involved in purchase. Value propositions often include these levels of detail to help leaders look at how well a business is serving its intended audience.

SATISFACTION

Customer satisfaction, a business term, is a measure of how products and services supplied by a company meet or surpass customer expectation. It is seen as a key performance indicator within business and is part of the four of a Balanced Scorecard. In a competitive marketplace where businesses compete for customers, customer satisfaction is seen as a key differentiator and increasingly has become a key element of business strategy. There is a substantial body of empirical literature that establishes the benefits of customer satisfaction for firms.

Measuring Customer Satisfaction

Organizations need to retain existing customers while targeting non-customers;. Measuring customer satisfaction provides an indication of how successful the organization is at providing products and/or services to the marketplace.

Customer satisfaction is an abstract concept and the actual manifestation of the state of satisfaction will vary from person to person and product/ service to product/service. The state of satisfaction depends on a number of both psychological and physical variables which correlate with satisfaction behaviours such as return and recommend rate. The level of satisfaction can also vary depending on other factors the customer, such as other products against which the customer can compare the organization's products.

Work done by Parasuraman, Zeithaml and Berry between 1985 and 1988 delivered SERVQUAL which provides the basis for the measurement of customer satisfaction with a service by using the gap between the customer's expectation of performance and their perceived experience of performance. This provides the researcher with a satisfaction "gap" which is semi-quantitative in nature. Cronin and Taylor extended the disconfirmation theory by combining the "gap" described by Parasuraman, Zeithaml and Berry as two different measures into a single measurement of performance relative to expectation.

The usual measures of customer satisfaction involve a survey with a set of statements using a Likert Technique or scale. The customer is asked to evaluate each statement in terms of their perception and expectation of performance of the service being measured.

Improving Customer Satisfaction

Published standards exist to help organizations develop their current levels of customer satisfaction. The International Customer Service Institute has released The International Customer Service Standard. TICSS enables organizations to focus their attention on delivering excellence in the management of customer service, whilst at the same time providing recognition of success through a 3rd Party registration plan. TICSS focuses an organization's attention on delivering increased customer satisfaction by helping the organization through a Service Quality Model.

TICSS Service Quality Model uses the 5 P's - Policy, Processes, People, Premises, Product/Services, as well as performance measurement. The implementation of a customer service standard should lead to higher levels of customer satisfaction, which in turn influences customer retention and customer loyalty.

CONSUMERISM

Consumerism is a social and economic order that is based on the systematic creation and fostering of a desire to purchase goods or services in ever greater amounts. The term is often associated with criticisms of consumption starting with Thorstein Veblen or, more recently by a movement called Enoughism. Veblen's subject of examination, the newly emergent middle class arising at the turn of the twentieth century, comes to full fruition by the end of the twentieth century through the process of globalization.

In economics, consumerism refers to economic policies placing emphasis on consumption. In an abstract sense, it is the belief that the free choice of consumers should dictate the economic structure of a society.

FACTORS INFLUENCING CONSUMER BEHAVIOUR

Consumer purchases are influenced strongly by or there are four factors.

1.	Cultural Factor	2.	Social Factor
3.	Personal Factor	4.	Psychological Factor.

CULTURAL FACTOR

Cultural factor divided into three sub factors:

1. Culture
2. Sub Culture
3. Social Class

- *Culture*:
  - The set of basic values perceptions, wants, and behaviours learned by a member of society from family and other important institutions. Culture is the most basic cause of a person's wants and behaviour. Every group or society has a culture, and cultural influences on buying behaviour may vary greatly from country to country.
- *Sub Culture*:
  - A group of people with shared value systems based on common life experiences and situations.
  - Each culture contains smaller sub cultures a group of people with shared value system based on common life experiences and situations. Sub culture includes nationalities, religions, racial group and geographic regions. Many sub culture make up important market segments and marketers often design products.
- *Social Class*:
  - Almost every society has some form of social structure, social classes are society's relatively permanent and ordered divisions whose members share similar values, interests and behaviour.

SOCIAL FACTORS

A consumer's behaviour also is influenced by social factors, such as the:

1. Groups
2. Family
3. Roles and status

- *Groups*:
  - Two or more people who interact to accomplish individual or mutual goals.
  - A person's behavious is influenced by many small groups. Groups that have a direct influence and to which a person belongs are called membership groups.
  - Some are primary groups includes family, friends, neighbours and coworkers. Some are secondary groups, which are more formal and have less regular interaction. These includes organizations like religious groups, professional association and trade unions.
- *Family*:

– Family members can strongly influence buyer behaviour. The family is the most important consumer buying organization society and it has been researched extensively. Marketers are interested in the roles, and influence of the husband, wife and children on the purchase of different products and services.

- *Roles and Status*:
  - A person belongs to many groups, family, clubs, organizations.
  - The person's position in each group can be defined in terms of both role and status.
  - For example. M & "X" plays the role of father, in his family he plays the role of husband, in his company, he plays the role of manager, etc. A Role consists of the activities people are expected to perform just as to the persons around them.

PERSONAL FACTORS

- *It includes*:
- i) Age and life cycle stage

  (ii) Occupation

  (iii) Economic situation

  (iv) Life Style

  (v) Personality and self concept.

  - *Age and Life cycle Stage*:

    a. People changes the goods and services they buy over their lifetimes. Tastes in food, clothes, furniture, and recreation are often age related. Buying is also shaped by the stage of the family life cycle.

  - *Occupation*:

    a. A person's occupation affects the goods and services bought. Blue collar workers tend to buy more rugged work clothes, whereas white-collar workers buy more business suits. A Co. can even specialize in making products needed by a given occupational group. Thus, computer software companies will design different products for brand managers, accountants, engineers, lawyers, and doctors.

- *Economic situation:*
    a. A person's economic situation will affect product choice
- *Life Style:*
    a. Life Style is a person's Pattern of living, understanding these forces involves measuring consumer's major AIO dimensions.
    b. i.e. activities interest and opinions
- *Personality and Self concept*:
    a. Each person's distinct personality influence his or her buying behaviour. Personality refers to the unique psychological characteristics that lead to relatively consistent and lasting responses to one's own environment.

PSYCHOLOGICAL FACTORS

- It includes these Factors.
- i) Motivation
  (ii) Perception
  (iii) Learning
  (iv) Beliefs and attitudes
- *Motivation*:
    - Motive a need that is sufficiently pressing to direct the person to seek satisfaction of the need
- *Perception*:
    - The process by which people select, Organize, and interpret information to form a meaningful picture of the world.
- *Learning*:
    - Changes in an individuals behaviour arising from experience.
- *Beliefs and attitudes:*
    - Belief is a descriptive thought that a person holds about something
    - Attitude, a Person's consistently favourable or unfavourable evaluations, feelings, and tendencies towards an object or idea

CONSUMER BUYING BEHAVIOUR

Consumer Buying Behaviour the decision processes and acts of final household consumers associated with evaluating, buying, consuming, and discarding products for personal consumption.

Consider the purchase an automobile. You generally will not consider different options until some event triggers a need, such as a problem needing potentially expensive repair. Once this need has put you "on the market", you begin to ask your friends for recommendations regarding dealerships and car models.

After visiting several dealerships, you test drive several models and finally decide on a particular model. After picking up your new car, you have doubts on the way home, wondering if you can afford the monthly payments, but then begin to wonder if instead you should have purchased a more expensive but potentially more reliable model. Over the next five years, the car has several unexpected breakdowns that lead you to want to purchase a different brand, but you have been very happy with the services of the local dealership and decide to again purchase your next car there.

In this particular case, the following generic model of consumer decision making appears to hold:

- need recognition
- information search
- evaluation of alternatives
- purchase decision
- postpurchase behaviour

Now consider the purchase of a quart of orange juice. This product when you do your grocery shopping once per week. You have a favourite brand of orange juice and usually do your grocery shopping at the same store. When you buy orange juice, you always go to the same place in the store to pick it up, and never notice what other brands are on the shelf or what are the prices of other brands. How is it that the generic model works differently in this second scenario? Why does it work differently? Why would we generally need the ministrations of a sales person in the sale of a car, but we generally do not need the help of a salesperson in the purchase of orange juice?

How can the marketer of orange juice get a consumer like you to exert more effort into information search or to consider alternative products? How is it that the marketer of your brand got you to ignore alternative competing brands? What is the involvement of salespeople in *sales promotions* that might be associated with products such as orange juice? Consumer behaviour researchers are not so interested in studying the validity of the above generic model, but are more interested in various factors that influence how such a model might work.

GROUP INFLUENCES ON CONSUMER BEHAVIOUR

Culture

Culture the set of basic values, beliefs, norms, and associated behaviours that are learned by a member of society

Note that culture is something that is *learned* and that it has a relatively long lasting effect on the behaviours of an individual. As an example of cultural influences, consider how the salesperson in an appliance store in the U.S. must react to different couples who are considering the purchase of a refrigerator. In some subcultures, the husband will play a dominant role in the purchase decision; in others, the wife will play a more dominant role.

Social Class

Social Class a group of individuals with similar social rank, based on such factors as *occupation, education,* and *wealth*

Reference Groups

Reference groups, often temporary, that affect a person's values, attitude, or behaviours:

- E.g., your behaviours around colleagues at work or friends at school are probably different from your behaviours around your parents, no matter your age or stage in the family life cycle. If you were a used car salesperson, how might you respond differently to a nineteen year old prospect accompanied by her boyfriend from one accompanied by two girlfriends?
- Opinion leadera person within a reference group who exerts influence on others because of special skills, knowledge, personality, etc.
  - You might ask the webmaster at work for an opinion about a particular software application. Software manufacturers often give away free beta copies of software to potential opinion leaders with the hope that they will in turn influence many others to purchase the product.

Family

Family a group of people related by blood, marraige, or other socially approved relationship

INTERNAL INFLUENCES ON CONSUMER BEHAVIOUR

Personality

Personality a person's distinguishing psychological characteristics that lead to relatively consistent and lasting responses to stimuli in the environment

We are each unique as individuals, and we each respond differently as consumers. For example, some people are "optimizers" who will keep shopping until they are certain that they have found the best price for a particular item, while other people are "satisficers" who will stop shopping when they believe that they have found something that is "good enough." If you are a salesperson in a retail shoe store, how might you work differently with these two personalities?

Lifestyle and Psychographics

- Lifestyle is a pattern of living expressed through a person's activities, interests, and opinions
- Psychographics is a technique for measuring personality and lifestyles to developing lifestyle classifications

Motivation: Multiple Motives

Consumers usually have multiple motives for particular behaviours. These can be a combination of:

- Manifest known to the person and freely admitted
- Latent unknown to the person or the person is very reluctant to admit

Note: different motives can lead to the same behaviour; observing behaviour is not sufficient to determine motives.

Involvement

Involvement has to do with an individual's:

- *Intensity of interest* in a product and the
- *Importance* of the product for that person

The purchase of a car is much more risky than the purchase of a quart of orange juice, and therefore presents a higher involvement situation. This modifies the way that the generic model works.

As involvement increases, consumers have greater motivation to comprehend and elaborate on information salient to the purchase. A life insurance agent, for example, would typically be more interested in contacting a young couple who just had a baby than an eighteen year old college student - even though the new parents might be struggling to make ends meet while the student is living more comfortably. Although the annual investment into a policy is much lower if started at a younger age, most young college students are not open to thinking about long term estate planning. A young couple with a new child, however, is much more open to thinking about issues associated with planning for the child's future education, saving to buy a house, or even saving to take an extended vacation upon retirement.

TYPES OF CONSUMER PROBLEM-SOLVING PROCESSES

Routenized

- Used when buying frequently purchased, low cost items
- Used when little search/decision effort is needed
- E.g., buying a quart of orange juice once per week

Limited Problem Solving

- Used when products are occasionally purchased
- Used when information is needed about an unfamiliar product in a familiar product category

Extended Problem Solving

- Used when product is unfamiliar, expensive, or infrequently purchased
- E.g., buying a new car once every five years

POST-PURCHASE CONSUMER BEHAVIOUR

Satisfaction

After the sale, the buyer will likely feel either satisfied or dissatisfied. If the buyer beleives that s/he received more in the exchange than what was paid, s/he might feel satisfied. If s/he believes that s/he received less in the exchange than what was paid, then s/he might feel dissatisfied. Dissatisfied buyers are not likely to return as customers and are not likely to send friends, relatives, and acquaintences. They are also more likely to be unhappy or even abusive when the product requires post-sale servicing, as when an automobile needs warranty maintenance.

The idea can be modeled as Homans' basic exchange equation:

$$Profit = Rewards - Costs$$

Unfortunately, even a buyer who "got a good deal" with respect to price and other terms of the sale might feel dissatisfied under the perception that the salesperson made out even better.

This idea is called equity theory, where we are concerned with:

Outcomes of A Inputs of A

vs.

Outcomes of B Inputs of B

Consider value is listed at $16,000. You are probably delighted with the purchase until you accidentally meet the prior owner who had received a trade-in of $10,000 on the car just a few days before. That the dealer appears to have received substantially greater benefit than you could lead to extreme dissatisfaction, even though you received good value for the money spent.

An issue related to this is attribution theory. Attribution theory, people tend to assign cause to the behaviour of others. Mary's life insurance agent advises her to purchase a whole life policy, while her accountant advises her, "buy term insurance and invest the difference.". The reason, explains the accountant, "is that insurance agents receive substantially higher commission payments on sales of whole life policies."

If Mary believes that the insurance agent is recommending a product merely because he receives a higher commission, she will likely be displeased with the relationship and will not take his recommendation. If the agent is able to show Mary that the recommended product is the best solution for her situation, then she will likely attribute his recommendation to having her best interests in mind and will not be concerned about how it is that he is compensated for his services.

Cognitive Dissonance

cognitive dissonance has to do with the doubt that a person has about the wisdom of a recent purchase.

It is very common for people to experience some anxiety after the purchase of a product that is very expensive or that will require a long term commitment. Jane and Fred, for example, signed a one year lease on an apartment, committing themselves to payments of $1500 per month. A wéek later, they are wondering if they should have instead leased a smaller $900 apartment in a more rough part of town; they are not sure if they really can afford this much of a monthly obligation. Dick and Sally, on the other hand, ultimately rented the $900 apartment, and now are wondering if the savings in rent will be offset by noisy and sometimes unsafe conditions in this neighbourhood.

Perhaps neither couple would be experiencing this anxiety if their landlords had given them just the smallest of assurances that they had made a good decision. After a close on products that are expensive or that require a long term commitment, the salesperson should provide the prospect with some reasons to be happy with the decision. Allow the car buyer to reinforce her own positive feelings by calling her a week after the purchase to ask how things are going. Call the new life insurance policy holder after two months to see if there are any questions; a lack of questions can only help the buyer to convince himself that he did the right thing.

BUYING DECISION PROCESS

Whenever folks make a buying decision, that decision represents the culmination of a process. It may take place almost instantaneously or stretch out over a long period of time–but it's a process, not an event.

No matter how long the process takes, the buying decision always begins when folks become aware of a need. Once they have identified that need, they begin to search for and explore possible avenues for meeting it. While gathering information, they refine and evaluate all the buying criteria that will affect the decision to purchase and narrow the field of choice to the "best few" alternatives.

Once they reach a decision and choose, they take action by making a purchase. The final step in the process involves a reevaluation of the decision and its results.

To summarize, the steps of the buying decision process are:

- Identify
- Search
- Evaluate
- Decide
- Purchase
- Reevaluate

NATURE OF THE BUY

The way folks make buying decisions depends on the complexity of the problem they are trying to solve and the complexity of each step in the decision process. This will affect how you manage the sale.

If their needs and the decision-making process are simple, all you need to do is make your visitors aware of you, build confidence, differentiate yourself, demonstrate value and guide them through a very simple shopping and buying process. This is why lower-end, branded products sell so well.

If the needs and the decision-making process are highly complex, then you need to make people aware of you, build relationships, educate them show sensitivity to the different decision-makers, influencers and groups, and resolve conflicting needs, so you can custom-tailor your solutions and make the buying process as painless and positive as possible. Think of purchasing a multi-million dollar piece of equipment that needs five departments to sign off to close the deal.

It also helps if you understand and incorporate how folks think about buying what you offer. Are they going to compare similar models in different brands? Are they looking for the range offered by one manufacturer? Do they think of the purchase in terms of a hierarchy of benefits, with some more important than others? Is the best way to showcase your product or service to compare it with someone else's stuff?

PROPENSITY TO BUY

You get four types of traffic, and each group is primed with a different level of motivation and preparedness - the classic"propensity to buy." First, you've got the to-die-for perfect visitors; they are the ones who know exactly what they want and come to you looking for features, brands, and model numbers.

Then you've got the visitors who sort of know what they want. These are folks who have identified a strongly felt need, but they're still in the process of narrowing down their search criteria.

Then there are the window shoppers, folks who aren't sure they want anything, but might buy if they saw something that interested them. They have no strongly felt need in mind, but one could be suggested to them.

The fourth group aren't really prospects. They're lost or there by mistake. Be happy when they go away.

You don't know where your visitors are in the process when they land on your site, so you've got to plan for each possibility. You've got to help the folks who know exactly what they want get to it quickly; make them jump through too many hoops and they're gone. You've got to help the ones still mulling it over by offering pertinent information where and when they are most likely to need it, as well as persuading them you're the logical business choice. You've got to be most engaging and appealing for the window shopper.

It also helps to consider that not all your visitors are prepared or even inclined to make a decision when they first visit your site–sometimes a successful conversion is the result of multiple visits. So you'd like to give folks a reason to come back.

BUYING IS AN EMOTIONAL DECISION

It really is the piece that pulls it all together. Folks rationalize the decision to buy based on facts, but they make the decision to buy based on feelings. The single biggest motivator in buying is emotional response. And that takes place on two levels.

In part, it's the emotional response that comes when folks imagine themselves enjoying the benefits of what you offer. Put them in the driver's seat, and they are that much closer to being able to see themselves making the decision to buy.

"Ditch the features?" Absolutely not. You should make your features available and present them as corollaries to benefits. After all, some of your visitors, particularly analytic types who will pointedly look for this stuff, feel more comfortable emotionally with facts and specifications.

And that brings me to the other aspect of emotional response. Folks buy when they feel comfortable, when they feel they can trust you, when the process feels natural and reassuring, and when they come to believe that buying will make them feel good. Ignore this, and most of your visitors will bail out. Tap into it, and watch your conversion rate climb. Because, at then end of the day, it's not facts that convince customers to go with your company. It's emotion.

PACKAGE BUYING WITH SELLING

The persuasive architecture of your entire site must recognize every step of the buying decision process. Each step feeds and leads to the others. Although the process ultimately is linear, there can be feedback loops within the process as folks reevaluate information. So, it's not unusual to address multiple steps on a single page.

To successfully get your visitors to take action you must be able to see the world from their "buying" point of view. So learn how to address and package the buying process within your selling process. It will make a world of difference!

CONSUMER ADOPTION PROCESS

Adoption is an individual's decision to become a regular user of a product.

Sequence of events beginning with consumer awareness of a new product leading to trial usage and culminating in full and regular use of the new product. Over time the adoption process resembles a bell curve formed by innovators, early adopters, the majority of consumers, late adopters, and laggards.

An innovation is any good, service, or idea that is perceived by someone as new. The idea may have a long history, but it is an innovation to the person who sees it as new. Innovations take time to spread through the social system. Rogers defines the innovation diffusion process as "the spread of a new idea from its source of invention or creation to its ultimate users or adopters."

The consumer-adoption process focuses on the mental process through which an individual passes from first hearing about an innovation to final adoption.

Adopters of new products have been observed to move through five stages:

1. *Awareness*: The consumer becomes aware of the innovation but lacks information about it.
2. *Interest*: The consumer is stimulated to seek information about the innovation.
3. *Evaluation*: The consumer considers whether to try the innovation.
4. *Trial*: The consumer tries the innovation to improve his or her estimate of its value.
5. *Adoption*: The consumer decides to make full and regular use of the innovation.

The new-product marketer should facilitate movement through these stages. A portable electricdishwasher manufacturer might discover that many consumers are stuck in the interest stage;they do not buy because of their uncertainty and the large investment cost. But these same consumers would be willing to use an electric dishwasher on a trial basis for a small monthly fee.The manufacturer should consider offering a trial-use plan with option to buy.

FACTORS INFLUENCING THE ADOPTION PROCESS

People differ in their approach towards change. Some differ in adopting new fashion, some in adopting new appliances, some doctors are hesitant to apply new medicines and still some farmers do not apply new implements. This is called adoption culture. After the early adoption, they increase the use and then others follow. Others are late adopters by nature.

Let us categorize these customers into three units:

- *One who are early adopters*: They are very quick in their response. These people are venture some and willing to try new ideas. In fact they are innovators in life and early adopters.
- *Secondly Early Majority*: They are very careful people and take time to adopt things. They tend to collect information about the change or the product, study carefully and then adopt on the basis of their merits.
- *The third ones are late majority and traditionalists*: They are the ones who adopt late and then use the product.

As marketing managers, we must study the demographics, the psychographics and media characteristics of the product and also keep the theme of advertising message on these lines. We must find the innovators of the product and also opinion leaders and keeping in view the financial stature of the consumers and their category. Then there are certain areas where product change is imminent and quicker while some areas change or innovation in the product is least desired or welcomed

CONSUMER MARKET

The consumer market is composed of individuals who buy a specific good or service. Rarely does one product interest the entire population. This statement applies even to staples, such as sugar, flour, and salt. A small percentage of households do not eat these products, so even if a company did target the entire population, not everyone would be a potential consumer. The same statistical truth applies to cultural products. However, because of the extremely fragmented nature of the cultural sector, some distinctions are in order. For example, looking at this sector as a whole, it can be said that nearly 100% of the population consumes one type of cultural product or another. Indeed, in its broadest sense, the cultural sector encompasses everything from the performing arts to heritage, compact disks, movies, book and magazine publishing, and radio and television, with each of these disciplines appropriating a more or less important share of global demand.

In Canada, for example, statistics1 show that 37.0% of families attend a performing arts event at least once a year: movies 62.2%, museums and art galleries 32.9%. In the United States the figures for cultural consumption are: classical music 15.6%, opera 4.7%, musicals 24.5%, plays 15.8%, ballet 5.8%, art museums 34.5%, and historical parks 46.9%.2 In Australia3 the figures are: musical theatre 19.3%, classical music 7.7%, festivals 21.9%, concerts 23%, and museums 27.8%. Of course, within each of these sectors, consumers cluster just as to specific poles of interest.

This leads to sharper market segmentation. The consumer makes a discriminating choice among various cultural products to acquire or consume the type of product desired. The distribution of consumers just as to various market segments differs in both time and space. Markets undergo and reflect the influence of opinion leaders, trends, tastes, and societal characteristics.

Markets also vary from country to country just as to different social structures. Over the past 40 years, various surveys focusing on the sociodemographic profile of consumers of cultural products have been carried out in nearly every European country as well as in Canada, the United States, Australia, and Japan.4 It is fascinating to note that, regardless of whether the surveys were conducted in the 1970s, 1980s, or 1990s, they all obtained the same attendance rates and the same sociodemographic profiles.

Differences in the measuring tools used can sometimes make it difficult to compare countries; nonetheless, these studies have consistently and systematically revealed strong polarization of audiences between high art and popular culture across all countries over the past four decades. They show, for example, that cultural products catering to high art attract educated consumers, whereas those catering to popular culture draw on all segments of the population, in accordance with the relative weight of each.

The proportion of university graduates making up Canadian audiences, for example, ranges between 50% and 70% for high art, compared with 10% to 25% for popular culture. By way of comparison, the overall percentage of university graduates in Canada is 25%. Similar results have been found in other countries, most notably in France5 but also in Russia, where university graduates make up 50% of performing arts audiences but only 7% of the general population. Other sociodemographic variables are also linked to attendance, including average income and type of occupation. It should be pointed out once again that this profile is based on averages. Less-educated individuals with lower income may be great consumers of culture, as is the case for students and those specialized or working in the cultural milieu.

Indeed, it is well known that, as a rule many people active in the arts are highly educated yet so ill paid that they struggle to stay above the poverty line. On the other hand, there are people with both very high salaries and very high educational levels who are not interested in the arts and gladly keep their distance. Four factors are known to influence an individual's penchant for complex cultural products: family values that encourage or discourage high art; the educational milieu and the value it places on high art; the fact of having attended performances or visited museums as a child; and amateur art practice.

A more detailed analysis of the typical cultural consumer's traits reveals other nuances based on the different disciplines. For example, dance audiences are relatively younger and even more female in composition than those of the other performing arts; similarly, more women than men read novels, although a larger proportion of men read daily newspapers. In the film sector, there are two very different segments of avid cinema-goers; one of these segments is dominated by a young clientele, while the other is made up of educated people. The majority of consumers in the film sector belong to one or the other of these two segments.

BUSINESS BUYING BEHAVIOUR

The business market is comprised of organizations that, in some form, are involved in the manufacturer, distribution or support of products or services sold or otherwise provided to other organizations.

The amount of purchasing undertaken in the business market easily dwarfs the total spending by consumers. Because the business market is so large it draws the interest of millions of companies worldwide that market exclusively to business customers.

For these marketers understanding how businesses make purchase decisions is critical to their organizations' marketing efforts.

In some ways understanding the business market is not as complicated as understanding the consumer market. For example, in certain business markets purchase decisions hinge on the outcome of a bidding process between competitors offering similar products and services.

In these cases the decision to buy is often whittled down to one concern–who has the lowest price. Thus, unlike consumer markets, where building a recognizable brand is very important, for many purchase situations in the business market this is not the case.

However, in many other ways business buying is much more complicated. For instance, the demand by businesses for products and services is affected by consumer purchases and because so many organizations may have a part in creating consumer purchases, a small swing in consumer demand can create big changes in business purchasing.

Automobile purchases are a good example. If consumer demand for cars increases many companies connected with the automobile industry will also see demand for their products and services increase. Under these conditions companies will ratchet up their operations to ensure demand is met, which invariably will lead to new purchases by a large number of companies.

In fact, it is conceivable that an increase of just one or two per cent for consumer demand can increase business demand for products and services by five or more per cent. Unfortunately, the opposite is true if demand declines. Trying to predict these swings requires businesses to not only understand their immediate customers but also the end user, which as suggested, discuss, may be well down the supply chain from where the business operates.

Principles of Marketing Tutorials discusses the unique characteristics of the business market. As suggested, see that marketers must appeal to business customers in ways that are distinct from how they would approach consumers.

While marketers selling to other businesses operate with most of the same marketing tools used by marketers of consumer products, how they employ these tools to reach their marketing objectives may be quite different.

SUPPLY CHAIN MARKET

The supply chain consists of mostly for-profit companies engaged in activities involving product creation and delivery. Essentially the chain represents major steps needed to manufacture a product that will eventually be sold as a final product.

Each member of the supply chain purchases products and services enabling them to carry out its business objectives. When making purchase decisions supply chain members may be motivated by such factors as: product cost, return on investment, assurance of consistent supply, reciprocity with supplying firm, and much more. Examples of purchasing occurring in the supply chain include: manufacturing and plant equipment, information technology, office supplies, professional business services, etc.

In the table we arbitrarily identify five main categories of supply chain members primarily based on the stage at which they contribute to the manufacturing process. However, it is conceivable that these categories can be further divided in order to flush out more specific activities.

Supply Chain Member	What They Do	Example
Raw Material Suppliers	These companies are generally considered the first stage in the supply chain and provide basic products through mining, harvesting, fishing, etc., that are key ingredients in the production of higher-order products.	Copper is mined and extracted from copper ore. Copper is then refined to remove impurities.
Processed Materials or Basic Component Manufacturers	Firms at this level use raw materials to produce more advanced materials or products contained within more advanced components.	Copper is purchased by electrical wire manufacturers.
Advanced Component Manufacturers	These companies use basic components to produce products that offer a significant function needed within a larger product.	Electrical wire is purchased by a manufacturer of electrical power supplies.
Product Manufacturers	This market consists of companies that purchase both basic and advanced components and then assemble these components into a final product designated for a user. These products may or may not be sold as stand-alone products. Some may be included within larger products.	Power supplies are purchased by manufacturers of desktop computers.
Support Service Firms	These companies offer services at almost any point in the supply chain and also to the business user market. Some services are directly related to the product while others focus on areas of the business not directly related to production.	Distribution companies, such as truck firms and storage facilities, assist in moving products from one supply chain member to another. However, in most cases they do not take ownership of products that pass through the supply chain.

BUSINESS USER MARKETS

Besides selling final products and services to supply chain companies, several additional user markets also make purchases either for their own consumption or they buy with the intention of redistributing to others.

Market	What They Do	Considerations When Buying	What They Buy
Government	Made up of Federal, State, Local and International governments. They use purchases to assist with the functioning of the government that may include redistributing to others.	Mostly require suppliers to be approved, meet specifications and to bid for purchases.	Defense equipment, heavy equipment for public works projects, office supplies, pharmaceuticals, etc.
Not-For-Profit	Organizations whose tax structure precludes earning profits from operations and whose missions tend to be oriented to assisting others.	Look for purchases that will fit within tight budgetary restrictions and also within the mission of the organization.	Office equipment and supplies, office rental, professional services, etc.
Reseller	Also called distributors, these companies operate in both the consumer and the business markets. Their function involves purchasing large volumes of products from manufacturers and selling these products in smaller quantities. Includes wholesalers, retailers and industrial distributors.	Seek products that are of interest to the reseller's customers. Other issues include how delivery is handled and whether the supplier offers incentives to help the reseller promote the product.	Consumer and industrial products to be redistributed to other businesses and co

In these purchase situations the buyer generally does not radically change the product from its form when it was purchased from a Product Manufacturer. While technically these markets are also part of the supply chain, members of the business user market do not, in most cases, engage or directly assist in production activities.

BUSINESS VS CONSUMER MARKETS

For marketers, the selling environment of business markets present uniquely different circumstances when compared to selling to consumers.

At the beginning of this tutorial we saw two ways in which consumer and business markets differ:

- Business markets are more likely to be price driven than brand driven, and
- Demand in business markets tends to be more volatile than consumer markets.

However, the two markets are dissimilar in other ways requiring marketers to take a different approach when selling to business customers than to consumers.

These differences include:

- How Decisions Are Made
- Existence of Experienced Purchasers
- Time Needed to Make Buying Decision
- Size of Purchases
- Number of Buyers
- Type of Promotional Effort Needed to Reach Buyer

BUYING DIFFERENCES

Buying Centre Decisions

In the consumer market a very large percentage of purchase decisions are made by a single person. As we discussed in the Consumer Buying Behaviour tutorial, there are situations in which multiple people may be involved in a consumer purchase decision, such as a child influencing a parent to choose a certain brand of cereal or a husband and wife deciding together to buy a house, but most of the time purchases are individual decisions. The business market is significantly different. While single person purchasing is not unusual, especially within a small company, a significant percentage of business buying, especially within larger organizations, requires the input of many.

In the marketing literature those associated with the purchase decision are known to be part of a Buying Centre, which consists of individuals within an organization that perform one or more of the following roles:

- *Buyer*: Responsible for dealing with suppliers and placing orders
- *Decider*: Has the power to make the final purchase decision
- *Influencer*: Has the ability to affect what is ordered such as setting order specifications
- *User*: Those who will actually use the product when it is received
- *Initiator*: Any Buying Centre member who is the first to determine that a need exists

- *Gatekeeper*: Anyone who controls access to other Buying Centre members

For marketers confronting a Buying Centre it is important to first identify who plays what role. Once identified the marketer must address the needs of each member, which may differ significantly. For instance, the Decider, who may be the company president wants to make sure the purchase will not negatively affect the company's bottom line while the Buyer wants to be assured the product will be delivered on time. Thus, the way each Buying Centre member is approached and marketed to requires careful planning in order to address the unique needs of each member.

Experienced Purchasers

As noted in the discussion of the Buying Centre, organizations often employ purchasing agents or professional buyers whose job is to negotiate the best deals for their company. Unlike consumers, who often lack information when making purchase decisions, professional buyers are generally as knowledgeable about the product and the industry as the marketer who is selling to them.

Decision Making Time

Depending on the product, business purchase decisions can drag on for an extensive period. Unlike consumer markets where impulse purchasing is rampant, the number of people involved in business purchase decisions results in decisions taking weeks, months or even years.

Size of Purchases

For products that are regularly used and frequently purchased, businesses will often buy a larger volume at one time compared to consumer purchases. Because of this business purchasers often demand price breaks for higher order levels.

Type of Promotions

Companies who primarily target consumers often use mass advertising methods to reach an often widely dispersed market. For business-to-business marketers the size of individual orders, along with a smaller number of buyers, makes person-to-person contact by sales representatives a more effective means of promotion.

TYPES OF BUSINESS PURCHASE DECISIONS

While it would appear business customers face the same four purchase situations faced by consumers, the nature of the business market has led many marketing academics to group business purchase situations into only three categories.

The reason is that the idea of a minor order may not hold as well in the business market, where buyers tend to place larger orders and where suppliers' marketing efforts are directed toward the most profitable buyers.

- *Straight Re-Purchase*: These purchase situations involve routine ordering. In most cases buyers simply reorder the same products or services that were previously purchased. In fact, many larger companies have programmed re-purchases into an automated ordering system that initiates electronic orders when inventory falls a certain pre-determined level. For the supplier benefiting from the re-purchase this situation is ideal since the purchaser is not looking to evaluate other products. For competitors who are not getting the order it may require extensive marketing efforts to persuade the buyer to consider other product or service options.
- *Modified Re-Purchase*: These purchases occur when products or services previously considered a straight re-purchase are for some reason now under a re-evaluation process. There are many reasons why a product is moved to the status of a modified re-purchase. Some of these reasons include: end of purchase contract period, change in who is involved in making the purchase, supplier is removed from an approved suppliers list, mandate from top level of organization to re-evaluate all purchasing, or strong marketing effort by competitors. In this circumstance the incumbent supplier faces the same challenges they may have faced when they initially convinced the buyer to make the purchase. For competitors the door is now open and they must work hard to make sure their message is heard by those in charge of the purchase decision.
- *New Task Purchase*: As the name suggests, these purchases are ones the buyer has never or rarely made before. In some ways new task purchases can be considered as either minor or major depending on the total cost or overall importance of the purchase. In either case the buyer will spend considerably more time evaluating alternatives. For example, if faced with a major new task purchase, which often involves complex items, such as computer systems, buildings, robotic assembly lines, etc., the purchase cycle from first recognizing the need to placement of the order may be months or even years.

8

Layout of Information: Impact on Management Research

It is not possible to set out here just one ideal way of organizing and laying out reports or papers. The tactics of arrangement and physical layout must be varied according to the task involved and the needs of the audience.

We tried to discuss the specific tactics of layout to be used in every type of report, paper, or other document, it would require almost a book by itself. So we propose here to discuss the best tactics for organizing and laying out detailed technical reports and papers, such as progress reports, project reports, and research papers.

THE INITIAL IMPACT

The first thing to realise is that your papers begin to produce a response from the readers-begin to work for or against you-as soon as they land on those readers' desks. Indeed, it is possible to argue that reports and papers begin to work for or against their writers even before that. Readers' over-all responses to papers are influenced by the ease with which they can identify the papers they want and retrieve them from libraries or information storage systems.

We begin by emphasizing that there are at least *two* broad groups of readers to consider; those who have asked for the paper, and those who have not been expecting the paper or report that has arrived.

The first group, who have asked for the report or paper to be sent to them, want to know immediately 'Is this the right paper?'; 'Does it have the information that I wanted?'; 'Should I read it now or later?'

The second group, who have not been expecting the paper, have at least four questions that run through their minds:

- What's this all about?
- Is it of relevance to me?
- Does it contain significant new information?
- Should I allocate time for reading it now?

Both groups are looking for *information* to help focus quickly on the orientation and content of the document. They want a prominent, succinct and apt title. They want to find quickly a terse but reliable summing up of the essence of the work, showing the points that touch their interests or needs-the reasons why the paper has come to them.

They want a clear summary of the ceases drawn from the work and of the recommendations consequent upon those ceases. If your paper is to get off to a good start, give your readers the information they want in the quickest and most accessible way.

Do you need to take all this trouble, especially when managers have asked you to write the paper, and your readers are being paid to read it? The answer is 'yes'; because no matter whether they are being paid to read your paper or not, your readers are unlikely to seize it with excitement and enthusiasm. All of us complain that we have too much to do, especially that we have too much paper to read. Any new document that arrives must compete for attention.

Consider our own response to most papers we receive. Do we settle down to careful reading at once? Usually not. We pick up the paper and weigh (sometimes literally!) and consider it. We look at its size and organization. We glance at its cover and 'headlines' and riffle quickly through to get a sense of its organization and density. We debate the attractiveness of reading the paper and-of great importance-we estimate the resources of time and effort that will be needed to deal with it. As we do this, an attitude to the paper begins to form-we begin to respond to it.

Our response-to-papers meter begins to register on a scale such as:

- That really so, how interesting!
- Looks very interesting.
- Interesting.
- Could just be interesting.
- I wonder if this is worth reading.
- Looks damned heavy going.
- Have I really got to read all this?

THE FRONT PAGE

The very appearance of a report or paper should begin the campaign to win the attention of both groups of readers. Does it look heavy, dauntingly thick and covered with dense black type? Does the design of the front page draw the reader's attention immediately to the answers to the questions that have crossed his or her mind?

Most readers who see the front page complain that their eyes are drawn immediately to information of secondary importance. Others notice first the heavy black prominence of the company's name in the top left-hand corner. Yet others see first the large part devoted to the distribution list. Most have to *search* for the title, which gives the main answer to the question: what is this chapter about?

Of course, a note on confidentiality, or the company's name, or the circulation list has every right to appear on the front page of a report. Those items are too prominent. Our point is that the secondary material has been given a prominence that it does not deserve-a prominence that *should* have been given to the title and the information of principal importance and use to the reader.

FACTORS THAT GIVE EMPHASIS

Three factors that are important in achieving prominence for items of information on a page: position on the page, size of the area allocated to the information, and size of the type faces used in the printing of the information. These three factors can be used alone or in various combinations to draw readers' eyes to those things that you wish to highlight.

To give the title of a paper maximum prominence, it is best to place it as near as possible to the position that breaks the page into ideal proportions-the 'golden section'. As *The Penguin Encylopaedia* states, the golden section is not easy to define exactly:

An ideal proportion used by architects and artists which cannot be resolved mathematically; expressed by a line divided so that the smaller part is to the greater as the greater is to the whole; very roughtly.

In classical times and during the Renaissance it was supposed to provide a key to the harmony of the universe, and architects and artists sought to compose their works in accordance with it.

In Western civilization, readers expect to find titles 'balanced' comfortably on the page, and this means that their eyes are inclined to go first to a position about one third of the way down from the top of the page and in the centre.

It helps if the title is in larger type than the rest of the information surrounding it on the front page; and if possible, it should be separated from all other information by ample areas of white space, which will make it stand out. Another device for giving emphasis is the use of underlining and ruling. But combination of several devices is usually overwhelming. Titles that are in large type and are clearly spaced do not need underlining as well.

Readers need to know a job number and a report number-where this chapter fits into a sequence of information. They need to know the date on which the paper was written, to know what currency it has. They will be helped by having a distribution list readily accessible on the front page, because it tells them who else has received the information and is therefore 'in the know'.

Though all persons reading internal documents should be well aware of the name of the organization for which they work, it is reasonable that the organization's name should appear on every document that is circulated.

A recognizable house style helps to build a sense of identity and 'belonging'. It is certainly important that readers should know which department, part or group the paper emerges from. Likewise, it is vital to know who has written and who has approved the circulation of the paper. And if a paper must be kept confidential, that is one of the first things readers must be told.

All these *are* relevant pieces of information and should, if possible, appear on the front page of the document; but they should be kept in subordinate positions so that the principal emphasis is always thrown on the title of the paper. This can be done without producing the cluttered effect. It is often possible to give readers even more information on the front page without the cluttering effect.

WORDING OF TITLES

We want to make two further points about titles, both designed to help make a sharp impact on readers: titles should be short, preferably on one line only; and they should specify exactly what the paper is talking about, not simply name a whole subject. First, they have to inform readers about what is in the document.

Second, they have to distinguish one document from another. If readers are flicking through piles of documents in their in-trays or in the reference part of a library, they want a brief title which can be taken in at a single glance, and which will distinguish one document from all the others.

POSITIONING THE SUMMARY

So far, we have been discussing what we call the orientation part of the report-the part that influences the readers' initial attitude to and interest in the paper. We have said that the summary plays an important part in this part. At this point in our discussion of how to organize information effectively, we wish simply to emphasize that most reports and papers need a summary on the title page or on the page immediately following.

And since the main aim of the summary is to emphasize what is new and interesting to potential readers, the principal emphasis in the summary should be on findings, ceases and recommendations. Of course, if your report is to be only one or two pages long, a separate title page and summary will seem over-elaborate. But even in those circumstances, get your paper off to a good start by ensuring that the heading of your first page is comfortably spaced and incorporates a sharp, focusing title.

If you decide against having a separate summary, at least bring your attention-catching information forward into a summarizing opening paragraph.

INTRODUCTORY MATERIAL

Once readers have been shown the pattern of ideas they are to be led through, it is useful to set out the background to the report in full. Readers who want a fully detailed account of your work find it helpful if you state in full the problem you were aiming to solve or the aspect you were setting out to investigate. Why was the work undertaken? What scope was given? What limitations of time, personnel and materials were imposed? It may help readers if you give an outline of previous relevant work at this point-a survey of the history of related work and a theoretical analysis of problems related to your topic. Anything that fills in the background up to the point at which the work began is relevant to the introductory part.

Any material that you now know as a result of having done the work that you are about to describe. A common source of distraction in introductions to reports is failure to distinguish what had been done *before* the work to be reported was started, and the inclusion of information that the writer could have known only after he had completed the work. Consider the following example:

This report relates to work on the active rudders on HMS Park Place during 1987. The work was undertaken because of problems in the past of ships losing propellers and breaking drive shafts. In the past this loss has been prevented by securing the active rudders to prevent rotation, but this was not satisfactory due to the time and effort required. To try and prevent further loss, a new design was instigated and at the same time, measurements were to be made of the various forces present when operating normally. These measurements were made on one of the modified shaft/propeller combinations and whereas the stresses measured would not be the same as the original shafts, the forces acting on the various components would be representative of the original system.

Corrosion affects the materials used in constructing chemical plants, the main areas of attack being crevices, welds, and bimetallic contacts. Undue stress and vibrations must be avoided. Many expensive materials can be profitably used as thin linings supported by cheaper, more corrosive, stronger materials. This technique decreases corrosion in plants which handle chlorides. The change can be hampered by cost, but as the technique improves, the cost will decrease. Linings of tantalum, zirconium and titanium are the most satisfactory.

The work to be reported in the paper was an exploration of which materials would be best for use as thin linings. Did the writer know before he started that linings of tantalum, zirconium and titanium would be most satisfactory? No, that is the cease he came to as a result of doing his work; but that became plain to the reader only after reading the whole report.

You will help yourself get the right perspective on writing an introduction if you consider that you are trying to say to your readers, 'this is the position as we saw it before we began our work'. That leads naturally into the body of the report in which you say, in effect, 'so this is what we did and this is what we discovered'. Here is an example of a better introduction:

Development Department is interested in the possibility of using resin cloth for electrical insulation. As overheating of electrical equipment could cause heating of the resin cloth, which could lead to the evolution of flammable gases from the resin, they asked us to investigate the pyrolysis products of the resin. We decided that it was necessary to approach this task in two stages:

- To establish a reliable analytical procedure;
- To identify and measure the products from pyrolysis of resin cloths A and B.

We could find no helpful literature on the thermal decomposition of resin cloths or on directly suitable analytical procedures. We therefore decided to attempt to modify the 'Rapid Combustion' method of Belcher and Ingram.

This report describes our experiments to establish a reliable analytical procedure. A later report will give details of the pyrolysis products from resin cloths A and B.

ACCOUNT OF THE WORK DONE

The account of the work you did will probably be the longest part in your report. It is difficult for us to discuss in general terms what should go in this part. The precise data that the reader will find helpful will vary according to such factors as whether you are describing a design, a survey procedure, a test method, or an experimental procedure. But here is a helpful check-list of what readers in an industrial setting will want to know in various types of papers.

WHAT READERS WILL WANT TO KNOW

- About new products: the potential uses, the risks, the commercial requirements, the technical requirements, if any more work needs to be done on problems, manpower requirements, financial requirements, material requirements, the probable life of the product or project, the relative importance of the product or project compared with other products or projects, and proposed schedules for development.
- About technical problems: just what the problem is, how big and important it is, whether it has arisen before and what has been done and by whom, whether the problem is temporary or permanent, whether the solution being put forward in the report is the only solution and if not, what others were considered and why they were rejected, what should be done now, who and what will be involved in the recommendations, and whether any redesign will be called for.
- About surveys of materials or processes: the properties, characteristics, and capabilities of the material, its limitations, whether its properties vary in varying conditions, where the material could be used and how, whether the materials are readily available or are to be made by the company, the costs of the

> materials or processes, the costs of plant required, if any, to handle the materials or processes, the materials and/or processes which the new materials or processes would compete with, how the new materials and processes would fit in with present company plans, processes, and future programme.

The way in which you arrange a description or explanation of your work will inevitably be related to your decisions about the aim and audience for your paper. There are many ways of organizing even an apparently simple description, depending on your readers' orientation or interests. For some readers, a description may be best arranged to guide them 'from the outside in'-reflecting the real order of perception as a person approaches an object for the first time; but for other readers, who have some understanding of the object you are describing, it may be better to write in a way that reflects the hierarchy of components-starting with the 'heart' of the machine or process, and gradually explaining how ancillary elements are related or how your work involved modifying customary structures or procedures.

If you have information to present about activities at three sites, A, B and C, and if you want to describe the ways in which you experimented with variations in manpower, machinery and materials, you have at least two patterns of organization available:

Arrangement 1

Site A	-manpower
	-machinery
	-materials
Site B	-manpower
	-machinery
	-materials
Site C	-manpower
	-machinery
	-materials

Arrangement 2

Manpower	-site A
	-site B
	-site C
Machinery	-site A
	-site B
	-site C
Materials	-site A
	-site B
	-site C

But we want to emphasize again here that your choice must be dictated by your readers' principal interests and by the particular impact you wish to make with your account.

ORDER OF ARRANGEMENT

In our discussions so far, we have been advocating that you arrange your reports and papers in order of importance *from the readers' point of view.* We have been advocating a *descending* order of importance, presenting the new, most important information in outline at the beginning of the paper, and giving the supporting evidence or detail afterwards. This is not simply to help focus and orientation. It is also because readers find it easier to assimilate detailed information if they have first been given a general framework into which to fit the detail.

Imagine a man who is called for jury duty, and finds himself watching a grave be-wigged figure rise to open the case: 'My Lord, the accused is a man of previous good character; he is married, My Lord, and has been married for eighteen years. He has three children, My Lord, lives in a detached house in a good part of town, and has worked for his present employer in the same capacity for over twenty years…' As the barrister drones on, ask yourself, is the defendant guilty or not?

The question is unanswerable, because much depends on whether he is accused of speeding or of murdering his wife. What the evidence is *for* determines our view of its importance. Unless we know what case we are trying, we cannot assess each item of information as we receive it. If it does not fit into a pattern or framework, it is rapidly lost in a confusion of formless detail. Yet such confusion is often caused by writers who give detailed evidence before stating their objectives and ceases. Readers do not know what the evidence is for, or where it is leading, and so are unable to make it do any work in their minds.

PYRAMIDS OF EVIDENCE

Evidence, in a document which is explaining, proving, or arguing a case, must be marshalled to support that case. And it will be of use to the reader only if he or she is clearly told what that case is. Too often writers let the evidence swamp the case. We must emphasize again that there is a difference between the order of discovery and the order of announcement. And that the thoroughness necessary to make and check discoveries is opposite to the parsimony needed to explain them without confusion.

We are aware that there are some types of writing that can make use of *ascending* order-starting with minor matters and gradually building to a striking climax. In theory, this technique can be psychologically effective: it makes use of the readers' curiosity and encourages them to read on to learn the final outcome. It is the detective story style, with clues dropped here and there to intrigue us and a final dramatic revelation of where responsibility and innocence really lie. But we think it is rarely appropriate for professional reports and papers to use this 'intriguing' technique. Perhaps if you have a particularly delicate topic to broach, it may be appropriate to approach it obliquely: but most readers of reports and papers are looking for a more open and rigorous approach. They will be at least suspicious and at worst hostile to your apparent reluctance to 'come to the point'.

Most reports and papers, then, will be best organized in a pyramid structure, in order of importance, with a summary at the top and a gradual expansion into greater detail within the body of the paper. The base of the pyramid will be your appendices, containing the most detailed information.

This arrangement has the advantage of making readily accessible the information wanted by the majority of readers. Readers can stop reading when they have obtained as much detail as they need. Perhaps only a few will read right through to the appendices. Your readership will probably be an inverted pyramid:

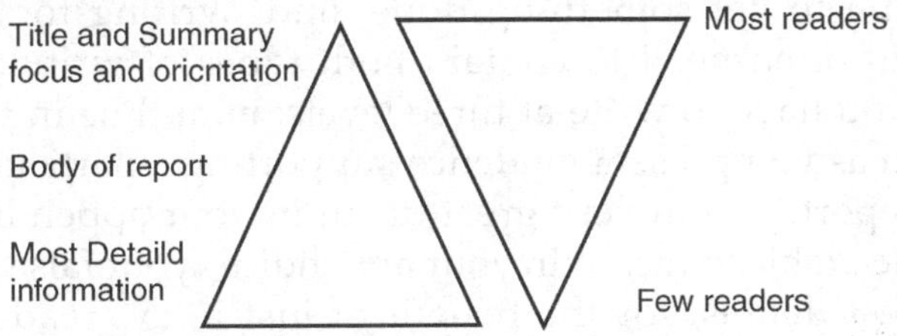

However, *within* your order of importance, it is possible to arrange parts of the account in many ways, to reflect, for example:

- Spatial or topographical arrangements;
- Experimental or manufacturing sequences;
- Fault-finding or operating sequences;
- Order of discovery;
- Existing patterns of information in libraries or other stores.

Each one of these ways of organizing a paper is 'logical' in its own terms. But the internal logic of such organizational structures is of little interest to readers. The logic which matters to them as they read is the logic of their understanding. This starts from the familiar (which may be the old process, or the desired end-product, or a familiar part of the machine which will be retained intact in modification), and moves onwards to the unfamiliar. Just what is familiar or unfamiliar depends on what the reader already knows, not what the *writer* knows. Many writers hand information over to their readers like a dinner-table guest passing a knife with the sharp end pointing outwards. Polite people turn it round, offering the comfortable handle first. So with information. In most cases it has to be turned round, so that the reader can grasp it comfortably.

AMOUNT OF DETAIL

The amount of detail in your account must also vary according to your purpose in writing and according to your audience. Are you aiming to assemble and write about all available information for permanent record or are you aiming simply to describe how and why you came to a particular set of ceases? In our experience, junior staff frequently misjudge what their supervisors want from them.

A major complaint from managers in business and industry is that new recruits still think they are writing school and university, emphasizing *how much* they know about a topic. Report-writing in business and industry is mainly a *management* activity, and not part of the academic activity of generating and making available new knowledge for anyone who may be interested.

Report-writing in business and industry should focus more sharply on what needs to be said in order *to get something done,* and details in reports and papers should be sorted and selected with that objective uppermost in mind.

Note, however, that it would be simplistic to set up too sharp a contrast between 'writing to get something done' and 'writing for the record'. A good paper will often need to contain both types of writing. Indeed, you may find that you have to write at three levels: in outline in your summary; in greater detail as you present evidence supporting a particular cease in the body of your report; and in very great detail in your appendices.

It may be desirable to record in your appendices your false starts, negative findings and test details, for the benefit of just a few readers who might otherwise waste time and money in the future by re-exploring ground you have covered already.

It is important to provide a clear signalling system within your report to help readers find the details they want-to find their way around. To do this, make liberal use of headings and sub-headings that performance as sign-posts signalling routes and announcing the content of parts.

You may feel that this uses more paper. But the disadvantage of increasing the amount of paper must be weighed against the advantage of making it possible for your reader to get a sense of rapid, comfortable progress through the story. Normally, this sense of comfortable progress will be helped by the division of the work into logically related, manageable parts, and by the liberal use of headings and sub-headings.

RESULTS AND FINDINGS

The results part in the body of your report should rarely by bulky. Bring forward into the results part just the main facts and figures that are necessary to support and explain the argument you are presenting. Do not 'clog up' the centre of the report with a mass of data that it is not essential for readers to consider as they follow the description or argument.

We are not saying that you should not present all your findings, negative and otherwise: we are suggesting that these findings *in detail* should be presented in appendices to the main report. In the main text, give the reader just the pieces of information that are necessary to make the argument logically acceptable and technically persuasive.

It is too easy to swamp a clear argument, which requires underpinning with carefully selected facts, with a mountain of detailed evidence. Readers should not be expected to repeat all the sifting the writer did in arriving at his or her ceases. Our experience is that the urge to be complete often leads writers to ignore the readers' need to have a *manageable* argument to grasp. *Less* evidence is usually needed if the reader is to *understand* the point. To record and discuss every result is overkill or in your filing cabinet.

DISCUSSION AND ANALYSIS

After the statement of your findings, it will be natural for you to discuss the ceases to which these lead. What is implied by the data that has emerged from your experiments, surveys or evaluations of material? In your discussion, you will state the inferences you draw from your observations. Drawing inferences means talking about results, not simply repeating them. Many report writers let themselves down badly at this point by failing to state implications, to recognize trends and changes, to draw attention to comparisons and contrasts, and to sum up differences. Repetition of readings should rarely be necessary: a discussion will normally require speculation about causes and effects, and analysis of implications for the future.

A discussion of what the facts imply must include a statement of the ceases drawn from the premises laid down. For this reason it is not essential in all reports to follow the discussion part by another part re-stating your ceases. A well-written report will have included the ceases and recommendations at the front in its summary; its ceases again in the course of its discussion; so it is not essential to state the ceases a third time after the discussion part. However, in a long and detailed report, it may be desirable to have a full statement of ceases in a separate part after the discussion within the body of the report, and to give a summary of the ceases at the beginning.

Footnotes

Distinguish between references and footnotes. References are statements that help readers find source material that is referred to in a text. Footnotes are additional comments, details or notes that the writer chooses to place outside the main stream of the account.

Footnotes at the bottom of the page are usually a sign that the writer has not thought out carefully what he or she wanted to say, or what importance to attach to each piece of information. Broadly speaking, if a piece of information is relevant to your readers' understanding of what is being said, that piece of information should be included within the main text, not slipped in at the bottom of the page.

The placing of items at the bottom of the page is an irritating distraction to readers, especially when they find that there is *no* additional information in the footnote or that it is information they did not need. After skipping to the bottom of the page, readers have to go back to the main text, find the appropriate place and pick up the threads of the argument as best they can. If the information you are tempted to put at the bottom of the page will be useful to your readers, put it in the main text. If the information is not important enough to be included in the text itself, that information is probably not worth including anywhere.

We are not arguing that all information is of equal importance. All writers occasionally find it helpful to offer their readers an 'aside' or parenthetical remark. But the most comfortable way to present such remarks is in parentheses, at least preserving the linear sequence for readers. Footnotes almost always introduce a sense of 'choppiness'. They should, therefore, be reserved for special circumstances.

PLACING OF ILLUSTRATIONS

Sometimes, you may feel that you can make your points most clearly by using non-verbal techniques of presentation. If so, place your tables or illustrations as close as possible in the text to the point at which you want readers to refer to them.

This will cause difficulties when you are producing a text simply in typescript. You will not always be able to include your graph, diagram or picture in a convenient place in the text. It may be necessary to collect all your graphs and figures in several separate pages at the end of a part of your report. If you do this, remember to tell your reader where the illustrations are. You can also consider presenting your illustrations on fold-out pages, to minimize the amount of turning to and fro that the reader has to do. Or, if you dislike this lay-out because fold-out pages can get tattered, consider the possibility of using two spiral bindings.

Beware of the temptation to include graphs and other illustrations in the body of your report simply because you have drawn them during the course of your work. Each time you are thinking about including an illustration, ask yourself whether that particular illustration will most effectively make the point you wish to press home to your reader. Are you being tempted to include the illustration simply to duplicate something that you have already said in words with adequate clarity? It is an irritating distraction for a reader to be encouraged to look at an illustration that provides no information in addition to that already in the prose text.

For example, one often reads statements such as 'the results show that as the temperature rose, the viscosity decreased, until at point X there was no further change. The reader then dutifully looks and after a few moments' scrutiny can see that as the temperature rose, the viscosity decreased, until at point X there was no further change. The reader, having gained no additional information from looking at the illustration, has then to go back and find the place in the prose text, pick up the threads of the argument and go ahead. Concentration on the argument has not been helped, rather hindered, by the writer's direction of the reader to look at the illustration.

Of course, if your readers *can* gain additional information by looking at the illustration, for example by extrapolating beyond given points or readings, then it will be beneficial for you to urge them to look at the illustration; but beware of the temptation to provide illustrations in scientific and technical papers simply to 'make it look scientific', or simply to show that you have been assiduous in drawing graphs and making tables as your work progressed.

Remember, too, that there is a difference between tables and graphs that are designed to make a point in an argument, and tables and graphs that are designed to make available a mass of information so that readers can scrutinize it at leisure. In this discussion of organization and lay-out of papers, we wish simply to emphasize that, wherever possible, masses of data and supporting. Give your reader a smooth, uninterrupted passage through the argument or description in the body of your report.

Appendices

Use appendices, then, to clear supporting information out of the way of the readers' concentration on the main theme. Is it necessary to include in the main text the specifications for materials and equipment used? Is it necessary to include in the main text your inspection-test data? Do you need to include in the main text the mathematical calculations by which you derived formulae? Do you need to include start-up procedures? Most material of this sort can reasonably be placed in an appendix where it is available if necessary but where it will not interfere with the progress of readers who do not need it.

STRUCTURE FOR OTHER TYPES OF DOCUMENTS

This discussion has concentrated on structure for reports and papers. The same structure, a pyramid starting with an incisive title, expanding gradually through a summary to the main story, and based on fully detailed appendices, normally works effectively for most other scientific and technical documents. In using the pyramid structure, you make it possible for readers to stop at various points on their way through the report, having accumulated as much as they need on their way up to that point. A well-written journal substance makes it possible for readers to do the same. It provides an effective, orienting title and summary. It then expands into full detail for those who want to know more about a procedure or survey method, or the advantages and disadvantages of various materials and activities. If the journal editor can find room for full details of matters such as specifications or experimental procedures, they are best left at the end for those readers whose interest continues to this level of detail.

Instruction sheets, specifications, and most other technical documents benefit from the same structure. A well-written set of instructions preferably starts with a statement of the overall aim of the procedure or an outline of the various steps or stages in the instructions. A well-written handbook for maintenance of equipment preferably starts with an orienting part which at least describes the remainder of the text.

Sales documentation is not the subject of our advice in this book-it calls for special techniques. But if you have to write technical information documents to be used in conjunction with sales literature, remember that new information is what readers are interested in.

They will not welcome a laborious repetition of first principles, known to everyone in the industry. Nor will they welcome having to wade through detailed descriptions of the mode of action of a type of machine they know very well. What *they do* want to know is how this particular product differs from familiar and established ones.

Other types of document include requests for capital, and recommendations for the purchase of machinery or services. Here, again, make sure readers know clearly *what* you want, before swamping them with details as to *why* you want it. Recognize that they may not want *full* details of all the alternatives, although they will need to be assured that you have checked all other possibilities before recommending one.

However, they do not want to re-do your job, and go through all the possibilities again themselves. For example, if you have eight possibilities to choose from, by all means give brief details of all eight in an appendix. But in the text, dismiss most of them quickly on the basis of their obvious inadequacies, and discuss in detail only two or three. This gives the assurance of a realistic choice, without the confusion of too much detail.

Even documents which group information according to physical location or manufacturing procedures are most effective if the whole document (and probably each part within it) starts with a summarizing sentence or paragraph outlining what is to come.

It is a basic tenet of all good communication that one starts by presenting an audience with some orientation material, an outline of the whole, before beginning to discuss the parts. Only in documents that aim at presenting a chronological account is it preferable to depart from an order of importance such as we have described; and even in such documents, it is probably best to start with some orienting information explaining why the historical account is being given.

First, choose an order for your information which works from main points downwards to details, and not the other way. Second, always be flexible in your choice of organization and lay-out. Resist the temptation to categorise each writing task, and then to squeeze and distort the information into a recognized and stereotyped format. Choose your path through the facts you have to communicate with a careful eye on the readers' convenience. Each task requires an individual structure.

THE USE OF HEADINGS AND NUMBERING

FORMAL AND INFORMATIVE HEADINGS

Usually, it helps if you make generous use of headings and sub-headings.

Headings break text into manageable parts, and help by increasing the 'white space' around the blocks of type, especially when the type is single-spaced. They also performance as signposts, pointing out what is to be found in each part. Formal headings such as *Problem,* or *Experimental,* or *Discussion* are neither informative nor useful, because they do not focus attention on the essence of the following paragraphs. Better headings, such as *Updating Operation Flow Charts* or *The Influence of Sunlight on Linings,* convey real information about the content of the part. In word-processed text, there are four ways in which the relative hierarchy of the headings can be shown:

- Numbering;
- Indenting;
- Using capitals and lower case letters;
- Bolding (use of heavy type). (In typewritten texts, underlining has to take the place of bolding.)

To ensure that readers grasp the relationships at a glance, documents that use all four systems are best. The usual hierarchy of size and letter forms is:

- Capitals Bolded (or Underlined)
- Capitals Not Bolded (or Underlined)
- Lower Case Bolded (or underlined)
- Lower case not bolded (or underlined)

A decimal numbering system helps further, but note the effect of the following layout:

- FIRST LEVEL HEADING
- SECOND LEVEL HEADING
- Third Level Heading
- Fourth level heading

Because a number like '7.2.1.2' is longer than the single '7' it seems more important. So it is preferable to use indenting as well, in order to complete the visual representation of the hierarchy of parts.

Some writers (or their typists or managers) will not use indentation because they believe that progressively increasing left-hand margins wastes paper. We think that nothing is a waste of paper that helps the reader. In any case, if the indentation is only two or three spaces each time, the margins never get very wide.

But if managers insist that indenting the text is wasteful, a good compromise is to indent the headings only, leaving all the text on the margin. The use of decimal numbering, differing weights of type, and indentation for the headings shows the reader the 'shape' of the information.

SYSTEMS OF NUMBERING

Three systems of numbering are widely used in business, industrial and research writing:

- The decimal system;

- Mixtures of numbers and letters;
- The HMSO system.

The *decimal system* is generally accepted as the clearest numbering system available. In this system, the headed parts and sub-parts only are numbered, not every paragraph. There can be any number of paragraphs in a part or sub-section.

When you have sub-divisions, your first sub-division number and heading should always come immediately after the division number and heading. Numbering to three or four places of decimals is usually a sign that grouping and sub-division of ideas need to be reviewed.

If you wish to set items in a list within your sub-sections, use simple numbers. Remember that the decimal numbering system is for *headings* only.

ALGORITHMS FOR COMPLEX POSSIBILITIES AND PROCEDURES

Another aspect of organization which we wish to discuss separately is the need to arrange information physically so that readers can easily find their route through a mass of information that must be made available, but will not all be relevant to all readers. It is often necessary to present information which has complex inter-relations, and to show how those inter-relations can lead to various outcomes. Similarly, it is often necessary to explain that various combinations of conditions can produce a particular state (perhaps a fault), and to explain that various actions must be taken according to which conditions exist.

From reading tax guides or instruction manuals for equipment, we all know that prose accounts of this sort of information can be extraordinarily complex. They often read like conundrums. Though the sentences may be short and simple, the complexity of the relations is confusing, principally because we have to read about all the possible situations. Normally, however, readers are interested in only one set of conditions, and wish to know the outcome from these only. They want the information presented in a way that will help them sort out the possible relationships or conditions and isolate the set relevant to their interests.

In these circumstances, it is not enough just to 'present' the complex information-to make a mass of data available to any reader prepared to work through it. For effective communication, the writer must enable readers to find their way quickly and easily to the decisions they need, which means helping them to ignore information not relevant to them. The writer must make the right information available for use, yet make minimum demands on the readers' time and attention.

Often, the best way to meet these objectives when writing about procedures is to use an algorithm. An algorithm is a carefully planned sequence of statements, questions or instructions arranged in a logical hierarchy and requiring readers to read only the starting item and such subsequent items of information as are relevant to their needs.

The most common forms of algorithms in engineering and scientific work are list-form algorithms, flow-charts (logical trees) and MAP layouts. All achieve the same purpose: they enable readers to concentrate on finding a clear path through a complex set of relationships or conditions by ignoring anything that does not apply to their situations. They

Before the adapter test can be carried out it is essential to check that there is a gap of 0.13 to 0.25 mm between the card reader lamp and the optic surface at the bottom of the lamp holder screw-hole.

If there is no gap or if the gap is not within the specified measurements, disconnect the card reader lamp terminals, screw the lamp out of the lamp holder and inspect the optic surface beneath the lamp holder screw-hole for dirt, dust or damage. If the optic surface is in good condition (shiny), the lamp can be reinstalled, ensuring that the gap between the lamp and the optic surface at the bottom of the lamp holder screw-hole is between 0.13 and 0.25 mm. Use a card strip to check this gap. If the optic surface is dirty or dusty, clean the surface with lint free cloth (and alcohol if necessary) and then reinstall the lamp, ensuring that the correct gap is present between the lamp and the optic surface. If the optic surface is not dirty or dusty but is in unsatisfactory condition for some other reason, exchange the fibre optic assembly and then reinstall the lamp, ensuring that the correct lamp-to-surface gap is present.

When the lamp is reinstalled, reconnect the lamp terminals. Then press the FAD button to signal that the card reader is ready for the adapter test. They reduce distraction caused by unwanted information and reduce the load on memory because readers do not have to hold in mind previous questions or previous decisions. Examples of a complex piece of prose, and of three algorithmic presentations of the same information are given. The original prose text is shown. The list form algorithm presents the same information using simple numbering. It is clear and to the point and takes less space than the flow chart or MAP layout. The need for the reader's eye to jump from item to item is, however, a disadvantage. The flow chart algorithm is equally explicit but takes more time to prepare and more space in the document.

It has, however, the advantage of using lines to guide the reader's eye from one item to the next. Also it can use different symbols (squares, rectangles, diamonds, circles) to emphasise the distinction between instructions, questions, comments and ceases. The MAP format is explicit and takes less space than a symbolic flow chart algorithm. It also has the great advantage that it can be produced entirely by typewriter. All the elements can be typed in from a normal alphanumeric keyboard. A disadvantage, however, is that it has less visual impact than a symbolic flow chart.

Complex, inter-related items of information are almost always communicated most efficiently to scientific and technical readers if presented in flow charts or logical trees, but once again it is necessary to emphasise that the most suitable choice of communication tactics will depend on the aim, audience and context of the document you are writing. Research has shown that the speed and accuracy with which readers can find their way through complex information vary according to:

- Whether each reader is able to decide easily which items of information are relevant and which irrelevant to his or her situation;
- Whether there are so many interdependent contingencies that some display formats are automatically precluded.

Wright and Reid explored the comparative effectiveness of presenting complex information in four ways-complex prose, a list of simple short sentences, a table, and a flow chart. Their main cease was that details of the user's background experience and situation influence the relative effectiveness of the different formats.

However, conveying exactly the same information, may nevertheless be better as a logical tree if it is being used on a do-it-yourself basis by the homespun car mechanic. These findings emphasize the need for writers to choose their visual tactics with as much thought about their aim and audience as they use in choosing their verbal tactics.

9

Feedback-Gathering Techniques: Action Research

Information about audience members is essential to any specialized communication campaign. A communicator must know about the receivers before he or she can design a message, choose a medium, or develop plans for the campaign. Several approaches to gathering audience information, concentrating on public opinion survey techniques. It reviews the procedures involved in opinion polling, but does not get into details of the process. What is involved and the steps typically followed by survey specialists are described. Public communicators with techniques of surveying. This will enable them to speak from an informed position and talk intelligently with survey specialists about audience research.

The role of assessment and evaluation in planning and determining the effect of a communication program. Although assessment generally precedes a communication campaign and evaluation typically follows it, the fact that both procedures involve similar research skills makes it convenient and useful to treat these topics together. In the present context, "assessment" refers to activities directed toward determining the status of selected beliefs, attitudes, and knowledge within some population. In short, issues of audience assessment refer to efforts to learn where people stand on some issue. Examples might include attitudes toward a service, a product, or the company producing them. Thus, assessment issues relate primarily to a desire to know what customers (or employees) know or feel about some issue of importance.

Evaluation procedures may involve some of the same data collection techniques used in the assessment phase of a communication campaign, but here the focus is directed specifically toward determining the impact of the communication effort, rather than "sizing up" the audience. There are a variety of approaches to evaluating the effectiveness of a communication program. Desired outcomes may include increments in knowledge (for example, understanding the strong points of a front wheel drive automobile), change of attitudes (for example, establishing favorable feelings toward a particular brand of cola), or modification of established behaviors (for example, changing employees' telephone usage patterns to minimize costs), and it is important that outcome measures mesh with the objectives of the communication campaign.

In a subsequent section, we review briefly five types of evaluations, all of which have important applications. The most important of these evaluation types, however, is the effectiveness evaluation, which involves determining the actual effect of the communication on the receiver. Effectiveness evaluation is central to all other types. If a particular approach does not have the desired effect on recipient knowledge (or attitudes or behaviors, depending upon the goals of the communicator), other considerations (like cost or convenience) become irrelevant.

AUDIENCE ASSESSMENT

Purpose

The purpose of an audience assessment is to determine the current status of some issue within a given population. An assessment might involve a determination of the degree of knowledge people have on some issue, their attitudes and beliefs regarding that issue, and their relevant day-to-day behaviors. Assessments can cover what respondents know, what they feel, and what they do. It is not necessary that an assessment cover all of these areas, and, in fact, interest most frequently involves people's feelings and attitudes about company-identified issues, employee- or customer-generated issues, or a combination of these. Whether the focus is on knowledge, attitudes, or behaviour, the objective of the assessment procedure is the same: to identify what people know, feel, do, or plan to do.

A good assessment program should provide a clear picture of the clientele and where this "public" stands on issues of importance to the company. This information serves two important roles in the process of communication. First of all, it provides a scientifically accurate picture of the views of the relevant public—customers, employees, or some other identified group. This often becomes important in confrontational settings, in which a self-appointed group purports to represent large contingents of the population and to be speaking on their behalf. Often, these assertions are based upon wishful thinking rather than fact, and a good assessment program can provide a real expression of the "people's will," which very well could be at odds with positions advocated by self-proclaimed public spokespersons.

The information gathered in an assessment effort also serves as an initial baseline against which subsequent change, prompted by a communication campaign, can be measured. For example, knowing before a media campaign was initiated that 55 percent of the population was in favor of some company action provides a convenient benchmark against which to evaluate the impact of the campaign.

The final use of an assessment is to permit one to tailor messages to specific audiences. At other points in this text, the significance of knowing one's audience is a factor in selecting the most effective communication. An audience assessment program permits one to achieve this knowledge of an audience and thus to design more effective communications. Knowing the proportion of a group that is opposed to, or in favor of, a position being advocated is extremely helpful, as is knowledge that some subgroup has a particular concern about an issue that is about to be addressed in a forthcoming campaign.

The major assessment techniques utilized in the assessment of customer attitudes and perceptions are public forums and consumer surveys. Variations on these two approaches are discussed. Because they are the most widely used approaches and clearly the most desirable, survey techniques are described in a systematic, step-by-step fashion, as they might be implemented by a business.

PUBLIC FORUMS

Public forums (hearings) usually are understood to be large, formal gatherings of people in which any person may express his or her viewpoint, sometimes by means of written testimony. These forums are used frequently by policymakers. Indeed, in some circumstances this form of public participation is mandated by law. When a contemplated policy change is likely to have a significant effect on employees, customers, or other interested groups (for example, when new production methods at a plant might have negative consequences for nearby residents), public forums scheduled at different times and in several communities (neighborhoods) could be used to elicit opinions of these groups regarding their feelings about the proposed changes—even though in most instances such information-gathering sessions are not mandated.

Public forums can also provide helpful suggestions for the implementation of a communication campaign. The participation of residents from different communities in public forums can yield a picture of the needs and values within differing communities, which in turn can be used in targeting individualized communications tailored precisely to these various communities.

In addition to the open public forum, it may be helpful in certain instances to make use of a smaller "key" informant sample of representatives from various company or community groups who might have influence in the problem area. Such key informant discussions can be helpful because they tend to be substantive and problem focused, especially if the sessions are structured to enhance this focus. The use of such samples also decreases the likelihood that a session will deteriorate into a generalized grievance hearing of individuals with limited understanding of the specific issue under consideration. Public forums and key informant samples serve different ends: A broad-based conference helps to legitimize a proposed course of action and increase program participa-tion; the involvement of key figures from various affected groups usually leads to a better understanding of the problem area.

Public forums have many limitations. They rarely represent a cross section of the population, and therefore provide a limited view of the total community. They also are limited in the kinds of information they can deliver. Data gathered in these forums are not collected systematically, nor do they lend themselves to the careful analysis possible with survey data.

To those experienced with public forums, it should not be surprising that they frequently amount to "window dressing" rather than actually serving the function of providing a valid picture of public perceptions. It is nearly always the case that views of the people in attendance at the meeting are not representative of the total community. Public forums are heavily attended by cliques and special interest groups and frequently lack broad community representation. People with "axes to grind" are more likely to be present than are average citizens, although even the smallest splinter groups are quick to claim vast constituencies just beyond the doors of the hearing room. Public speaking skills are at a premium in such circumstances, effectively barring many less articulate individuals from expressing their views and from having them reflected within the meeting itself. The power of vocal, but unrepresentative, groups can be restricted sometimes through the use of information checklists.

Information Checklists

A checklist of public forum agenda items can be circulated to provide a summary of the sentiment of members attending a meeting. The information checklist functions as a kind of survey, although it is limited to those who actually attend the forum. Since it is a survey, the rules pertaining to the construction of survey instruments, discussed in a subsequent section, apply. Careful attention must be directed toward item construction, scaling, etc., to ensure the reliability and validity of the checklist. Information checklists are easy to use and inexpensive, and they yield quantifiable data; as such, they offer some resistance to manipulation by organized groups. However, checklists also suffer from certain shortcomings, owing to their limited capacity in allowing only reactive participation and superficial discussion of relevant issues. Even if checklists measured perfectly the views of the people in the hall, the information that they yield would not likely be representative of the total population.

In practice, the forum leader administers a brief (that is, ten or fewer items) questionnaire at the beginning of a meeting to determine sentiment within the group on the main issues. Knowing that 70 percent of the group was opposed to, or in favor of, the site for a new generating plant would be helpful in evaluating the testimony offered in the forum.

Despite their limitations, public forums can be expected to retain an important position in audience assessment programs. Public forums have a long tradition, dating at least from the time of the early Quaker meetings, and this long history coincides with our democratic sensibilities regarding citizen participation. Since public forums will continue to play an important role in the dissemination of information, as well as being a vehicle for the expression of public sentiment, it is critical that any technique for improving their information potential be explored.

The information checklist approach summarized above is but one technique that can improve the quality of data; there are other structural changes that can yield even more dramatic improvements over a verbal free-for-all in which only the strident are heard and represented. Two such modifications are discussed here; in other contexts they have proven to be effective in generating participation and in providing data that accurately assess the attitudes of customers or employees.

TECHNIQUES FOR IMPROVING PUBLIC FORUMS

Nominal Groups Technique

One of the more prominent organizational strategies for improving the structure of forums is the nominal groups technique (NGT). This method was designed originally to enhance the capability of focusing on the development of ideas and priorities; consequently, it is well suited for identifying consensus positions of popular opinion. It also has been used in citizen participation efforts aimed at needs assessment and in generating potential problem solutions. The NGT also is useful as a preemptive communication approach for identifying potential problem areas before they become serious.

With the NGT, participants first generate independent responses to openended questions posed by the forum leader. Once the independent responses are completed, participants are divided into small groups in which their ideas are presented and recorded by a group facilitator. These ideas are clarified and elaborated within the context of the small group and then rated independently by each participant. The facilitator directs discussion of the points only in order to clarify each nominated issue (concern). Debate on various issues is avoided by emphasizing the elaboration of various concerns and predicted outcomes of different courses of action. These are then followed by private, independent rankings of their relative importance and probabilities of occurrence.

In short, the NGT permits the identification of important issues that should be addressed in subsequent communication efforts, without raising contention within the group. Indeed, the small group process can be pursued interactively until consensus emerges around some core of significant issues. At the conclusion of the process, the organization conducting the public forum should have an accurate assessment of the attitudes and positions of those in attendance at the public forum. The independent generation of ideas precludes domination by special interest groups and does not favor more verbally skilled participants.

Anonymous rating by participants of each item generated by the group allows adequate representation of diverse values and ideas. This anonymous rating technique contributes to the expression of ideas unhampered by fear of criticism. Thus, a major advantage of the NGT is the capability it provides for identifying problem dimensions in a non threatening manner; critical issues are identified and innovative solutions may be suggested.

By way of example, let us consider a situation in which an organization is contemplating a major policy change (for example, because of international competitive pressures, a union is considering wage concessions in order to save jobs). Union leaders must know the likely reaction of their "public" (the rank and file) to this change in order to plan an effective communication campaign.

In the NGT approach, all participants at the public forum would independently list their reactions and concerns regarding the wage proposal. No discussions would be allowed at this point; small groups would be formed from people at the forum and generated problems would be listed on large posters so they could remain in plain sight for all to see. Within the groups the identified problems would be discussed only for clarification, with no regard to merit or relevance. Participants then could rate problems on a fivepoint scale, ranging from very important to very unimportant, and an average scale score would be obtained for each identified problem. The problems obtaining the highest average scores would then be retained and addressed in a communication campaign.

As a second, more specific example, consider a company contemplating a site for a new manufacturing plant. Generated problems resulting from the small groups might include new jobs, safety, property value changes, esthetics of the new building, necessity for the new plant, and consequences to the environment. These problems would be listed on posters and discussed only to ensure that the issue was represented accurately. Participants in private would rate these six issues on scales (for example, 1 = very unimportant, 2 = unimportant, 3 = neither important nor unimportant, 4 = important, 5 = very important), and an average importance rating would be computed for each issue. The top one or two issues, say, new jobs and property value changes, would be identified, and company communications would focus on these important issues rather than on matters that were found to be of little interest.

The NGT thus combines the advantages of focused concentration (provided by the independent task) with the sharing of knowledge and experience, increased capacity for synthesis of ideas, and enhanced motivation provided by the small group activities. It is designed to produce the maximum amount of high-quality data with the least amount of interpersonal conflict. Recent research, in fact, has shown the NGT to be superior to more traditional individual and group brainstorming approaches in terms of both number and quality of ideas generated, as well as the satisfaction of the participants.

Dialectical Scanning

A second innovative approach, the technique of dialectical scanning, also can be helpful in identifying important and controversial issues around which discussion and communication should be centered. The intent of dialectical scanning is similar to that of the NGT, in that the use of controlled face-to-face interaction permits the convener of the forum to arrive at an understanding of areas of concern and potential conflict without generating conflict within the meeting itself.

Dialectical scanning helps identify areas of potential conflict regarding some policy or course of action and focuses debate only on issues that are truly controversial within the forum group. It contrasts sharply with the NGT by emphasizing rather than minimizing controversy, and thus should be used primarily in situations where the possibility of polarizing the group attending the forum is not seen as a danger.

A skilled convener is critical to the success of this technique. He or she has the important role of directing the group's interaction toward problem identification in such a way that identified problems are amenable to systematic discussion and generation of potential solutions. Participation takes place in stages during a single, large group session in which the principal activity is to collect and then progressively sharpen issues of controversy within the group. The trend is toward progressive clarity of the actual issue of controversy.

Dialectical scanning as a technique to elicit participation and to clarify the attitudes of a community toward some proposed policy might include the following stages. The convener begins with a presentation of the proposed course of action to those attending the meeting (for example, private citizens, relevant agencies, labour or management groups, and/or representatives of the business community).

Following this initial presentation describing the proposed policy change, the convener moves the group into the initial stage of dialectical scanning: the identification of points of agreement and disagreement on the issue presented by the convener. No attempt is made to resolve conflicts that may appear in the initial expression of opinions. Instead, agreement is sought regarding whether conflicts actually exist and whether opposing arguments are correctly aligned with their opposites. The initial task for the group is simply to identify conflict areas and to "agree to disagree" on these various points of conflict. A tree diagram is then used to portray points of disagreement graphically for each controversial item.

Returning to the example of the choice of a site for a new plant, the contrast between dialectical scanning and the NGT becomes clear. The forum convener might begin by proposing that building a new plant on the proposed site was justified because new production capacity was necessary, new jobs would be created, property values would not suffer, and the plant would be safe and physically attractive and would have a negligible impact on the environment. The next step would involve the systematic identification of issues within those contentions that are sources of conflict. If the sources of conflict were the beliefs that "there will be no new jobs" versus "there will be new jobs" and "property values will not decrease," these would be diagramed for the group.

Differences and disagreements are discussed during the second stage of dialectical scanning. The theory underlying dialectical scanning holds that differences and resulting conflicts generally stem from one of three sets of circumstances: (1) factual misunderstanding, (2) difference about assumptions concerning cause-and-effect relationships, or (3) differences in values. In resolving these conflicts, it is important that discussion be focused on the actual source of the conflict. Consequently, one must identify "where" people actually disagree. Of these three types of conflict areas, probably the easiest to deal with are factual misunderstandings and discrepancies in cause-and-effect relationships.

Factual misunderstandings leading to unwarranted fears concerning an innovative program might be dispelled by an accurate depiction of the circumstances and procedures involved in the new program. Further, the extent of the factual misunderstanding can be estimated for the general population, and correcting these erroneous beliefs could be a goal for a communication campaign.

Within the meeting itself, expert (that is, credible) sources can be helpful when conflicts arise from assumptions about cause-and-effect relationships associated with the focal problem. Increased familiarity with the processes involved in a problem area may contribute to more accurate prediction of the potential effects of a contemplated change. Known effects that differ from the erroneous expectations of people who are unfamiliar with the results of previous experiences suggest that an information campaign might be helpful. Such a campaign might shape audience beliefs so they better matched the realities of the situation.

Value differences provide the third likely source of disagreement. A major virtue of the dialectical scanning approach is its capacity to make value differences salient, so that they can be resolved whenever possible. The overt confrontation of value differences decreases the amount of time likely to be spent on pointless appeals to logical arguments when logic does not provide the underpinning of the difference in beliefs. When the source of the conflict is a difference in values, it can be helpful to bring the value-laden aspects of the change in policy into the open. To the extent that a policy conflicts with someone's value of conservation, logical arguments regarding the cost savings of the contemplated move would be largely ineffective. A more effective approach would involve addressing the value itself, and in instances where the value was not really threatened, to make that point clear.

The primary advantage of dialectical scanning is the deliberate attempt to confront values surrounding the controversial issue. Not only does the approach serve to expose all participants of the public forum to the diversity of potentially held opinions, but it also provides those in charge of educational and communication efforts with an insight into these same issues. Not incidentally, the technique can foster commitment to decisions reached by the participants at the public forum.

The weakness of dialectical scanning stems from the characteristic that is also its primary strength, namely, the focus on disagreement. One possible negative consequence of employing dialectical scanning is that forum participants may become polarized around issues that might have been dormant and unacknowledged previously.

This polarization could be harmful to the relationship between the company and its customers if the public forum is widely attended or its outcome carried over into the broader community.

An ineffective leader might well exacerbate the polarization within the group, so there is some risk associated with the technique. To be on the safe side, it might be wise to implement dialectical scanning procedures in instances where the public forum is aimed more at identifying issues of conflict, but where polarizing the particular group in attendance is not seen as a problem.

Arranging a series of small public meetings throughout the customer area affected by a policy could be an effective means of identifying the content of conflict-producing issues as well as their nature (for example, if the basis of the conflict is factual or value laden). Values that, when brought into focus, have a tendency to polarize the group might be left dormant; but the old adage to "let sleeping dogs lie" requires that we first know where these animals are located.

SURVEYS

Although it requires more sophistication and is more demanding of the research skills of the person(s) conducting the assessment program, a survey typically yields much higher-quality data than does a public forum. The need for solid information on customer and employee attitudes has led many companies to adopt survey procedures. In this section we review some of the basic features of survey methodology in the context of a simplified, "cookbook" approach that covers the major concepts but omits much of the specific detail.

Our purpose here is to acquaint the reader with techniques used in survey research. This review will enable him or her to work more closely with professional researchers. We do not purport that this information is sufficient to enable the reader to conduct a survey without technical assistance.

Briefly stated, initiating a survey requires answers to three basic questions: About whom do we want to know? What information do we wish? How can we best derive this information? In answering these questions, the survey researcher is addressing the issues of sampling, instrumentation, and datagathering procedures (for example, interviewing). Each of these issues is discussed below.

Sampling

There is no need to question all members of a population. Instead, we select certain members of the population to get a picture of the entire population. We call the process "sampling." Indeed, scientific sampling typically yields results that are superior to those arrived at by attempting, but failing, to contact everyone in a population. The task of selecting a sample involves technical concepts and skills that cannot be taught in the context of a brief treatment of the subject. Thus, in this section we will review only general concepts.

To begin, it may be helpful to define certain terms and then present an example of a sampling procedure. A sample is a segment or part of the entire group from which it is drawn. The entire group from which the sample is chosen is called the "population," and a good sample should be representative of this population. The sample also should be adequate in size in order to yield usable results. Under certain circumstances a sample may not be representative and is referred to as a "biased sample."

This bias could be due to a number of factors including initial selection problems, selective response, imperfect instruments, and defective technique. For example, a survey based on returns of mailed questionnaires might begin with a representative sample, but selective factors governing return rates might result in a biased sample. Individuals in certain income brackets, for instance, might be more likely to respond than others. "Protest" voters, for example, tend to be more frequently represented in such samples.

In certain circumstances we may be interested in ensuring that members of some subgroup are represented in our sample in the same proportion that they exist in the total population. Such a subgroup is often referred to as a "stratum" and is defined by one or more characteristics that set this group apart from other segments of the population (for example, male/female, employed/unemployed, black/white). Two techniques for representing such strata are noted below in the discussion of probability and nonprobability approaches to sampling.

Representative Sampling

Representative sampling utilizes randomizing techniques for selecting individuals who will participate in a study. Representative sampling is more demanding than nonrepresentative sampling, but the value of the data for drawing conclusions about the total population is superior and justifies the additional effort. Four major approaches to representative sampling are discussed below.

Simple Random Sampling

Random sampling does not mean haphazard, careless, or unplanned sampling. Rather, every effort should be made to control the choice of participants so that every person has the same probability of being included in the sample. An easy technique for securing random samples is the use of tables of random numbers. By first numbering cases, beginning at some random point in the table and then moving in a given direction, the survey researcher can select individuals corresponding to the numbers until his or her sample is complete.

With large groups it is likely that a computer will be required for selecting a sample. It should be noted, however, that this approach theoretically is inapplicable if the population is not specified easily. Fortunately for many companies, however, lists of clients, customers, or employees from which to select a sample are readily available.

Stratified Random Sampling

In stratified random sampling, the population first is divided into two or more strata (for example, age, income, and sex might be used as stratification factors). A simple random sample is taken from each stratum, and the subsamples are then joined to form the total sample. In general, the size of each subsample is proportional to the number of cases in each classification within the population. For example, if 40 percent of the population in an area is below the poverty level, the sample should reflect this proportion.

Sampling by Regular Intervals (Systematic Sampling)

Another procedure involves selecting cases at regular intervals from a series, alphabetical list, or any other arbitrary arrangement. The first case is selected at random, and then cases are chosen at set intervals (for example, every fifth listing), the size of the intervals being determined by the desired number of individuals to be included in the sample. Obviously, this technique can be used only when there is a complete listing of the population available.

For example, systematic sampling could be used when selecting from all company employees, because we would have a complete list for this population. One caution is that before selecting individuals from a list, it is important to make certain that there is no systematic pattern in the list (for example, clustering together of certain types of customers) or other distortion in the arrangement of people that would bias the sample.

Cluster Sampling

Cluster sampling is helpful primarily when researchers will be interviewing people in a face-to-face setting. It is not useful with telephone or mail-out surveys.

This procedure moves through a series of stages from general to more specific units (for example, blocks to houses to individuals) until the sampler finally comes to the population elements that provide the desired sample.

This ultimate set of elements (individuals) is identified by first sampling in terms of randomly selected larger groupings- the clusters.

For example, suppose you wish to survey small-town homeowners in Iowa. First, prepare a list of small Iowa towns, then select a simple or stratified random sample of these communities. Next, list the homeowners from the chosen communities and sample them.

The survey instruments would be administered only to this final sample. As this example suggests, cluster sampling frequently involves combinations of the other approaches as well. One advantage to this form of sampling is that, at least initially, the complete list of potential respondents is not necessary. From our example, we would not need the names of every small-town Iowan—only those from the towns that ultimately made it into the sample.

GENERAL PROCEDURES FOR TWO SAMPLES

To derive an adequate picture of customer or employee attitudes, it is wise to implement representative sampling procedures. The most straightforward approaches are the simple random sample and the somewhat more complicated systematic random sample. Both of these must meet certain criteria, however, that may be difficult to obtain since they require a complete list of the population, and for systematic random sampling the order of respondents in the list must also be random. Two examples follow.

Systematic Random Sample

In a systematic random sample, we begin with a list of the total population whose responses we wish to estimate. Preferably this list would be alphabetically arranged and sequentially numbered. Using this list and the following procedure, one could draw a representative sample of the population.

- Decide on the size of the sample. Textbooks on statistics provide criteria for estimating adequate sample size, given the amount of measurement error an investigator will tolerate. Generally, a large sample reduces the amount of error. However, a small sample is more economical in terms of interviewer time and energy. Generally, a sample of four to five hundred people is sufficient for most purposes.
- After deciding on the size of the sample, calculate a "skip interval." If, for example, a sample of four hundred people is to be chosen from a population of ten thousand, the skip interval would be 400/10,000, or 1 in 2.
- After calculating a skip interval, choose a random starting point on the list. Do this by drawing a random number from a table of random numbers. If the last five digits of the random number fall in the range from one to ten thousand, then the customer corresponding to this number can be used as the starting point of the sample.

- Starting with the customer whose number corresponds to the random number, draw every *k*th (twenty-fifth) person from the list until a sample of four hundred has been compiled. If the list ends before the sample is complete, the skip interval is carried from the end of the list to the very beginning. Sampling is then continued until, as in this example, four hundred persons have been drawn.

Simple Random Sample

Although procedures for drawing a simple random sample are applicable to any specifiable (finite) population, we limit our discussion to the specific example of drawing a small sample from a large metropolitan telephone book. Obviously, a sample of phone numbers represents only the population of people who have phones with listed numbers-not the total population in some locale.

For many surveys, however, a phone sample can be an adequate approximation of the total population, even though not all individuals have telephones. The specific steps for arriving at the sample are as follow:

- First, find the total number of columns in the phone book.
- Find an average number of names in a column.
- Decide on the total sample size.
- From a table of random numbers, draw a series of random numbers equal to the total sample size, plus about 10 percent extra. For this list the random numbers will be smaller than the total number of columns in the phone book.
- From the same table of random numbers, draw a second series of numbers equal to the total sample size, plus about 10 percent extra. For this list the random numbers should approximate the average number of names in a column.
- Each number in the first list corresponds to a column in the phone book. Numbers in the second list correspond to a name in that column. Systematically find each phone number specified by the joint application of these two lists of random numbers.
- If the phone number belongs to a business or office, throw it out and replace it with another number specified from your list. This is the main reason for having the additional 10 percent extra numbers.

Although somewhat simplified, these two examples are indicative of the types of processes involved in selecting a sample for a survey. They are often painstaking, but when used properly they deliver a sample that will reflect, within recognized limits, views of the entire population. Most recently, survey researchers have been using a procedure called "random digit dial."

This sampling technique uses computer programs to select telephone numbers from designated communities. It is complex, but accurate, and has become the procedure of choice. Research consultants will no doubt suggest random digit dial techniques for most telephone surveys.

Once a sample has been selected, we must construct an instrument for measuring the knowledge, attitudes, or behavioral intentions of interest. The next section contains a brief guide for constructing two common forms of survey questions, as well as suggestions for evaluating potential questions.

NONREPRESENTATIVE SAMPLING

In limited instances, surveys may be conducted on nonrandom samples. Such samples have the advantage of being easily assembled, and they can be a convenient source of new ideas. Surveys based on nonrepresentative samples provide anecdotal information. Findings can never be extended to the entire population. We can only discuss the respondents and never suggest their answers reflect a larger group. The primary problem with nonrandom samples is that there is no way of determining the extent to which the information they provide is representative of population values. Therefore, use of nonrepresentative samples is limited to pretest application and case studies. Three types of nonrandom samples are described below.

Accidental Sampling

In accidental sampling the sampler simply reaches out and takes the cases that come to hand, continuing the process until the sample reaches a designated size. For example, a researcher might interview individuals as they enter a department store. The obvious danger, of course, is that the people coming into the store might be atypical of the company's population of customers. Thus, their responses might prove highly misleading. Accidental samples are most useful in uncovering preliminary issues for further study.

Quota Sampling

Quota sampling guarantees the inclusion in the sample of diverse subgroups of the population and ensures that these groups are taken in proportion to their representation in the population. For instance, the sampler might take an equal number of men and women who enter the company's business office. However, respondents are typically chosen haphazardly or at the convenience of the researcher, rather than randomly, and this lack of randomization compromises the trustworthiness of the resultant information.

Purposive Sampling

The basic assumption behind purposive sampling is that with good judgment and an appropriate strategy, one can hand pick the cases to be included in a sample and thus develop samples that are satisfactory in relation to the needs of the survey. This assumption is obviously tenuous. An example would be where a sampler selected individuals whom he or she regarded as typical customers and consequently representative of the population of all customers. To the extent that the sampler's estimate is incorrect, the results of the survey will prove biased.

CONSTRUCTING AN INSTRUMENT

Before actually beginning to construct questions, one should have a clear idea of the purposes of the research. Critical concepts should be well defined and objectives carefully specified. A literature review of related survey studies may help define the problem and provide preliminary ideas about question format and wording. Above all, the item writer must be clear about what information he or she wishes, and all questionnaire items should flow from this informational objective.

One issue that must always be confronted in developing a measuring instument involves the degree of structure that is imposed on potential answers to questions. For example, a close-ended opinion item could take the following form: "Would you argue in favor of Proposal X? 1—Yes, 2—No." On the other hand, an open-ended item would ask: "What do you think about Proposal X?" Questions of this latter type are called "open ended" or "free response." They are particularly useful in exploratory phases of research, when one is not sure of the particular responses or range of responses that questions might elicit. There also are several disadvantages to unstructured questions, since they often yield unwieldy, time-consuming responses that can be difficult to analyse in a meaningful manner.

Structured questions always have a set of fixed alternatives for answers. In a sense the respondents classify themselves according to a set of established categories that are provided them in the questionnaire. Such questions are easier to administer, score, and analyse than are unstructured questions; but they preclude the possibility of obtaining original, unexpected information that might prove valuable. There are several types of answer formats for structured questions. The dichotomous form is probably the simplest, requiring a choice between only two categories (that is, yes or no). The multiplechoice structured question provides the respondent with several alternatives.

Using scaled responses also permits some determination of intensity. For example, "How desirable do you feel Program X will be?"

- Very desirable
- Somewhat desirable
- Somewhat undesirable
- Very undesirable

Obviously, the choice of categories is important. In particular, alternative answers should be clear, should contain only one idea, and should have both positive and negative evaluations. Furthermore, the extremes should be anchored with words such as "always," "never," "very," etc. Items must be both positively and negatively worded to avoid confounding with "yea saying" (the tendency to agree with any positively worded statement) and the danger of the instrument appearing to be a "sales tool" rather than a scientific tool.Another approach that has been used in structuring questions for attitude assessment is the semantic differential approach. With a semantic differential, the individual is asked to evaluate a topic on a set of seven-point scales whose extremes are defined by adjective pairs that have opposite meanings. For example, "Please evaluate Program X."

		Very	Quite	Some-				
What		neutral	Some-					
What		quite	very					
Bad		—	—	—	—	—	—	Good
Valuable	—	—	—	—	—	—	—	Worthless

In addition to issues of format, it is important to pay attention to the specific wording of questions. The researcher should adhere to following guidelines when constructing question items.

- Avoid unclear questions.
  - Questions should specify their exact referent. Instead of "Have you seen the Municipal Transportation Department's television ad?" the question should be, "Have you seen the new 'Ride the Bus' television ad?"
  - Sentences should be short, direct, and simple; that is, they should contain one complete thought.
  - Universals such as "all or never" should be avoided other than for anchoring extreme answer alternatives in a structured questionnaire.
- Make questions relevant to most respondents. When attitudes are requested on a topic about which few have thought or about which they are uninterested, the results are not likely to be very useful.
- Avoid loaded questions or those that make one response seem obviously more desirable. For example, "Do you favor increased nuclear power, or the much safer solar power?" "Do you agree or disagree with the position of Adolf Hitler when he stated that..."
- Use only words that will be understood by respondents. Questionnaire items should be precise so that the respondent understands the specific issues that the items are addressing.
- Avoid double negatives, which serve only to confuse respondents.
- Attitude statements should be stated as opinions, not as if they are factual or worded so that they could be interpreted as factual.
- Short items are best. The respondent should be able to read an item quickly, understand its intent, and select or provide an answer to it without difficulty.

INTERVIEWING

The idea of approaching complete strangers and asking a series of unusual questions can be frightening. After some practice, however, and a few days in the field, initial anxieties usually are allayed. Taking time for careful rehearsal and the development of a series of stock answers to problem questions often proves useful. The manner of serf-presentation of an interviewer profoundly affects the quantity and quality of responses. A friendly, competent, and business-like interviewer usually elicits from the interviewee a favorable, cooperative reaction to participating in the study.

We now review a variety of basic interviewing techniques that have proved effective in past practice. One should adhere to these techniques whether the interview is being conducted over the phone or in person. A good interviewer maintains the following presentation:

Neutral

The interviewer's job is to record information regardless of whether it is bad, good, boring, or exciting. Special care must be taken never to suggest an answer or to reveal one's own opinions. To ensure reliable results, questions should be asked exactly as they are worded, in the same order every time.

Casual

Do not approach the assignment too earnestly or too grimly, lest respondents become defensive. Interviews should be enjoyable for both interviewers and respondents, because interviewers are providing respondents with an opportunity to express themselves on important matters.

Conversational

The interviewer always should use an informal, natural way of speaking that puts the respondent at ease. This does not mean that the interviewer should lose control of the interview; simply that he or she should be comfortable handling any interruptions or objections that might occur. Stock answers to problem questions given in an offhand tone of voice, as though the objection had been given a hundred times before, will keep the interview moving even with difficult respondents.

Friendly. It is important to put the respondent at ease by seeming sympathetic and understanding, at the same time emphasizing that there are no "correct" answers.

In addition to issues pertaining to rapport between the interviewer and respondent, the second major area where difficulties may appear involves the recording and scoring of responses. In an effort to be relaxed and conversational, many people will alter questions and record answers in a haphazard manner. Unless the interview instrument is used consistently across interviewers and respondents, any data obtained will be meaningless. A list of nine principles for the accurate administration and scoring of the questionnaire is given below.

- Usually the first meaningful reaction to a question is the important or true one. Do not record any changes in an answer to a past question if you have already gone on to other items.

- Do not record a "don't know" answer too quickly. People say "I don't know" when stalling for time to formulate their response. The phrase may be merely an introduction to a meaningful comment, to give the person time to think.
- When straight "yes" or "no" answers are accompanied by qualifications such as "yes, if..." or "yes, but not,..." record the comments regardless of whether space has been provided for them. Later they may reveal something important about the question that was not anticipated.
- Record comments or remarks just as they are given. The exact words people use to describe their feelings are important, and the interviewer should keep interpretations of persons' remarks to a minimum.
- Get specific comments, not vague, meaningless generalities like "I like it because it's good" or "It's okay." Ask "why" in such cases.
- Keep talking as you write. Ask the second question as you record the response to the first. In face-to-face interviews, keep eye contact with the person and do the writing unobtrusively. This deportment is one key to the informal atmosphere essential to successful interviews.
- Focus the respondents' attention on the questions. If they wish to talk about some other topic, plainly but firmly steer them back to the questions. Smile and say, "That's interesting. Now what would you say about this question?"
- Record all answers yourself; never allow the respondent to do so. A related point is that you never should take a friend or anyone else along when you are interviewing. Never allow anyone other than the designated respondent to answer your questions.
- Get all the information required on the interview schedule. In other words, ask every question and record every answer—in the correct sequence. It also is helpful to check over the questionnaire before leaving the respondent's presence in the event an item was omitted.

EVALUATION

The assessment and evaluation components of communi-cation programs are tied logically and procedurally. For example, a company might survey its customers regarding some new course of action. Then, it might implement a communication campaign to change customer attitudes in a way that facilitates the implementation of this new policy. Later, it might reexamine the customer attitudes in an effort to determine the impact (that is, effectiveness) of the communication campaign. By assessing repeatedly an audience's views and evaluating the impact of successive communication campaigns over time, the next step in the campaign typically becomes quite clear.

Despite this procedural overlap, it is important to distinguish between the activities of assessment and evaluation. In our view, assessment is carried out before any attempts at manipulation or treatment. It is a procedure to determine whether some form of intervention is needed or to inform the researcher of the type of intervention that is likely to meet with the most success. Evaluation refers to the set of procedures focused on a determination of the success or failure of the intervention. It is quite possible to do a preliminary assessment of an audience without evaluating the effectiveness of a message. Further, it may be possible to evaluate the impact of a communication without assessing attitude change among the audience. As we have observed, assessment and evaluation programs have different aims, functions, and procedures. By keeping these differences in mind, we avoid the unfortunate muddling of these two distinct components.

A communication campaign might be devoted entirely to a knowledge objective, in which case the program would focus on attempts to increase customers' or employees' understanding of some issue, without making an effort to alter their attitudes. For example, a social services organization might present a program aimed simply at informing potential clients of an available service. Evaluation of the effectiveness of the ad would be in terms of whether the public learned the factual information in the communication; knowledge measures, rather than attitude scales, would be employed for this purpose. Indications of public awareness could be gained through questionnaire measures or through the monitoring of the number of individuals making use of the service before, and after, the advertising campaign aired.

Although campaigns to enhance knowledge do occur, advertising programs that focus exclusively, or primarily, on the attitudes of customers are by far the most frequent. Indeed, the link between communication and attitudes is so firmly established that we cite other possible foci (namely, behaviour change and knowledge) here only to prevent them from being entirely overlooked.

Attitudes are seen as central predispositions that influence our behaviour in predictable ways. Given the centrality of attitudes in the view of most communication specialists, it is clear why evaluation of communication efforts typically focuses on attitudes and attitude change. In order to evaluate a communication program, there must be a high degree of correspondence between the objectives of the program and the outcome measures that are used to evaluate that program. If the principal thrust of the communication is toward changing attitudes, the outcome measures used to evaluate the program must measure important attitudes that are relevant to its objectives.

OBJECTIVES

Unless a communication program has clear, quantifiable objectives, its effectiveness is very difficult to evaluate. To the extent that objectives are diffuse and vaguely stated, their attainment will be difficult to determine.

Thus, the first activity in any communication program, an activity that will govern all subsequent matters, is the clear statement of exactly what one wishes to accomplish.

All decisions and procedures should flow from the objectives behind the communication. Objectives usually are stated in terms of intended effects in the people who will be exposed to the communication. These changes may involve increases or decreases in relevant attitudes, behavioral intentions, or behaviors; but whatever the case, we are talking about audience change as the desired outcome.

Unfortunately, many communication specialists fail to operate according to clearly specified objectives. Those in charge of the communication campaign may have difficulty defining both the nature of the problem and the goals being sought, as well as the desired level of audience response. Realistic, precise goal setting should always precede deliberations about the more technical aspects of evaluation. By specifying objectives early in the communication evaluation process, an evaluator is better able to consider the planning and design of evaluation activities. In addition, clarifying communication objectives has the added advantage of preventing confusion among the staff assigned to this task. Imprecise goal statements often confuse staff members who misinterpret stated goals and may, as a result, pursue divergent goals. Specifying communication objectives clearly not only serves the purpose of beginning an effective evaluation process, but also may provide a means by which staff activities can be coordinated.

As we all know, each communication program has many different goals or objectives besides the enhancement of company image. However, regardless of what objective or objectives a communication program has adopted for its audience, evaluating achievement of these objectives requires that each objective be measurable.

TYPES OF MEASUREMENT SCALES

Measurements can occur in a number of different ways, but the major methods of measurement involve the use of one of three types of scales: nominal, ordinal, and interval.

Nominal Scales

Nominal scales are used simply to distinguish one class of objects, activities, or people from another class or classes. For example, a small firm might classify its customers into one of three groups (high, moderate, low) according to their dollar volume of business activity. Occasionally in evaluation activities, numbers are assigned to the different values on the nominal scale. In other words, low dollar volume could equal

- Moderate
- High
- However, these numbers serve only to distinguish between the different categories. They carry no further meaning.

Ordinal Scales

When using an ordinal scale, the numbers that are assigned to different people or things have further implications. When assigning numbers according to an ordinal scale, the objects receiving numbers are ranked from one to however many are involved. The *Fortune 500* is a well-known example of an ordinal scale. Here, the top five hundred U.S. companies are ordered from largest to smallest (though "small," in this case, is obviously a relative term). This qualification is important, because it shows that while the numbers in ordinal scales have more meaning than those of nominal scales, they are not an accurate measure of the value in question (in this case, company worth). The ordinal scale does tell us that the company ranked number one is larger than the one ranked number eight, for example, but the size of the difference between successive numbers is not necessarily equal. We would not, for instance, be justified in saying that the difference between company number 1 and number 2 is equal to the difference between company number 499 and number 500. To make those types of assertions, we have to move to a more sophisticated type of scale.

Interval Scales

The interval scale is the most sophisticated of the three types discussed here. Interval scales not only distinguish between the persons or things to be measured, it ranks those items and provides a measure of the relative difference between them. In interval scales, then, the difference between three and four is the same as the difference between one and two. Measured in terms of dollars, businesses' profitability is an example of an interval measure. Differences between businesses are interval, in that the unit of measure (dollars) means the same thing at all points along the scale. A $1 million difference in profitability between firm numbers 400 and 399 means the same thing as a $1 million difference between firm numbers 100 and 101.

MEASURE CHARACTERISTICS

There are two important technical concepts pertaining to the value of a measuring procedure for generating solid data. These two concepts are called "reliability" and "validity." Reliability of an instrument refers to the ability of that instrument to report consistently the same measurement information when the instrument is applied and reapplied to a particular thing, person, or activity. That is, a very reliable instrument should place the respondent at about the same level (high, medium, low) each time it is used. One example of a reliable item on a questionnaire might be "How frequently do you attend religious services?" If respondents were given that item to answer three different times in one day, it is very likely that they would write the same answer each time—the instrument would assign them the same value consistently. Such an item would be designated as consistent or reliable. As a practical matter, longer instruments that utilize several items to measure the same concept tend to be more reliable than brief or single-item measures.

There are mathematical procedures for computing the reliability of a particular measure or instrument. When worked to solution, the appropriate mathematical formula yields a "reliability coefficient" that expresses the reliability of the measure. The procedures for determining the reliability coefficient are less significant here than is a general understanding of the concept of reliability.

A test having low reliability means that the test will not yield a similar score upon retest, while a questionnaire that is perfectly reliable will yield the same information consistently when one measures the same thing. If ten individuals complete a perfectly reliable questionnaire on July 30, they will all answer the questions exactly the same way they did on July 10, as long as none of the questions measure things that actually could have changed over that period of time. Since there are two sources of unreliability in survey research—the survey instrument and the interviewer—the overall reliability of the survey technique is dependent on both of these factors.

The most frequently used method of measuring questionnaire reliability is called the "test-retest technique." This technique is used to demonstrate reliability over time. When using the test-retest method, the investigator must first select a sample of people for whom the questionnaire was developed (for example, owners of small businesses, low-income people, renters, etc.).

It is important to remember that a questionnaire that is reliable for one of these groups will not necessarily be reliable for another; consequently, people who complete the questionnaire during the pilot test for reliability must be the same kind of people who will be completing the questionnaire in the actual full-scale evaluation. The basic procedure involves administering the questionnaire on one day and having the responses on this first test correlated with answers received on identical questionnaires at some later time (typically one to three weeks later).

A second type of reliability is associated with the data gatherer (interviewer). In instances where the questionnaire will be administered verbally (that is, in an interview survey) and participant responses recorded by an interviewer, it is possible for human error to decrease the reliability of the overall measurement procedures.

Through training, we can be reasonably assured that interviewers will present the questions in the same fashion, but the scoring of respondent answers seldom receives the same attention. Having several would-be interviewers score responses to the survey instrument that have been tape recorded is not only a good training device, but by pressing for high reliability among interviewers, the investigator can increase the reliability of survey results. A similar procedure might be applied to telephone interviews by using a phone with an amplifier. As the respondent answers the interviewer's questions, several staff members on the other line could record these answers on their own separate interviewing forms. After interviewing several people in this manner, one could compare the interview forms of the different interview staff members and determine the reliability of the interview recording system.

Reliability is important in large part because it puts a limit on the even more important characteristic of validity. Validity in evaluation means something close to what in common language usage we call "accuracy." To the extent that an electric meter is accurate, it is a valid measure of the amount of electrical energy utilized by a home or business.

As with reliability, validity is expressed as a validity coefficient. In theory, validity coefficients are rather straightforward expressions of the relationship between some measure that is being used to predict a later outcome and that actual outcome. In other words, if we develop a survey measure with which to predict how people will vote on some issue, the instrument must be highly correlated with actual voting behaviour in order to be valid. Although the concept of validity is rather simple, in practice it is often difficult to obtain the type of outcome data that allow us to validate a survey instrument thoroughly.

One approach to validation that sometimes is helpful is the "known groups technique," in which the scores of one group known to be high on an issue can be compared with scores of another group known to be low on that issue. To be valid, the "high" group should score high in the attitude survey and the "low" group should score significantly lower on the same instrument. For example, an attitude questionnaire regarding the performance of Democratic and Republican congresspersons should result in very different sets of scores if administered to the Young Democrats and the Young Republicans at the local university.

Thus, the known groups approach involves comparisons between two groups known to be different on the dimension measured by the survey, and the survey is deemed to be valid to the extent that it accurately categorizes individuals as high or low on the issue. Unfortunately, in some instances, known groups are unavailable. In the absence of easily measured outcome variables, which would permit an estimate of the predictive validity of the instrument, the investigator may have to settle for high reliability coupled with convincing logic that the items *ought* to predict effectively (that is, face validity).

TYPES OF EVALUATION

When any two people talk about evaluating some program or, in this case, a communication campaign, it is a rare instance when they are actually talking about the same activities. This is not to say that either of them is incorrect, but rather to imply that a wide range of approaches and activities falls under the general rubric of evaluation. In order to clarify matters, it may be helpful to review briefly different approaches to evaluation and to offer a categorization system for these different approaches. For purposes of arriving at a common language for discussing evaluation, let us distinguish among five types of evaluation strategies. These five types do not exhaust all possibilities, but they do cover the most widely used types of evaluation.

Nominal Evaluation

A nominal evaluation refers to the extent to which activities were executed in accord with the original proposal for the communication program. The question is simply whether the communication program was conducted as planned. In other words, if the original proposal called for four television spots, advertising on three radio stations, and quarter-page newspaper ads, a nominal evaluation would simply look at whether or not these activities actually occurred.

The basic question addressed in the evaluation is whether people actually did what they indicated they would and whether the communication campaign was conducted as planned. A nominal evaluation is the lowest level in sophistication, and it amounts to little more than a check on contract compliance. This type of evaluation obviously is only a first step, since it is clear that even though a communication effort has complied with its original plan, it still might not have changed audience attitudes.

Effort Evaluation

An effort evaluation is largely what the name implies; issues such as the number of customers reached, customer-to-staff ratios, and person/time accounting procedures are the typical techniques used in this type of evaluation. The evaluator is asking the questions:

"How hard does this group work, and how many people do they reach?" The evaluation data amount to tallies of the number of people exposed to a message. The prime issue for an effort evaluation is efficiency, that is, reaching the maximum number of people with the least commitment of company resources.

A company that stresses effort evaluation to the exclusion of other approaches may be expected to produce communication campaigns in which large numbers of people are reached inexpensively. The use of "bill stuffers" is an example in which all customers can be reached, and the cost is limited to production of a single piece of paper.

The mailing costs remain essentially the same so the communication effort is inexpensive. This fact probably accounts for the recent increases in the number of companies, particularly the oil and credit card companies, that are including mail-order advertisements for various gadgets with their monthly billings.

It is unfortunate, given their low cost, that bill stuffers are relatively ineffective means for communicating to customers. An effort evaluation does not ask such questions as whether people read the various flyers included with their bills, but rather how many customers had the message in their hands and at what cost.

Unless the communication produces some change in the customer, any cost is too much, and there is always the possibility of having an effect opposite to the one intended. The annoyance attendant to digging through several flyers to find one's monthly billing probably does not serve as an effective springboard for changing one's attitude in a direction more favorable to the biller.

Process Evaluation

The process evaluation is concerned with the effectiveness of administrative and operational procedures. The focus of this technique is not on some outcome, but on how decisions are made and how communication programs are implemented. Aspects of the "management by objectives" perspective would be included under the process evaluation category. Issues such as information flow within the division of the company devoted to communication, linkages between the various units within that group, and overall organizational structure are the principal areas of attention. Thus, the focus tends to be internal and descriptive.

A process evaluation essentially involves a logical examination of existing procedures, linkages, and the flow of both information and authority within an organization. The perspective is one of organizational development, and the goal is efficiency of operation within the unit. This sort of evaluation is of obvious value, but improving the administrative flow of the communication unit within the company is no guarantee of effective marketing or public relations programs.

Cost/Benefit Evaluation

The cost/benefit approach to evaluation is an effort to compare various procedures and programs in terms of their rate of return, given an equal commitment of resources. The challenge for one who is undertaking a cost/benefit evaluation is to develop a common metric for the cost and benefit components of the equation. The cost may be derived from program budgets very easily, but benefits can be more difficult to quantify, particularly in terms of dollars and cents. Often in the absence of hard data on benefits, the cost/benefit analysis becomes a thinly disguised effort evaluation in which all programs are seen as equally effective, or ineffective, and the focus is strictly on cost.

The cost/benefit evaluation can be done only after a good deal of prior research has demonstrated the relative merits of different communication approaches. Unless there is some accumulation of prior evidence, it may be difficult a priori to predict the amount of audience change occurring in response to a communication campaign. Although cost/benefit evaluations have tremendous inherent appeal because they pose the question of how much performance we get per dollar, in practice they often are more selfdeceptive than helpful. Indeed, unless other types of evaluations have been conducted, the benefit side of the equation is always a mystery, and the cost/ benefit analysis amounts to a second-rate evaluation effort with an overly pretentious name.

Effectiveness Evaluation

In an effectiveness evaluation of a communication program, one is concerned with the impact of the communication on the audience, both individually and collectively. This technique is probably the most significant form of evaluation, because without a clear demonstration of an effect on the people receiving the communication, the other types of evaluation are largely irrelevant. Undertaking a cost/benefit analysis or process evaluation prior to a demonstration of the effectiveness of the communication program is of limited value. If the communication does not influence the audience in some way, issues regarding the cost of that communication are of minimal interest.

In short, an effectiveness evaluation is the most important of the five types discussed here, since it provides a necessary base for other evaluative efforts. Unless a communication program has a demonstrated capability for altering its target (namely, knowledge, attitudes, behaviour), then the other aspects of evaluation are unimportant. On the other hand, the discovery of an effective communication approach makes the other types of evaluation of immediate concern.

It is a basic assumption that the most pressing need of those interested in evaluating communication programs is an understanding of how one might evaluate the effectiveness of a communication.

Determining the impact of a communication, or a series of communications, is really the keystone to planning and conducting public communication programs.

POST-ONLY DESIGN

The comparison in the post-only design is between what we observe, possibly with a survey or questionnaire following some communication, and what we think would have been the case without that communication. This type of comparison is obviously rather informal and amounts to a kind of case study in which we compare our projections of the future with something we actually measure and attribute all discrepancies to the communication campaign.

An example might involve a company that is interested in changing the formula of its established soft drink and anticipates some resistance to this plan. In response to anticipated difficulties, the company engages the services of a prominent public relations firm for several hundred thousand dollars. After an all-out media blitz extolling the virtues of the new, improved cola, the consulting firm proudly reports that rather than the anticipated resistance, 65 percent of the people surveyed are supportive of the innovation. Since the company is more interested in cola sales than surveys, it is well satisfied with the results of the communication program, and it will never occur to the executives to ask whether any of these communication and evaluation efforts were necessary. Whether the anticipated resistance was a reality is unknown. Indeed, it is possible that the communication campaign actually reduced public support, but these are questions that cannot be answered from the post-only design.

PRE-POST DESIGN

In the pre-post design, some initial measure of audience (that is, customer) attitudes on some issue is made, followed by a communication campaign that in turn is followed by the administration of another measure similar to the first. The comparison between the before and after measures is taken as an indicant of the amount of change in the audience's attitudes that is attributable to the communication. A somewhat tenuous assumption that the investigator must make is that nothing else of relevance to customer attitudes occurred during the interval between the pre- and postcommunication measures, and that the pretest did not change the attitudes by itself.

Let us return to our soft drink example. In an effort to retain traditional profit margins and keep its stockholders happy, the company wishes to maintain its current customer base and add to this base through the modification of its mainstay soft drink. Being sensitive to the sometimes whimsical nature of consumer preferences, the firm does an initial series of comparison taste tests, pitting its new drink against the old, and finds an approximately even split in customer sentiment. The firm, of course, is not satisfied with this roughly equivalent response, and thus launches a communications effort designed to swing public sentiment to the side of the new drink.

Two months after the introduction of the drink, both sales and a survey of public sentiment show that opposition to the new drink substantially outweighs support. The company concludes that the communication efforts were a failure and reassigns those involved in the campaign, without taking time to consider the fact that factors extraneous to the ad campaign might have been responsible for this outcome. Hostile advertising campaigns from competitors, a change in weather resulting in a general decrease in soft drink consumption, a downturn in the economy, etc., might, in fact, be responsible for declining sales. The effectiveness of the communication campaign remains unknown. Indeed, public reaction might have been much worse without it. Given the shortcomings of the evaluation design, we cannot determine which, if any, of these alternatives is correct.

The pre-post design is intuitively attractive, and we see it used widely for selling products from muscle-building courses to car wax. Unfortunately, attitudes are more easily influenced than muscles by factors in the day-today environment; as a consequence, this design does not permit strong causal arguments regarding attitude change. The next successive level of sophistication in evaluation design involves identifying another (comparison) group of people who were exposed to all of the various factors operating in a natural environment except the communication campaign, and then making comparisons between that group and the group who received the communication.

PRETEST-POSTTEST-CONTROL GROUP DESIGN

The pretest-posttest-control group evaluation design calls for a true experiment, and thus it permits one to make strong assertion regarding causation. In the simplest instance, the communication campaign is compared against nothing, in that we examine the attitudes of two groups before and after only one of these groups has received the communication. If the two groups were initially equivalent, then any changes noted for the group receiving the communication, over and above those occurring for the group that was not exposed to the communication, should be attributable to the communication. This is the classic sort of experiment we have all seen, and it is a very powerful evaluation tool. Indeed, in instances where it is possible to select at random those who will receive the communication and those who will not, it is the best evaluation strategy available. In instances where this is not possible, the interrupted time-series procedure discussed below is another possibility.

The procedure for conducting an evaluation in accordance with the pretestposttest-control group design involves the following steps. First, we have to construct by random selection two comparison groups from some larger sample. This randomization is necessary to ensure that the groups are initially equivalent. Both groups are pretested, and one group receives the communication campaign, while the other does not. The comparison in this design, in contrast to the other designs, is between two groups, rather than a repeated examination of a single group over time. The term "group" here means anything from a small contingent of twenty people or so to an entire community. The size of the sample is less significant than is the fact that all the people in it were selected randomly. It also is noteworthy that there is no necessary restriction that limits the design simply to two groups; several communication approaches could be attempted at various locales, and they all could be compared with each other as well as with the absence of any campaign. By using radio in one area, television in another, newspapers in a third, a mix of all of these in a fourth, and nothing in a fifth, a company could get some reasonable estimate of the effectiveness of these various treatments. Variations in the effectiveness of different types of bill stuffers might also be studied through this type of design.

An example of this design in practice was provided by a study undertaken in Michigan to determine the effectiveness of television spots sponsored by the state Department of Energy and aimed at facilitating self-help conservation practices by Michigan citizens. An important aspect of the spots was a message urging viewers to contact an energy hot line for free advice by a team of engineers and other experts in energy conservation. The objective of this study was to determine the effectiveness of television spots for inducing viewers to contact the energy office and generally to foster better public relations.

In order to conduct this study, two geographic areas with very similar characteristics were necessary; further, it was important that these two areas not share a common television station. Two areas were located, each containing three towns of moderate size (100,000 to 200,000 population) and large rural areas surrounding these communities. It was decided by a coin flip that area X would receive the television campaign for a one-month period, while the campaign was withheld from area Y television stations.

Frequency of calls from the two areas was noted, as well as the number of people in area X indicating that they were calling as a consequence of the television spot. At the conclusion of the month-long period, the television spot also was implemented on area Y channels to ensure these residents were not denied a helpful service. The findings of this study indicated that the television spots were highly effective in generating interest in conservation activities and promoting the energy hot line.

By staggering start-up dates for communication efforts in different locales systematically, a company can determine the effectiveness of different messages without denying the message from any of its customers. By exposing certain groups selectively to a communication approach and then comparing them with groups who have not received the communication, one can finetune a communication for maximum impact.

INTERRUPTED TIME-SERIES DESIGN

In certain instances it may not be feasible to initiate comparisons between different groups in order to evaluate the effectiveness of a communication for changing the target group. For a company serving an area where all individuals have equal access to the same communication media, conducting an actual experiment may be difficult. An alternative approach is to compare people in the group with themselves over time, but in such a way that one avoids the problems inherent in the pretest-posttest evaluation design. The interrupted time-series design involves taking several measures of the outcome variable (that is, knowledge, attitude, or behaviour) before the media campaign is initiated and several measures after the campaign.

If the campaign is to be initiated immediately and appropriate records are available, it may be possible to use historical (for example, archival) records to arrive at the necessary baseline information. By measuring several times before and after the communication, the investigator is in a more solid position to argue that any changes occurring right after the communication campaign were indeed the result of the campaign, and not of some chance event.

Consider a simple example, the case of a large, independent retailer whose customers reside primarily in a single metropolitan area. Establishing comparison groups is seen as a virtual impossibility, yet the company is keenly interested in evaluating the effects of a multimedia communication program on usage of its in-house credit card. A random sample of customers is selected from the company's master list of card holders, and their monthly charges over each of the last thirty-six months can be determined from company records.

An average for each month can then be computed for the sample of customers selected. At this point the information campaign would be implemented, and average card usage would be recorded for a period of time (say, the next twelve consecutive months).

Data for the first three years provide a baseline against which one can compare customer behaviour following the communication campaign. Sharp increases or decreases in customer activity can be attributed to the communication efforts of the retailer.

Monthly variations can be controlled by comparison with previous years' charge figures. For example, it seems likely that the average customer would charge more during the Christmas season than in February.

Using previous years' data to offset the cyclical nature of such activity is an additional advantage conferred by the interrupted time-series design. This design and other quasi-experimental designs, in general, can make good use of archival data in answering questions about the impact of a communication campaign that might not be answerable strictly by experimental means.

10

Product and Brand Policies: Information and Management Research

In a competitive private enterprise economy, the men who prosper most are those who best succeed in satisfying the wants and needs of markets. In marketing products to consumers, the profit system tends to reward those who do the best job of offering goods or services which most adequately or most economically satisfy the previously ungratified wants of sovereign consumers who, by the distribution of their current consumption expenditures among a wide range of available free choices, guide the future ownership and control of the means of production. Similarly, in industrial marketing, the wide range of alternatives available to purchasers with respect to sources of supply and types of materials or equipment to use dictates a customer-oriented approach to product policy.

POLICIES OF PRODUCT DEVELOPMENT AND MODIFICATION

The development of new products and the modification of existing products to conform with dynamic changes in market demand are matters of major policy decision in many kinds of companies—manufacturing firms, wholesale and retail middlemen, and service industry enterprises.

Broad and Narrow Conceptions of Product

Fundamental to a sound programme of product policies is a realistic conception of the meaning of product. A narrow and erroneous conception of product is to regard its essence as a physical thing and to think of it in terms of physical attributes, such as form, shape, dimensions, component parts, or materials used in construction. In a broad and meaningful sense a product is not a physical thing but consists of the satisfactions that may be derived from its use or consumption. These consist not merely of the basic function or purpose for which a product is conceived, such as the making of a beverage from coffee or the accomplishment of transportation by means of the automobile. They include also a wide variety of intangible or subjective considerations, such as convenience in use, esthetic qualities, symbolic meanings, and other satisfaction-yielding attributes which may be explicitly recognized or subconsciously experienced by users.

A narrow, industry-oriented conception of product can be disastrous from a marketing standpoint, as illustrated by the following examples: The relative decline of railroads as a transportation agency is explained largely by the belief on the part of railroad managements that they were in the *railroad* business. Actually, there was increasing demand for transportation, but the need was fulfilled by others because railroads conceived their product narrowly ("railroad transportation") rather than broadly ("movement service"). Leading motion picture companies in Hollywood failed or encountered serious financial difficulties with the growth of television. Industry executives had believed that they were in the "motion picture" business when truly their product was "entertainment." Certain oil companies developed a substantial market in connection with oil heating, but then lost most of this market with the growth of gas heating. This is attributed to industry-oriented feelings that oil companies were in the "oil business." A broader conception of the product as a source of energy would have enabled such companies to develop the gas industry themselves rather than see their market diminish as the result of activities of innovating gas transmission companies.

Nature and Scope of Product Policies

Many discussions of product policy and planning are rather provincial when implying that such policies are unique or peculiar to *manufacturing* companies and that the concern is with the development of *new* products. Every business firm markets some product or products. A bank offering a new type of savings or checking account is offering a new product. So also is the laundromat which installs self-service, coin-operated dry cleaning equipment. When a retailer or wholesaler decides to add a new category of merchandise (e.g., selling power lawnmowers in a drugstore) this is a product decision for the organization in question.

Product policies are concerned not only with the adding of new products but with the dropping of old ones and with the modification of existing products on a continuing or intermittent basis. They serve as guides in determining what classes of products or what specific items shall be manufactured or handled for resale, and what the specific characteristics of these items shall be.

The task of planning the composition of a product line and adjusting it to the ever changing pattern of consumer demand is often referred to as *merchandising,* especially in large manufacturing, wholesaling, and retailing companies. Since the so-called merchandising activities of retail and wholesale middlemen have been indicated in earlier parts of this text, the treatment of product policies in this section is approached primarily from the viewpoint of the manufacturing company inasmuch as it poses the most complex situation; however, the principles in the ensuing discussion apply to middlemen as well, except for considerations relating directly to form utility production and, in the case of retailers, those concerned with obtaining distribution through other resellers in the distribution channel.

Among large manufacturing companies, product policies are one of the most significant responsibilities of the top management executives. These persons are commonly assisted in policy formulation by staff officials who devote their attention to the job of product development and product planning. *Product development* embraces the work of technical research and engineering design; *product planning,* on the other hand, is concerned with estimates of the magnitude of potential markets, estimates of sales volume, budgeting of costs, and other matters relating to the economics of modifying a product line.

Motives for New Product Development

It is often assumed that new products are added to those already manufactured or handled for resale because of short- or long-run *profit* considerations. This is an oversimplification since profitability is an important factor in all types of business decisions and is an essential requirement to be met for long-run continuation of a non subsidized business in a private enterprise economy. The businessman's interest in new product development can be better explained by underlying motives of a much more specific nature.

First is the motive of *survival* which is not peculiar to the subject of new product development nor to business generally but is a universal struggle characteristic of all aspects of civilization. In many industries and trades, a large per cent of all products sold did not exist five or ten years previously. Notable are the fields of electronics, chemicals, packaged food, and beauty aids. The struggle for survival is illustrated by an Ohio manufacturing company that had a successful beginning by developing and marketing industrial ceramic products used in the manufacture of glass dinnerware. As consumer acceptance of glass diminished, owing to developments in the plastics industry, this firm saw its major market practically disappear and was forced into a search for new products to preserve existence.

Second, new product developments are commonly a means of *growth,* another pervasive human goal. Few companies can long survive in a static level of activity; they either forge ahead or fade away. Growth in the absolute sense is always more limited with a restricted or fixed product line than is the case when altogether new opportunities are available from time to time.

Third, many companies are interested in new product development as a means of maintaining or enlarging *share of market position.* This is growth in a relative sense and has received much more consideration in recent years than mere absolute growth. Department stores, when judging their performance on the basis of absolute growth (year-to-year sales increases), were lulled into a sense of false security which collapsed with the realization that they were not maintaining their share of market, as defined by per cent of total retail store sales or total sales of all goods commonly sold by such enterprises. New products or major modifications of existing product lines are often an essential requirement for maintaining competitive position. This is especially important in the apparel trades, where all companies in a given industry must quickly adapt to changes in the popularity of general and specific fashions or suffer drastic consequences. It is also of exceptional import in the field of consumer durable goods where competitive product improvements or innovations are introduced with frequency or regularity.

Fourth, many product changes are forced by *changes in related industries.* The petroleum refining and automobile manufacturing industries constitute, an outstanding example of close interrelationships in product developments. Increases in the compression ratios of newer models of automotive engines necessitate higher octane motor fuels. Thus the ability of the automotive industry to market automobiles with more powerful engines is limited, in part, by the ability of the petroleum industry to supply the required fuels. Competition within the petroleum industry is so intense, however, that each major refiner attempts to take the lead in supplying grades or qualities of motor fuels that meet the requirements of the most advanced automotive power plants.

Fifth, *diversification of risks* by serving different needs or markets is often a motivating circumstance. To illustrate, the Bell & Howell Company which originally specialized in motion picture cameras and projectors found that it was vulnerable to business fluctuations. Business was stabilized and risks more widely distributed by expanding into microfilming, tape recording, high-fidelity phonograph equipment, and other lines. A desire to achieve *temporal stability* is another important consideration. To illustrate, at one time the sales pattern of the McGraw Electric Company, manufacturer of Toastmaster and other electrical appliances, experienced undesirable seasonal peaks and valleys and was unfavorably influenced by cyclical factors. This was offset by a long-range planned programme of expansion which involved the manufacture of transformers, transmission equipment, circuit breakers, and other items marketed to public utility companies. By entering the industrial market, the company achieved greater temporal stability, both seasonal and cyclical.

Criteria of Product Acceptability

After a new product has been decided upon by a manufacturing company, much expense is usually incurred over a considerable period of time for field surveys of consumer demand, estimates of competitive activity and potential markets, preliminary and final design specifications, engineering and marketing tests, and design and marketing plan modifications, all of which are commonly done prior to large-scale manufacture and marketing. The success of most new products cannot be judged entirely by the volume of initial sales. For goods of high or normal replacement frequency, the ultimate test is whether business users or ultimate consumers are willing to make repeat purchases. Consequently, it often takes as much as six months, frequently as much as two or three years, before the success of a product innovation can be judged properly.

Of the many thousands of new products introduced annually, only a small percentage is successful. It is shown that within a relatively small sample of companies familiar to a well-known business-consulting organization, each seriously contemplated new product idea moves through a series of management decisions, and about one-half of the new product conceptions is discarded during each step of the process. The result is that one successful new product emerges from the original fund of some 40 presumably meritorious product conceptions. Since this chart is based on the experience of relatively large companies, most of which have specific product development and planning programs, it undoubtedly portrays an overly optimistic situation. Other research has indicated that products introduced to the market without careful market analysis, planned development, and thorough market testing have a much higher mortality rate. In the light of this experience, it is understandable why progressive companies approach the introduction of new products with great caution, evaluating new ideas in the light of various criteria, the most important of which are discussed below.

Marginal Cost and Revenue Approach

From the standpoint of economic analysis, a firm is better off by adding a new product only when the expected net revenue from the sale of that product will exceed the amount of cost incurred in doing so. Such expectations are usually most favorable when there are certain fixed costs which can be shared by all products, old and new. When any kind of fixed cost can be spread over a wider sales volume base, it may be said that previously some "excess capacity" existed. This is true in the sense that it would cost the company less to manufacture and market the new product than it would cost some other firms that might be set up to do so alone. Excess capacity may involve the incomplete utilization of managerial skills, manufacturing facilities, distributive facilities, advertising, or financial resources. It is, however, rather difficult to formulate accurate estimates of probable revenue from the sale of a new product, especially in view of the fact that competitive activity is likely to be increased as a result of the introduction of a new product into the field. Thus, probable marginal revenue can only be approximated. Elaborate budgets are likely to be prepared only if the new product meets certain other indicated common-sense standards of acceptability.

Distinctive Know-How. Sometimes a main factor in determining the acceptability of a new product is that it requires or can benefit considerably from the distinctive know-how that constitutes a company's differential advantage within its industry. This criterion may be illustrated with reference to the Clevite Corporation, which has a number of major divisions in the industrial markets for bronze bushings, bearings, technical instruments, transistors, and other electronic products. The principle which guides policy on new products has been described by the company president as follows: "In a 'component' business like ours, we try to select products that will enable us to use fully the specialized technological, engineering, and manufacturing skills that we have and that are not readily available to competitors."

Full-Line Marketing. When a company has a full line of products, relative to the number of related products successfully marketed by its more important rivals, it has substantial advantages in terms of advertising impact, personal selling costs, economies in physical distribution, and ability to obtain and maintain a superior organization of wholesale and retail outlets in its channels of distribution. Such considerations have prompted a number of mergers and consolidations within the major appliance industry since 1946. Manufacturers of only one or a few appliances have found it increasingly difficult to compete with others who sell a wide range of such products. Certain specialized manufacturers have discontinued business, while others have sold their facilities to other manufacturers who were in the process of developing a complete line.

Substantial economies in physical distribution functions are achieved by full-line marketing organizations that can move mixed- or pool-car shipments under common freight classifications, thus obtaining the benefit of minimum freight shipment costs. In the paper industry, for example, there are a number of manufacturers of a diverse line of wrapping papers, meat packaging materials, egg cartons, towels, napkins, cups, plates, ice cream containers, etc. Even though individual products in the line may usually be sold in small volume and could be shipped ordinarily only at l.c.l. rates, wholesalers and large industrial users can consolidate their requirements and purchase a mixture of such items in carload quantities, thereby obtaining maximum transportation economies.

Common Channel of Distribution. Ability to utilize the facilities of a sales organization more fully often explains attempts to market additional products which can be moved through the same channel of distribution. In part this is related to the examples cited above, but may be considered as a separate point in that distinctive know-how or productline relationship need not be involved. So long as the new product is sold to the same class of buyers and can be handled by the same marketing organization, it is more acceptable than when new marketing institutions must be sought out for it. Plough, Inc. is a company that has expanded substantially by acquiring other companies engaged in the manufacture of packaged convenience goods, most of which can be marketed.

A new product requiring marketing effort through a new or strange channel is rarely introduced by a company unless it can be done upon such a large and promising scale that a separate organization can be economically developed solely for the marketing of such product. Dow Chemical Co., for example, encountered serious difficulties when it entered the consumer goods field with a new product, Saran Wrap, and attempted to market the item through its established industrial sales organization. Experience eventually proved that an entirely separate marketing organization was essential for developing the product's potential sales.

Manufacturing Considerations. While marketing factors tend to dominate policies related to new product development, the most desirable avenues of approach are frequently indicated by manufacturing considerations. Sometimes this means that an acceptable new product is one for which existing manufacturing or processing facilities can be used. Thus, an Ohio manufacturer of wooden gift boxes of the kind used for sets of silverware entered the field of small occasional tables. As a result of declining sales trends in wooden gift boxes, there was idle manufacturing capacity. Small tables could be made with the same type of raw material and by utilizing manufacturing equipment already installed and in operation. The new product also helped to iron out seasonal peaks and valleys in production previously experienced.

Some companies look for new products that can be manufactured from the same types of materials or from by-products. Most of the major meat packing companies have become important manufacturers and marketers of pharmaceutical products, which have been developed out of research to utilize all possible by-products of the meat manufacturing process. The idea of making new products with common raw material ingredients is most prevalent among vertically integrated companies that control raw material sources, that can profit from an expansion in the market for such a basic raw material, or that can exploit fully the differential between basic material cost and price of finished product made from it. This has been especially common within the petroleum refining, rubber, and chemical industries.

Acquiring New Products by Merger: Legal Limitations

One approach to product diversification or expansion is research, development, and marketing planning within the company. Another approach, especially popular in recent years, has been the acquisition of products by purchase of other companies with established products. It has been estimated that 40 per cent of the mergers occurring in the late 1950's were prompted by considerations of product line diversification. The marketing and new product implications of corporate acquisitions and consolidations are of such magnitude that they are a continuing topic of discussion in the business press.

General Dynamics Corporation, for example, increased its sales 4.3 times between 1950 and 1959 largely by product diversification achieved through acquisition of companies in the airplane, guided missile, submarine, nuclear energy, and electronics industries. The Warner-Lambert Pharmaceutical Co. was formed as a result of the merger of the Lambert Pharmaceutical Co., manufacturers of Listerine Products, and the William R. Warner Co., a leading toilet goods and cosmetics manufacturer. The Gillette Co., formerly a specialized manufacturer of razors and razor blades, diversified by acquiring the Toni line of home permanents and the Paper Mate line of pens. The Elgin National Watch Co. expanded into the field of miniature electronics and precision instruments by purchasing Neomatic Inc., American Microphone Company, and Advance Electric & Relay Co.

When there is a close relationship between the products marketed by the two companies involved in a merger, there is a possibility that the acquisition of the one by the other may be in violation of the federal Clayton Act which, as amended in 1950, provides that:

No corporation engaged in commerce shall acquire, directly or indirectly, the whole or any part of the stock or other share capital and no corporation subject to the jurisdiction of the Federal Trade Commission shall acquire the whole or any part of the assets of another corporation engaged also in commerce, where in any line of commerce in any section of the country, the effect of such acquisition may be substantially to lessen competition, or tend to create a monopoly.

This law, which is enforced both by the U.S. Department of Justice and the Federal Trade Commission, requires findings and conclusions not of *actual* anticompetitive effects, but *merely* of a *reasonable probability* of a substantial lessening of competition or tendency toward monopoly. As explained in the House of Representatives report on this legislation, such an effect may arise in various ways, including the "elimination in whole or in material part of the competitive activity of an enterprise which has been a substantial factor in competition, increase in the relative size of the enterprise making the acquisition to such a point that its advantage over its competitors threatens to be decisive, undue reduction in the number of competing enterprises, or establishment of relationships between buyers and sellers which deprive their rivals of a fair opportunity to compete."

Whether the Clayton Act has or has not been violated in the case of a specific merger or consolidation depends not upon any absolute rule or generalization, but upon findings of fact and interpretations in the light of specific situations. An illustration of the type of merger alleged by the Federal Trade Commission to be a prima-facie violation of Section 7 of the Clayton Act is provided by the case of Pillsbury Mills, Inc. In 1951 and 1952, Pillsbury acquired the assets of two of its principal competitors, namely, Ballard and Ballard Company and Duff's Baking Mix Division of American Home Products Corporation. The companies acquired by Pillsbury had been in substantial competition with it prior to the acquisition. As a consequence of the merger, Pillsbury's share of the market in the southeastern part of the United States increased substantially. For bakery flour, its sales in this region increased by 40 per cent; for mixes, by 78 per cent; for family flour, by 154 per cent; and for feed, by 775 per cent. These changes occurred in an industry in which the number of mills had been declining and a larger per cent of industry sales was being realized by a steadily declining number of companies.

Modifications of Existing Products

There appears to be no uniform rule governing the number of items that can be marketed by any one organization. For the first 70 years of its history, Coca-Cola Co. was a conspicuous example of a rigid "one product in one package policy." During the 1950's, however, it modified its product line by introducing new sizes and types of containers and by marketing other types of flavored beverages. The H. J. Heinz Company in the food field and the Eli Lilly and Co. in the drug trade are wellknown companies with relatively long lines of products, but in both cases the products are closely related in terms of final use and channel of distribution through which they are marketed. Other companies such as Textron-American, Inc. have provided a wide range of products without any close or discernible relationship among many of them. Regardless of the number of items in a company's line, or its policies regarding the contraction or expansion of its line, it is faced with continuing questions relating to modifications of its existing products. In the competitive struggle to maximize sales volume and profits by providing products which will better satisfy consumer wants and desires, modifications of both consumer and industrial products are almost continuous.

Forms of Product Modification

Modifications of existing products take a wide variety of specific forms. *Style change which creates fashion obsolescence* is a popular form of modification—one often cited by critics of our marketing system as a source of waste and dissatisfaction, but one which is credited by many proponents of private competitive enterprise as a major explanation of high levels of employment, family income, and living standards. Planned timing of changes in pre-existing models is the basis for many product changes in durable and nondurable goods, as illustrated by certain aspects of annual model changes in automobiles and fashion changes from season to season, and even within seasons, in ready-to-wear apparel.

Certain *design changes* are primarily *related to utility* rather than to fashion obsolescence. Automatic washing machines with lint filtering features were a popularly accepted modification in 1956 because such features solved a problem which was a common source of consumer dissatisfaction. Many features in automotive design are related to utility as well as fashion as in the case, for example, of automatic transmissions, turn signal indicators, factory installed air conditioning, power steering, and power brakes.

Changes in the types of *materials* used in manufacture is another form of modification. In order to reach wider markets, manufacturers of television sets used mass-produced plastic cabinets because these were much more economical than the wood cabinets which were used almost exclusively in the models first manufactured by the industry. New ingredients used in peanut butter and certain cheese products have made it easier to spread them on bread or crackers. The use of foam rubber in upholstered furniture has had an important influence upon the quality, appearance, and cost of many items in this category.

Developing new *uses* for or changed *attitudes* about products is a form of product modification when the product is conceived broadly in terms of its satisfaction-yielding potentiality. For example, sales of pancake mixes were diminishing owing to diet-consciousness and trends to slenderizing foods. A leading advertising agency developed a successful new promotional campaign built upon new uses, including simple summer suppers, waffle recipe ideas, and novel pancakes. These applications were essentially new from the standpoint of consumers who were accustomed to pancakes only as a hearty breakfast item. The Overhead Door Co., manufacturer of garage doors, was losing sales because of intensive competition from new firms in its field. It developed and successfully promoted the concept of installing a second overhead door at the rear of the garage, thus converting garage space into a patio, a shaded breezeway, or game area in warm weather months. In this manner, the same product, as defined by its physical attributes, became a modified product in the sense of a component of a part of a residence that satisfied hitherto ungratified wants.

Packaging

An additional type of product modification that warrants separate attention is packaging. For many types of consumer and industrial goods, this is one of the most important problems of product policy. While the activity of packaging is of ancient lineage, a realization of the various purposes served by well-planned packaging and their relationship to other aspects of marketing strategy is of recent origin. Various objectives that may be attained through packaging have been identified as follows:

- Protecting the product
- Adapting to production line conditions
- Promoting the sale of the product
- Changing product density (i.e., changing the ratio of product volume to package volume)
- Convenience, or facilitating the use of the product
- Having reuse value for the consumer

Any kind of package may contribute something to the attainment of all of the foregoing objectives, but each will do so to varying degrees. The problem of packaging policy is to make decisions that will result in the best over-all contribution of packaging to total marketing effort.

While certain types of containers, such as glass flasks and bottles, were known in early times, they served a strictly utilitarian purpose of holding and protecting contents. Such was the primary objective of packaging until the development of modern manufacturing methods and transportation services. Today, content protection is still a major objective. A manufacturer may be required to use corrugated shipping containers of certain minimum bursting strength to satisfy transportation regulations, but he may decide to use much stronger materials to permit high stacking of merchandise by means of modern materials handling equipment in wholesale warehouses. Product protection often remains an objective at the point of final use, as illustrated by the preservation of freshness of a partially used loaf of bread.

In the early years of marketing packaged merchandise; packaging was primarily an extension of the manufacturing function in industry. While it was recognized that some attributes of packages could enhance one's market position, most decisions about packaging were made from the standpoint of types of materials that could be used in connection with manufacturing and assembling processes in factories. A type of wrapping material with ideal product protection characteristics might, for example, be found impractical from the standpoint of slowing down the production line in the factory because of the necessity of operating packaging machines at slow rates. In recent years the trend has been to improve packaging machinery so that it will handle wanted types of packaging materials, thus providing a desired reversal of emphasis.

Under modern conditions of self-service merchandising, the package has become a standard unit of sale that must speak as a silent salesman for itself. Especially in the case of convenience goods, the graphic arts are drawn upon to call attention to the product, identify it, and make it more attractive. The package is also commonly the means of conveying descriptive and use information to the final buyer, in connection with the discussion of labeling. Because of the influence of non rational considerations in purchasing, particularly in the case of items commonly bought on the basis of impulse, the question of desirable symbolism, coloring, shape, and form is the subject of much motivational research activity. The sales promotion aspects of packaging are indeed numerous and varied. For example, a manufacturer of breakfast cereals may decide to introduce a new package size for a popular item, hoping that retailers will stock both sizes rather than just one, and with the result of more shelf space exposure to the consumer at the point of final sale. If both sizes are accepted by the trade and by consumers, there is a possibility of greater total sales, but if the sales of the new package are largely at the expense of the old, there will be negative effects in other aspects as, for example, manufacturing considerations, packaging material costs, or, perhaps, product density in warehouse storage.

The matter of product density is a packaging function characterized by the greatest conflicts relating to other objectives. For example, a cylinder is an efficient packaging material for liquids, and a given quantity of liquid can be packaged in cylindrical form with the use of a smaller amount of packaging material than is the case with any other shape. When, however, a number of cylinders are packed in a shipping carton, there is considerable wasted space, and lower product density for transporting and storage purposes than if rectangular containers had been used. On the other hand, a sales promotion decision to use a long neck type of bottle for a brand of salad dressing may lower product density for storage and display purposes and greatly increase the cost of packaging material. Such disadvantages may, however, be offset by greater distinctiveness on the retail store shelf, and the shape of the container may suggest the existence of a greater physical volume of contents than actually is available. The design of a package for the purpose of misleading the buyer about its contents raises significant ethical or moral questions; moreover, deception of this kind is likely to be illegal under the provisions of the Wheeler Lea Amendment to the Federal Trade Commission Act.

Many packages are designed to facilitate the use of the product after purchase. In some cases the nature of the package is such that it is a very large component of total product cost in which case it is also likely to be the outstanding feature from a user benefit viewpoint. Illustrative of modern innovations of this type are aerosol containers used for a number of products such as insecticides and shaving cream and polyethylene squeeze bottles introduced in connection with Stopette deodorant but now used for many liquid and powder products, chiefly in the cosmetic and toilet goods industries. Other anticipated developments of a similar nature are plastic squeeze containers that will measure and dispense food ingredients by the teaspoonful, and pressure dispensers that will provide exact doses of medicines. The reuse value of a package is often a promotable feature in the case of certain consumer products, as illustrated by olives sold in cocktail glasses and vegetable shortening marketed in decorative cans for subsequent use as kitchen canisters. As a general rule, designing a package to do other jobs well tends to minimize its reuse value, with the result that this function has diminished somewhat with growing appreciation of the marketing significance of other attributes of packaging.

Introducing New or Modified Products

The introduction of new products or substantially modified existing products poses a number of complicated management problems which can be but briefly suggested in this general treatment of marketing. Unless modifications are regular and expected by the trade, as in the case of annual model changes for automobiles and certain major appliances, the timing of the introduction is a major problem. Although modifications are sometimes used as a device to offset a declining or depressed sales situation, it is generally regarded as preferable to plan for the introduction of modifications at times when cyclical or seasonal factors indicate that the market will be highly responsive. Plans must be laid sufficiently in advance so that wholesalers and dealers are notified and are not caught with large inventories which will become obsolete. Arrangements must be made for personal selling and for physical distribution in advance of widespread consumer advertising and sales promotional activities. Problems of physical distribution are often very great. If a new model or new packaging is to be introduced through advertising on a given date, all wholesalers and all retailers handling the product must be supplied with a normal stock quantity almost simultaneously. Such a requirement places a heavy strain upon physical facilities of the manufacturer and his warehousing and shipping organization and calls for the most careful advance planning. The introduction of new products or significant product modifications is normally accompanied by unusual amounts of advertising and sales promotion efforts which must be carefully planned and integrated with other plans for personal selling and physical distribution.

BRAND POLICIES

One of the most distinctive features of modern marketing is the wide use of brands by manufacturers and distributors and the general acceptance of or preference for branded items upon the part of most consumers. At this point, certain purposes and methods of demand creation and some of the problems connected with the sale of branded merchandise are considered.

Reasons for Brands

One of the principal reasons for the use of a brand name is that it helps the purchaser to *identify* products. While identification is sometimes accomplished by other means, such as trademarks or unusual containers, brand names are the principal instruments. Second, brands actually *protect the buyer.* As long as a purchaser continues to buy branded articles, the manufacturer of which is known, he is protected as to standards of quality and to some extent in the matter of price. At least he knows what he has been paying for the article and can form a judgment as to a fair price in a new situation. Third, brands protect their owners by giving them a certain measure of *control over the demand* for the products. It is frequently the goal of a manufacturer of a branded article to make his product superior at a given price and so well known that thousands or millions of consumers and other buyers will insist on that brand or at least prefer it to others. Many manufacturers and wholesalers have gained consumer *preference* for their brands, but probably the majority have only succeeded in securing consumer *acceptance.* A fourth reason is that a brand name is a necessary adjunct to any form of demand creation activity in which *appeals to selective buying motives* are stressed. Thus, selective or competitive selling effort and brands are mutually interdependent.

Fifth, the use of a brand name enables a manufacturer to add different products to his lines, for it *facilitates the introduction of new items* inconsequence of the prestige derived from his existing brand. Finally, in the case of technical products of high unit value, a brand name *aids in stressing repairs or other related services.* Prospective buyers of automobiles, adding machines, typewriters, cash registers, and other such devices are much more inclined to buy a particular item if they know that they can secure certain types of repair service at convenient places and at moderate charges.

Types of Brands

An examination of the different brands on the market discloses two distinct types. First, there are brands adopted and sponsored by manufacturers, and commonly known either as *manufacturers'* or *national brands.* The latter designation tends to emphasize the fact that the most successful brands that have been adopted by manufacturers and pushed aggressively have been generally advertised on a national scale, although many manufacturers' brands are promoted and distributed only on a regional basis.

Second, many brands are the property right of middlemen in the channel of distribution. Such brands may be sponsored by retailers, wholesalers, or cooperative buying groups. In any event, they are collectively designated as *private brands* or as *distributor brands.* While some private brands are nationally known, such as those used by Sears, Roebuck and Company and the Great Atlantic & Pacific Tea Co., the prevailing tendency is for private brands to be restricted to local or regional influence.

Manufacturers' Brand Policies

Most manufacturers, and certainly almost all of the larger ones, have recognized the wisdom of adopting brands. Nevertheless there are still many who, for one reason or another, do not brand or advertise their products.

Marketing Unbranded Goods

Prominent among the reasons for marketing unbranded goods is a lack of appreciation for the value of established brands and absence of initiative or financial resources necessary to establish a selling and advertising organization. Many a manufacturer is willing to sell all or part of his output on an unbranded basis and for a variety of reasons.

In selling unbranded goods, a manufacturer finds it possible to cater to purchasers who are anxious to secure supplies for private branding. This may sometimes afford an outlet for surplus goods even when a manufacturer markets his own established brand. He may have overestimated the demand for his trademarked article and manufactured more than could be absorbed by his market. To prevent depreciation from obsolescence and physical deterioration and to save interest on the capital tied up in extra inventories, he may be glad to dispose of his surplus for sale under a private label, so long as his own brand remains protected. Some manufacturers sell only first-class products under their own brand and dispose of imperfect and inferior goods to wholesalers or retailers who label them with their private brands. It should not be inferred, however, that all private brands are inferior. On the contrary, many private brands are of superior quality.

Unbranded goods make it easier for a manufacturer to shade his prices when warranted by general business conditions or other pertinent factors. Previous purchasers, because of lack of knowledge as to the exact sources of supply from which lower-priced goods have been procured by their competitors, are not likely to resent the practice. A manufacturer of branded goods, on the other hand, feels an obligation to maintain selling prices even when added stimulation to business through lowered prices may be deemed advisable, merely because customers still have large quantities of his products on hand for which the established price has been charged.

Manufacturers of unbranded goods are, however, subject to a number of disadvantages. They are not in a strong strategic position, especially if products can be readily duplicated. Unless the manufacturer enjoys peculiar manufacturing advantages, his business is precarious and may easily be lost. He must frequently compete strictly on a price basis and hence may lose to a more efficient competitor and suddenly find himself without a market. One of the chief interests of middlemen who purchase goods for private branding is in securing them at lowest prices. They will therefore purchase wherever they can secure the greatest economies, for little prestige attaches to any one source of unbranded merchandise except that which arises from rendering superior service and integrity.

Blanket Versus Individual Brands

When a manufacturer has two or more products which are to be branded, it becomes necessary to decide whether the same brand, commonly referred to as a *house* or *blanket* brand, should be used for all or whether separate brands should be adopted for individual items. Probably the majority of manufacturers who produce several articles of similar quality use one blanket brand or trademark for all items in the line, as illustrated by Heinz, Libby, or Del Monte food products, Elizabeth Arden or Pond's cosmetics, Johnson & Johnson first aid and toilet goods items, and Parker or Ever sharp pens and pencils. Individual rather than blanket brands are used, however, by a number of the country's most important manufacturers including Procter & Gamble Company, the International Shoe Company, Lever Brothers and Unilever, Ltd., and the General Motors Corporation.

A blanket or house brand enables the buyer to identify all the products bearing that mark, aids in establishing consumer recognition, and extends the prestige of the whole line to the individual items in the family. This facilitates the introduction of new items. Several products can be called to the attention of consumers in a single advertisement, with major attention being focused either on one of the items featured or on the brand itself.

Yet the adoption of a house brand presents some very difficult problems. In the first place, the same standard of quality must be maintained for all products. Should a single product prove inferior in quality to that of the general group, it is likely to impair the reputation of the entire line. Second, care must be exercised to see that the products are allied in some way. A blanket brand cannot be advantageously applied to commodities for which association may not prove desirable, as in the case of soaps and cooking fats or glue and hams. A third precaution is that a blanket brand does not lend itself to the same degree of aggressive selling and cannot be so highly individualized as a trademark that is applied to a single product. This probably constitutes the single most important objection to blanket or house brands. For example, "Crisco" certainly means more to the average housewife than any blanket brand like "Heinz," merely because the former applies to a single product, the association of which is complete as soon as the name is seen or pronounced, while the latter refers to a line of food products with a more or less vague frame of reference.

Multiple Brands and Market Segmentation

Many manufacturers have a policy of marketing several brands of similar products. This is commonly a strategy to appeal to different segments of the market which may be differentiated in a variety of ways, such as interest in price, preference for a particular channel of distribution, reactions to different kinds of brand images, or desire for slightly differentiated physical attributes of product.

One common purpose of introducing a second brand of a similar product is to meet price competition. During periods of business recession, it may be possible to stimulate sales by marketing lower priced items. In other cases, the need for a lower priced brand arises from keen competition in the field. A "fighting brand" is then adopted, with the express purpose of meeting all price competition. This may or may not involve a change in quality or in channels of distribution.

Another reason for several brands of a given product or class of goods may be the desire to satisfy different outlets. Some middlemen may demand a less expensive brand, and their business may be sufficiently extensive to justify its adoption. The International Shoe Company, for example, through its different manufacturing plants, produces a number of brands so that all types of stores may be served with shoes varying in price from the lowest to almost the highest. The establishment of a lower priced brand also enables manufacturers to dispose of imperfect and inferior merchandise without jeopardizing the prestige of their regular brands.

Another example of market segmentation is provided by the Procter & Gamble Company, which markets multiple brands of toothpaste, vegetable shortenings, packaged household soaps and detergents, as well as multiple brands of other types of products. It has been reported that the theory which underlies the company's strategy is that no one detergent or shampoo will satisfy every housewife and that the best way to increase the company's share of a particular commodity market is to launch a second or a third brand to appeal to different segments of that market. A new brand may differ only slightly in actual performance from some established brand, but it must have some distinctive characteristic that can be dramatized in advertising. According to advertising appeals commonly used, "Tide gets clothes cleaner," Cheer gets them "whiter," and Oxydol gets them "detergent clean... and bleach-white. Thus, the company has a major specific selling appeal identified with each of several individual products and can offer to each customer something which is most in line with specific buying interests. For similar reasons General Foods Corp., introduced a third brand of instant coffee, "Yuban," at a time when its two previously established brands, "Maxwell House," and "Sanka," were reputed to hold a competitive position amounting to 55 per cent of the total instant coffee market.

Related examples are to be found in the cigarette manufacturing industry. Most of the major manufacturers have a variety of brands. Illustrative is Philip Morris, Inc. which markets the following brands, several of which are available in different packages or lengths: Alpine, English Ovals, Benson & Hedges, Parliament, Philip Morris, and Marlboro. By this diversity of brands, the company is able to serve all segments of the market—consumers who wish exclusiveness in price and package, those who like ordinary cigarettes, long sizes, filters, or menthol flavour.

Branding Materials and Parts

There is a growing tendency among manufacturers of materials and parts to perpetuate the identity of their products by means of branding. The commonest examples of such attempts are to be found in the production of batteries for automobiles, and of automobile bearings, bodies, tires, and other equipment. Radio and television equipment and numerous accessories, including tubes, transistors, and other parts, are thus branded and advertised. Manufacturers of rubber heels have attempted to identify their product as a means of influencing shoe manufacturers to use a specified brand. In many such cases there are two distinct markets for the product: first, the manufacturer, who uses the product as a part of the original equipment, and second, the consumer, who buys it for replacement purposes.

Branding not only may occasionally force a manufacturer of the finished product to purchase the branded part or material but will make it possible for dealers and service stations to be identified with the part, so that necessary services involving repairs, inspection, and installation may be rendered satisfactorily. This in turn results in purchasing such parts for replacement purposes by brand, especially when the product is of a relatively high unit value or high replacement frequency. The branding of textile fibers, yarns, and cloth has become of increasing significance since the advent of man-made or synthetic fibers. Among brand names commonly featured in trade and consumer advertising for apparel are Dacron, Milium, Helenca, Dynel, Celanese, Acrilan, and Chromspun. Even among natural fibre cloth, it is fairly common to find brand name advertising in consumer publications for such materials as Aberfoyle cotton, Harris Tweed, and Forstmann woolens.

In many instances these branded materials are identified by labels on finished items of apparel and constitute an important selling feature of the product, although the use of such brand names in this manner has been somewhat complicated by the Textile Fibre Products Identification Act, which became effective in 1960 and which requires the disclosure of the generic name of each fibre-whether natural or man-made-in a textile product, along with its respective percentage of total fibre weight. For purposes of the law, a blouse could not be described as "made of 65% Dacron" (a brand name) "and 35% cotton" but would have to be designated as "made of 65% polyester" "and 35% cotton.

Private Brand Policies of Middlemen

Most manufacturers of nationally advertised goods are strongly opposed to the marketing of private brands by middlemen in their channel of distribution, yet at the same time many of them also serve as a source of supply of private branded merchandise, thereby disposing of surplus goods or achieving certain economies of scale that would not be attainable if sales were confined to their own branded items.

Regional and national wholesalers, commonly use private brands in order to compete with local wholesalers whose establishments may be located nearer to customers. In retailing, the marketing of private brands of some products is a common policy among mail order companies, department store ownership groups, food chains, automotive accessory chains, certain drug chains, multiunit organizations in the alcoholic beverage trades in some states, and other largescale organizations. Many cooperative buying groups, voluntary chains, and resident buying offices also have extensive private brand programs. Not so widely recognized is the extent to which manufacturers procure merchandise made by others for distribution under their own private brands. Illustrative is the practice of large tire companies that purchase certain automotive accessory products for resale as part of their merchandise line. Another example consists of major oil companies that buy tires, batteries, and other products for resale under their own private brand name in their controlled service station outlets.

In the true sense, such manufacturers that buy merchandise for distribution under their private brands are acting in the capacity of wholesalers and/or retailers of the products, and thus their activities of this kind are to be considered as failing within the scope and analysis of private brand policies of middlemen. While most large-scale middlemen are anxious to obtain the potential advantages of a private brand merchandising programme, many of them are loath to incur the displeasure of manufacturers of national brands which account for the bulk of total sales volume in most merchandise categories. In the food trade, for example, annual studies indicate that major manufacturers' brands account for about 75 per cent of sales of packaged food products, with the remainder divided among so-called "minor brands," including both private and local manufacturers' brands.

In the marketing of shopping and specialty consumer goods and industrial equipment and supply items, most wholesale and retail middlemen are somewhat more reluctant to engage in a private branding programme.

For such products, it is easier for the manufacturer to follow policies of selective distribution at all levels in the channel, and he is most likely to avoid the selection of outlets that compete directly with the sale of his own products by means of private brands when equally suitable alternatives are available.

So far as the public is concerned, arguments have been advanced by its advocates to the effect that private branding has beneficial results. Opponents naturally deride the plan and represent it as detrimental to the general welfare of the consumer. It is often alleged that distributors' brands are less reliable than manufacturers' brands and that they involve a tremendous multiplicity in brands. This is said to be confusing to the public. Moreover, manufacturers of major brands and their advertising agencies are quick to point out that most distributors of private brands are parasitical in the sense that they do not engage in product research and development activity and do not help to enlarge markets by stimulating primary demand. Owing to the controversial nature of the whole question of private brands, it is essential to consider the reasons for such policies from the standpoint of middlemen and to ascertain the prerequisites for successful promotion of private-brand merchandise.

Reasons for Private Branding

Two major reasons for private branding are peculiar to wholesalers. One of these may be designated as self-preservation. Direct sale to retailers has been most common among manufacturers of highly advertised lines of products. Many wholesalers, consequently, entertain the fear that as soon as they develop a sufficient volume of sales on a manufac-turer's line, he may establish his own integrated wholesaling system. Wholesalers with brands of their own are in a better position to compete with direct-selling manufacturers. Second, private brands are often established by wholesalers as a means of protection against their own salesmen. Many wholesalers' salesmen are aggressive individuals who know their trade intimately and secure much of their business because of their impressive personality rather than on the basis of the reputation of the house they represent.

This knowledge enhances the salesman's bargaining power, of which he sometimes takes full advantage. He may thus threaten to join a competitor if his demands are disregarded and divert the bulk of his trade from his present employer. When the wholesaler develops a market for his own exclusive brands, his salesmen's activities intensify demand for these products, thereby diminishing the danger of losing trade when a popular salesman severs connections with the house.

A number of additional reasons may be advanced to explain the private brand activities of middlemen both at the wholesale and retail levels of distribution. For one thing, middlemen are interested in private brands because they often afford an opportunity for a larger gross margin of profit. Some manufacturers of heavily advertised brands have cut middlemen's discounts to a minimum and attempt to justify such action by the argument that, since they have created the demand for the product, the merchant does not have to exert much selling effort and therefore is adequately compensated by a narrower margin.

The ability to control repeat business is an important reason for private brands. Some manufacturers' brands, except those distributed through exclusive agencies, are sold by competing outlets, customers may purchase them from a number of sources. The private brand is, however, available only from the merchant who controls it.

Third, private brands are used to avoid direct price competition. Price competition is generally keenest among sellers of highly advertised national brands who stress price as a patronage appeal.

A private brand distributor may carry such items only for completeness of stock and attempt to develop business for his own brand which, for practical purposes, is not directly comparable with lines handled by competitors. A fourth reason is that private brands permit greater freedom in pricing. Prices of products bearing manufacturers' brands are frequently fixed by manufacturers in a desire to maintain resale prices. Under such circumstances a middleman has limited freedom to vary prices even when trade and other conditions would seem to warrant price cutting.

When a merchant affixes his own brand to the merchandise, he is perfectly free, within certain legal bounds, to price his goods in accordance with the dictates of his judgment. In a period of poor business, or in territories in which keen competition prevails, a variation in price may be a determining factor in the volume of business ultimately secured.

Fifth, middlemen operating on a large scale are frequently able to take over all or a substantial portion of the output of certain manufacturing companies. This often results in an unusually strong bargaining position, with the result that the procurer of private branded merchandise buys at prices much lower than would apply in purchasing nationally advertised goods of similar quality.

Finally, private branding permits greater freedom in the selection of sources of supply. Goods are often bought on a specification basis. Thus the buyer may have nearly an unlimited number of sources of supply for certain common and easily manufactured items, as compared with a single source in the case of goods branded by the manufacturer.

Prerequisites to a Successful Private Brand Policy

To secure satisfactory results from marketing private brand merchandise, two important requirements must be met. First, the middleman must assume full responsibility for the quality of the product bearing that brand. This necessitates purchasing in large quantities in order to insure a regular supply and strict uniformity in quality. Experience has shown that, in order to maintain a uniform quality of his product and to secure economies in buying requisite to success in the undertaking, goods must be purchased in larger quantities than when dealing entirely in nationally advertised goods. Larger stocks must be carried, so that private brands usually have a slower rate of turnover than manufacturers' brands of similar goods.

A second merchandising problem arising from the handling of private brands relates to the assumption of the task of demand creation. Successful utilization of a private brand necessitates the establishment of a sales promotion department and the organization of a more aggressive sales force, closely resembling the type of salesmanship used by specialty manufacturers. Salesmen must be trained to render such special assistance to retailers as will induce the latter to cooperate in promoting sales of the private 'brand merchandise. In retail stores, additional promotional effort and more intensive personal selling is a requirement to induce consumers to purchase private brands rather than the major manufac-turers' brands which already have substantial acceptance.

Outlook for Private Branding

During the late 1950's and early 1960's several environmental conditions were closely related to the opportunity and outlook for private branding. First, reduced gross margins on major advertised brands of many consumer products resulted from aggressive price cutting attributed to the growth of "low margin" or discount house retailers and to the retaliatory tactics of established organizations. This has led to greater interest in private brands as an opportunity for realizing satisfactory gross margins.

Second, various lines of retail trade have been characterized by greater concentration of sales among fewer companies. This has been especially important in the department store field, among food chains, and in the automotive accessory store trade. Thus, the growth of the largest companies in such fields has placed them in a better position to develop private brand programs. Finally, in many industries excess manufacturing capacity exists. Internal pressure to maintain or increase sales volume has encouraged a larger number of manufacturers to accept business from middlemen for their private branding programs. Since these circumstances are not likely to be reversed in the foreseeable future, the outlook for at least moderate growth in private branding appears promising.

11

Management Research: Theories of Problem-Solving and Decision Making

Mental imagery and related processes can be quickly and effectively applied to the management of many types of problems within organizations. Human resource professionals can train employees to use imaginal processes to scan problem dynamics and to develop a rich list of alternatives to test for problem solution.

While people sometimes resist using their imagery in problem-solving, once familiar with the techniques, they usually overcome their resistance. Just as is true in other applications, trainer competency in the development and presentation of imaginal scripts and scenarios is critical in making imaginal techniques powerful tools in problem-solving and decision making. Scripts show various ways that these techniques can be integrated with more traditional and rational means of problem-solving and decision making.

PREVENTING PROBLEMS

In today's turbulent societal and business environment, organizations face challenges and search for opportunities in their environments. Very few organizations are immune from influences of such things as the possibility of another fuel crisis, the federal budget deficit, international trade imbalances, the value of the dollar in reference to foreign currency, or the precarious geopolitical situation in the Middle East. Organizations that ignore these environmental realities, impact on their operations and strategies are suffering from a form of corporate myopia.

Organizations that actively scan their environments, anticipate emergent problems and take advantage of opportunities that may arise over time. These are the organizations that will survive and prosper in the information age of the future. To survive, organizational members must be taught to appreciate and alter their mental models of the future so that surprises are prepared for before their impact on the organization.

Your organization's environment includes all of the political, legal, economic, international, sociocultural, value-based, technological, geopolitical, and demographic trends and changes that affect its ability to function effectively and efficiently over your strategic planning horizon. Twenty years ago, there was more stability in this environment than there is today. As time passes, the social environment will become more complex and will present all organizations with novel problems that demand creative and anticipatory problem-solving skills. For example, we can no longer assume away the rest of the world economically. Most current business decisions are affected by international events; we truly live in a world economy.

One of the key functions of the HRM unit is to serve as a scanning unit that watches the environment for patterns of change that affect the organization. The HRM unit is in contact with many sources of current information about the future and the market place. This responsibility falls to the HRM unit because it works with the human dimension of organizational functioning. One creative way to accomplish the problem definition task is to use imaginal techniques to develop clear and explicit scenarios of the future as well as strategies your organization can apply to the hypothetical, but potential future environment. Further, you can share this expertise with other managers and planners, so that the total organization expands and articulates its visions of the future in preparation for that future.

For example, one problem that organizations will face in the future is the problem of recruiting qualified personnel. As the age of the population goes up, as the number of entering workers goes down, and as the technological sophistication of work increases, organizations will face the critical problem of finding, attracting, and maintaining competent work forces. If traditional manpower planning methods are used solely, one may find that these techniques don't function in the future environment defined by emerging trends.

However, if HRM personnel are schooled in the use of creative, projective problem-solving, they can build scenarios of future conditions, how conditions will affect manpower planning over time, and how the organization can adapt its recruitment and selection techniques to accommodate these trends. In other words, imagery can be used to supplement traditional manpower planning, but not to replace it. In this example, the planning group would take part in a process that involves the following procedures.

- Consensual Definition of the Problem: Herein, the group discusses the nature of the problem that is anticipated and develops consensus about the dynamics, of the problem. A suitable definition here would be: "How do we acquire talented and qualified employees in the future as the number of qualified applicants decreases and as the technological requirements of the workplace increase?" This definition presupposes that the HRM staff have prescreened the problem by using available forecasting and trend analysis information.

- Individual Problem Brainstorming: After arriving at consensus on the nature of the problem, staff can be placed in a relaxed state and given imaginal cues to promote creative scanning of the problem and the potential ways that the problem can be solved. A possible script for this activity might go something like this.

Take a moment now to close your eyes, stretch out, and let relaxation 7 flow throughout your body. Become aware of any physical or emotional sources of tension or anxiety that you may be experiencing. As you scan your mind and body, imagine yourself converting negative or tense energies into black balloons — see yourself blowing these balloons up and watching them sail away from you, carrying both tension and routinized thinking with them. You are totally relaxed and open to using your imaginal and creative talents to handle the problem we are studying. Now envision yourself as adept and creative at problem-solving. See yourself as able to handle the most complex future problem in an intelligent and creative manner. See yourself as using your creative problem-solving skills to deal with our current problem.

Now imagine that you're responsible for recruitment and selection of competent personnel five years from now. Imagine that you have carefully scanned the employment environment as you ponder how to attract and retain employees so that we remain effective and profitable in the future. Envision the types of employees we will need to meet the challenges of this dynamic future. What types of skills and abilities will we need? What types of attitudes and characteristics will you be looking for in your employees?" What information sources and recruiting channels will you use to find potential employees who best fit the needs of the organization. How will you influence prospective employees to see our organization as the type of place in which they prosper.

Take a moment now to reflect on your ideas and impressions. Try not to edit or screen any of your ideas. Where you have created an interesting idea, take some time now to play with the idea. Relax and let your creative powers help you further develop potential solutions to this future problem. View the problem as an opportunity for you to exercise your creative problem solving skills on a challenge. That's good. Now, take another moment to collect your varied images and thoughts. Shortly we'll come back together as a group to look at the issue through the multiple and creative visions we have generated.

Be confident that your ideas will contribute to our overall problem solving efforts. [Pause.] Once again, try not to edit or delete your thoughts. Imagine yourself as ready to record and share your good ideas. Imagine yourself writing your ideas down on a mental notebook for safekeeping and sharing." This script gives personnel the opportunity to evaluate freely the problem from a variety of views and to share their ideas with others. It also gives them practice in reframing their conceptions of the problem and building freely creative depictions of potential solution paths.

- Reconstitution: Herein, the group would come back together and share collective experiences, insights, and ideas generated during the imaginal script exercise. Someone in the group would record the ideas and at the close of this exercise would reiterate the ideas to the group. This reiteration would serve as the basis for the fourth step in this process. This process of "expanded effort" generates a great number of potential ideas that may be creative and feasible solutions' options. Research has shown that the more elabourate the information generation process, the greater the degree of creativity and originality that is promoted.
- Free Imaginal Excursion: During this phase, staff uses the collective creativity of the group as a basis for further elabourating potential problem solutions. All staff have an expanded view of the problem from others' perspectives; they will use this broad-based cognitive structure to further study and solve the problem. A short, provocative image set allows staff to once again access and explore their creative ideas. Consider the following script.

  Once again, take a relaxed attitude and posture. Place yourself in a creative state and review the materials we have just covered. You have expressed your ideas from the first script. Take a moment to review these ideas. Now take another moment to review the ideas of your colleagues. That's good. Now, once again, place yourself in the position of recruiting and selecting employees ten years from now. Given all of the ideas that you have now experienced, how would you go about recruiting and selecting new employees for the firm in this dynamic future? Take a few moments now to develop a scenario for managing this problem.. Try not to be limiting or judgmental in developing your strategy.
- Problem Elabouration and Solution: After bringing staff back into the present and once again elabourating ideas, staff evaluates the various options that are present and develops an anticipatory recruiting strategy for dealing with work force changes of the future. Your strategies may focus on either training current personnel to be more adaptive in the future, or you may focus on an increase in manpower scanning efforts, which you decide is critical to recruitment and selection in the competitive future. The important process within this step is to consolidate the various perspectives on the problem and to generate strategies that take into account the dynamics that have previously been identified.

Problems can only be identified and proactively managed if they are anticipated by and considered within the mental models that organizational personnel hold about the future. These mental models are the recurrent images, depictions, and scenarios that we hold of our organizations and the action paths of these organizations. Mental models are highly imaginal in nature and can best be reviewed, modified, and improved by educating personnel to work comfortably with these models during imaginal practice sessions. If the mental models of personnel are overly focused on the short-term present, the likelihood that the organization can anticipate and manage very different future problems is greatly inhibited. Only by encouraging and rewarding people for envisioning the future can we actually begin to deal with the probable contingencies that will emerge.

Frequently, personnel are so tied to self-limiting and reactive future images of their organizations that little true anticipatory mindwork is done to prepare the organization for its challenges or its opportunities. In order to promote more long-term thinking, you can help educate other personnel in anticipatory-projective imaginal exercises that allow them to move beyond the routinized thinking that often governs many facets of organizations.

Our research has clearly shown that matching an inappropriate problem solving approach with a creative or challenging problem leads to less productivity and creativity in problem-solving. If we are to adapt a method of preventative problem-solving in the future, we must activate the imaginal powers of personnel to depict, alter, and improve our organization's response to inevitable changes. Unique problems cannot be solved through retrospection or through routinization. Such problems are solved when individuals go beyond habitual thinking patterns. Problem-solving is a skill area. As with any other skill area, acquisition and use of sound methods in problem-solving occurs through practice.

ORGANIZATIONAL PRODUCTIVITY

As with anticipatory and preventative problem-solving, creative problem-solving will be a characteristic process within the successful organization of the future. In fact, anticipatory problem-solving is closely related to the creative process, and allows the creative individual both to define the creative process and to define the problem more vividly. Creativity seems a mystery to most of us. We often assume that only a very few talented people are fortunate to have this wondrous human capacity. We reward creativity with accolades and large paychecks. We all secretly wish that we were more creative. Many consulting organizations offer "surefire" programmemes and techniques that will enhance creativity in a two-day (or so) seminar.

While all of this is understandable, it is unfortunate. Creativity is an innate cognitive process that is available to most healthy individuals when and it they choose to prioritize creativity as a skill area to be developed. Mental imagery is an important component of creativity and a process that is available to everyone in order to recognize and apply in personal and professional activities. Recent research has shown that individuals who have vivid and controllable imagery also have higher degrees of creative expression than individuals with less vivid imaginal experiences. The ability to build and elabourate imaginal mindsets and scenarios is a learned skill for many people and something that they have consciously applied in their life.

Research also shows that by merely telling someone that they either are creative (by reputation) or should "be creative" in a problem-solving context improves the number and quality of their ideas or problem responses. This suggests that even superficial manipulation of the creative self-image of an individual can have positive effects on creative performance. Finally, historical and anecdotal reports on the creative works of Einstein, Edison, Kekule, Wordsworth, Whitman, and many other artists, writers, and statespersons consistently indicate that they utilized and manipulated their imaginal processes to deal with problems that required creative or innovative solutions. These results are important to keep in mind, especially since we too often see creativity as a talent of the few rather than as a potential that most of us can have.

The Creative Self-image

Enhancing creative problem-solving involves recognizing the importance of self-image to one's creative behaviour. For instance, if you define yourself as a creative individual, you will eagerly undertake challenging tasks that allow you to become more creative and adept at flexible methods of problem-solving. Likewise, if you mentally model yourself as uncreative, you will avoid unique, novel, or challenging tasks and will rely on routinized problem-solving methods to solve a limited set of predictable problems. In other words, the self-fulfilling prophesy contributes to creativity. Recall at this point that a mental model is the depiction, mental picture, or image set that an individual maintains and uses as a reference guide for choice and action.

One's self-image is the mental model of self that guides the individual in dealing with reality. Creativity is one aspect of this mental model that most of us define both from our own experiences and from the evaluations of significant others in our lives and work. By helping your organization's employees recognize and perceive their abilities to be creative, you help them to reframe their self-images so that their problem-solving improves. Several examples of brief imaginal techniques are provided in the following examples to show how the creative self-image can be enhanced.

After inducing a state of relaxation in staff or trainees, the following script can be used to help them re-frame their internal imaginal models of self. Now that you are relaxed and free of tension, you will explore your creativity. You will scan your past, your present, and your future to picture your ability to be creative. As much as possible, relax during these excursions and develop a picture of yourself as a creative and contributing member of our team. Think of how you've dealt with problems in the past. Envision how you wish to deal with problems in the future. That's good — you are relaxed. The ability to relax helps you be more creative.

Try to remember to relax each and every time that you are faced with a task that requires creativity and innovation. Now it is time for us to begin our travels. Take a moment and return to a specific point in time in your past when you accomplished something that made you feel especially creative. Take your time in locating this event or period -there is no hurry. Have you found that event? Good. Take a moment and re-live that event or period in your life as vividly as you can. Place yourself in that timeframe and re-experience the actions, feelings, and consequences of your creativity. Envision yourself in that time and space demonstrating and using your innate creativity. As much as possible, recall all that you can of that experience.

Now that you have relived that event, how did you feel about yourself at that time? What did it feel like to be creative and innovative? How did you use your innate creativity? What were your personal and professional rewards for being creative? You have clear evidence that you have been creative in the past. Now we are going to change our focus to the present. As you maintain a state of quiet relaxed attentiveness, begin to scan the challenges and opportunities that you face today. What tasks currently require your creative or innovative attention? Be specific in defining these tasks. Now select one of the most important and difficult tasks that you face today. Why is this your most important task? Why does this task require your creativity and innovation? How are you planning to manage this task?

Now as clearly as possible, imagine yourself carrying out this task in a very creative manner. Actually rehearse how you will manage this task so that your creativity is applied to it. See and experience yourself analyzing the task [pause], thinking creatively about the task, and acting in a creative fashion as you succeed in accomplishing the task. That was good — you now have envisioned yourself behaving creatively in the present. What are the consequences of behaving creatively? How do you feel about yourself when you apply your creativity to problems? How do your feelings about and images of yourself change when you behave creatively. Now it is time for you to project yourself into the future.

During this exercise, it is important that you begin to see yourself as creative and flexible in your problem-solving and decision making. Your self-image — that mental picture you hold of yourself -influences your creativity. It is critical that you perceive yourself as creative in your thinking and actions. Creative individuals, like yourself, maintain a creative self-image. Now, totally relax. Imagine yourself as creative and innovative in the future. As vividly as possible, see yourself as able to access and apply creativity as you need it. Think of creativity as a big pot from which you can scoop with a ladle when you need to do so. Envision yourself as able to use your mental imagery to help you solve problems.

See yourself as able to tolerate the frustration and ambiguity that often surrounds innovative tasks. Experience yourself as a flexible thinker — a thinker who can generate many ideas; a problem-solver who creates many unique ideas and solutions to problems; an individual who can think in many categories. Begin to build a new self-image of creativity. Hold this image and return to build it often. Use new experiences as challenges to test your creativity. Build a clear picture of yourself as easily able to think and act in creative ways. This script, of course, will not make an employee more creative. It will reshape and reframe the thinking and self-imagery of the individual so that he/she comes to think and act in ways that promote flexible, creative production. Such a script, or derivations of this script, would be used a number of times in imaginal practice contexts to help the individual with the reframing process.

The key point to recall is that as an employee comes to see him/herself as more creative, he/she will begin to behave in ways that demonstrate more creativity. This script uses several critical imaginal formats that are important not only to self-image enhancement, but to other training venues within your organization. First, when you have individuals recall and depict past experiences, you are helping them use episodic recall imagery. Such memory recall and depiction provides a framework for the individual to use when dealing with present or anticipated problems.

Usually, episodic recall allows the individual to specify instances that are analogous to the present context of problem-solving. By so doing, some of the strangeness or ambiguity of the current problem is reduced. Additionally, recall allows the individual to review past actions in relationship to the present so that potential courses of action may be transferred to the present. Episodic recall imagery is largely based on accessing and replaying details of experience from long-term memory.

Second, this script made use of behavioural or covert rehearsal, a technique that has been widely applied in both therapeutic and training realms. This technique involves cuing an individual to project him/herself into a future condition, state, or scenario and asking that they rehearse the best way to manage a problem. You also ask them to imagine the consequences of adapting the given behavioural or problem-solving approach. Such rehearsal generates productive awareness and readiness for problems and helps the individual stylize potential choice and action paths for the future.

Finally, this script provides a number of questions and suggestions to the individual. These cuing mechanisms influence the expectancies of the individual relative to the present and the future. Research continues to show that one's expectancies about an event or problem greatly influence the eventual success or failure of one's efforts. By shaping the self-expectancies of the individual, you can help bring about an image of him/herself as capable of dealing with problems in more creative ways. This, of course, contributes to reframing the individual's self image.

Overall, to engender more creative behaviour, a good starting point remains the self-imagery of your organization's employees. If they cannot come to see themselves as creative, it is highly unlikely that they will adapt creative and flexible means for managing problems. Such a programmeme could then be reinforced with organizational reward and incentive systems that contribute to the development of a creative culture in the organization.

DIVERGENT THINKING SKILLS

Two skill areas are critical in solving problems today — convergent and divergent thinking. Imagine this problem: how do we reduce our trucking costs from Orlando to Memphis by finding the route that is fastest, with cheapest fuel prices, and least patrolled by the police? In this problem we are searching for the best solution to a problem that is defined by three conditions that must be met. Our solution must take into account these three conditions and is, in fact, boundaried by these conditions. We are working in a problem context of the type where IF fast, cheap, unpatrolled, THEN route A. We are seeking to reduce our options. We want the best logical solution. We use analysis, facts, and figures to draw our final conclusion. This type of problem requires *convergent thinking skills*.

Convergent thinking involves the ability to analytically and evaluatively view a dynamic problem to select or create the single, best solution or response. Herein, the individual converges on the solution that fits the demands of the problem (fast, cheap, unpatrolled). During convergent thinking, the analytical faculties of the individual are used to weigh the costs versus benefits or the threats versus *opportunities* that can result from a selected solution or action path. In this way, convergent thinking is consistent with logical, linear, or sequential thinking. This means of problem-solving and thinking is predominantly taught and used in American educational and business systems. It is an approach to problem-solving that works best in well-defined problem contexts where there is plenty of relevant information.

However, with unique or novel problems where there is limited information, convergent thinking and problem-solving falters because it cannot accommodate a lack of rationality in the problem context. Further, convergent problem-solving, by nature, is reductionistic — it excludes facts and variables that are not immediately relevant or apparent to the development of the single, optimal solution. Since the problems we will face in the future are likely to be unique and novel, convergent problem-solving skills may not be so useful as they have been in the relatively stable and predictable past. Convergent problem-solving may also lack power in the future because imaginal and intuitive processes are ignored in lieu of rational and empirical approaches to problem-solving. Since imaginal and intuitive processes are closely linked to creativity, the convergent problem-solver may be inhibiting his/her ability to think creatively.

Now, imagine this problem; how do we provide for the ongoing personal and professional development of our staff? In this problem, there probably isn't any one best way, since the needs of staff will vary as will their commitment to personal and professional development. Further, there is no single, time-tested method for evolving and promoting training and development. Lastly, the skills that are required of workers will change with increasing technological progress. Many skills that will be essential in the future do not even exist today. While the problem may seem deceptively easy to manage, it is one that many organizations will face in the future. To deal effectively with this problem, you must project yourself into a future context and imaginally evaluate the dynamics of the problem. This is a problem where divergent thinking skills are best applied.

Divergent thinking skills involve three basic abilities that can be taught. The first ability is *imaginal fluency*. Imaginal fluency involves the ability to use imagination and creativity to generate multiple potential problem responses, solutions, or ideas. Research has shown repeatedly that the individual who demonstrates imaginal fluency also demonstrates the second key area of divergent thinking, *originality*. Originality is what we often associate with pure creativity. It is the ability to develop unique or novel perspectives, solutions, or ideas. Finally, divergent thinking involves *flexibility* or the ability to think in many categories and to make shifts from one category of thinking to another in search of an idea, response, or solution to a problem. Fluency, originality, and flexibility lead to more adept and creative problem-solving.

Specified below is a script that can help you and your employees build scenarios to apply to this problem. This script promotes fluent, original, and flexible thought relative to the previously identified problem. Now that you are relaxed and attentive, we are going to project ourselves into the future. We are going to place ourselves in this organization ten years from now. Take a moment now to re-orient your thinking to the future. You have done projective exercises before. Use your previous imaginal abilities on this problem. Take a moment now to establish a future mindset. The problem we are considering is one that we have talked about often in staff meetings — how do we provide for the on-going personal and professional development of our employees in the future?

This is a familiar yet difficult problem. It requires that we think in a long-term perspective. The script we will experience will help us do this and will help us generate many creative ideas about managing this problem. During the script, allow yourself to think flexibly. "Try to ignore any personal censorship you have about your ideas. When we are dealing with the future all ideas have value. Imagine yourself coming to work ten years from now. Take a moment to scan your environment. What type of day is it? How do you feel about the day?

As completely as possible, fill in the details of what it will be like for you to come to work ten years in the future. Envision what your office will look like. Think of the office machines you see. What will be on your mind as you come to work that day ten years from now? Take a moment now to build a scenario of this event. Sketch out in your imagination that day and your thoughts and feelings. That is good. You are ready to deal with the problem that has been mentioned. You will deal with it from a future perspective that you have created. Again, avoid censoring the ideas that come to mind — all ideas are appropriate.

The problem our organization faces is how to provide relevant and meaningful training and development for our employees in the future. Allow your imagination to scan that problem freely for a moment. What ideas pop to mind? What spontaneous insights do you have? If none appear, relax and let your creativity come forward. In order to meet the training needs of our employees in the future, we must know our employees. We are going to explore the needs, values, and skills of our employees ten years from now. Let your imagination place you in our organization ten years from now. In your own mind, imagine how the firm will look.

How will things be different from now? Take mental notes of your images and impressions. Take a moment to envision our workplace ten years from now. Now you have imagined yourself going to work and looking around the shop ten years down the road. Imagine that you are invisible to everyone in the firm. You can come and go as you please. This gives you great flexibility to observe and make mental notes on our future employees. You will take this opportunity to gather impressions of your firm's employees You will be asked to focus on several things during this experience. As much as possible, let your imaginations direct your thoughts. Make mental notes of your impressions as they evolve. That's good, let's begin.

As you invisibly float through the organization, begin imagining that you encounter and observe various employees at work. As much as possible, use your imagination to answer the following key questions. As you observe the operations in the firm, how are these future employees alike and different from current employees? Take a moment to imaginally develop likenesses and differences between today's worker and tomorrow's worker. Don't censor your thinking. That's good. Make mental notes as your impressions evolve.

This script would continue along these lines until your staff had imaginally developed impressions of the needs, values, skills, and attitudes of both new and continuing workers in the firm. By training your staff to break context and explore the long-term nature of this and other problems, you reduce their routinized problem thinking. You also increase the impressions that are relevant to developing programmemes for future training. A second script might focus on the evolution of programmemes that fit with the orientations of the workers. A short script of this follows. This script would, of course, be presented after impressions from the earlier script were aggregated.

Now that we have collectively envisioned the needs, values, skills, and attitudes of our future workers, we must build programmemes for them that sustain their motivation and development. This will be somewhat easier since we now have a clear vision of what our work force may be like in the future. We will use the information gathered in our previous script to build a potential programmeming strategy for the short-term and the long-term. Once again, use your imagination and creativity to build programmeme ideas that address the needs, values, skills, and attitudes of our workers over time. Feel confident that your ideas are worthwhile.

Given our previous brainstorming, imagine and review our present programmemes and think of how these could be adapted to the future. Every idea is worthwhile — so eliminate self-censorship and make clear mental notes of your ideas. Try to develop as many ideas as you can. The first programmeming area you'll consider is career planning. Take a moment and think about our current programmeme. What parts of the programmeme are most valuable and should be continued? Likewise, what parts should be eliminated in the future? How should the programmeme be adapted to meet the needs, values, skills, and attitudes of the future work force? Take a moment now to scan the career planning realm. Develop as many ideas as you can to improve the effectiveness and relevancy of this area in the future. That's good — make mental notes of your ideas. We'll now move on to recruitment and selection.

Relevant scripts, similar to the one in the above example, can then be written for recruitment and selection, compensation, training, performance appraisal, and the other functional areas of your HRM department. The key to writing these scripts is to encourage your personnel to apply information and impressions from previous scripts to the remodeling of the various areas. Varying the script approach for each area will reduce monotony. For instance, if you wanted to explore the area of an Employee Assistance, you might use a script such as this:

We will now turn to our employee assistance programmeme. We have envisioned what our workers will be like in the future. We have a clear picture of their needs, values, skills, and attitudes. We also know that stress will increase in the future. Our current EAP programmeme helps our employees work with to solve stress and other counseling problems. Take a moment to reflect upon our current programmeme. What areas do you think are effective? What areas will need expansion or enhancement in the future? As you think about this, envision the types of future personal problems our workers will have. As you generate ideas, also think of programmemes and activities that the EAP can use to meet these problems. Don't constrain your thinking. "That's good, make mental notes of your impressions -we'll now share our ideas.

These scripts would promote fluency, flexibility, and originality of thinking. Over time and with increased exposure to imaginal techniques, your staff's ability to apply these processes to tough problems will grow. Convergent and divergent thinking abilities are both necessary for effective problem-solving. Both areas can be enhanced through a variety of imaginal scripts such as those above. Beyond this, one can use other techniques to enhance creativity and problem-solving effectiveness.

We'll explore a few of these techniques now:

- *Timeouts*: In lieu of coffee breaks, you may want to introduce a timeout option in your firm. Evidence has shown that most employees spend only thirty-five to forty-five minutes of productive activity per hour of work. Thus, within an eight-hour workday, approximately two hours are wasted. In order to gain back some of this precious time, you can set up one or two regular break periods during the day when employees can either listen to relaxation tapes or be involved in focused imagery exercises. In either case, employees will become more acclimated to imaginal processes and techniques as they are given opportunities to practice. Focused imagery sessions might deal with relevant topics such as career planning, stress reduction, dietary adjustment, or other areas that are relevant to members of your team.
- *Gaming*: A third way to promote general creativity and problem-solving effectiveness is through "gaming." This approach may take the form of transforming a problem into a distant but analogous context, or it may involve having employees work with various problems that demand creative fluency, originality, and flexibility. Several types of games can be used that involve reconceptualizing problems in terms other than those commonly used for problem definition.

For example, one might envision the problem of recruiting as getting animals aboard the ark. The problem then becomes one that is out-of-context and open to new ways of viewing the situation. Thomas Gordon's Synectics has many transformational approaches to gaming with problems. Games may also take on the ambiance of a competition with the team generating the most creative yet feasible approach to a problem winning a prize. Creativity is often fueled by humour, and humour can often be promoted through generating a game atmosphere during serious problem-solving. Remember, creativity is not just an innate talent, it is a skill arena that can be recognized and improved through practice.

CONFLICT AND NEGOTIATIONS

Conflict and negotiation events engender much stress in organizations. As the world becomes more complex and as individuals compete for fewer resources, the potential for conflict will increase within and between organizations. Social psychological research has long shown that when groups are in conflict, they tend to distort perceptions (or mental models) of themselves and their adversaries. In fact, these distortions of reality aggravate conflict situations and often inhibit attempts at negotiation and resolution. Various imaginal techniques can be applied within conflict situations to help competing individuals and groups: (1) correct distorted mental models; (2) re-envision relationships and interpersonal dynamics; and (3) develop strategies for conflict management and future cooperation.

An example from recent history may illustrate how conflict is difficult to handle in organizations. The well-publicized demise of Frank Borman at Eastern Airlines represents the consequences of a conflict that was improperly managed because neither Borman nor the involved union officials could transcend their routinized images to develop a collabourative plan of problem resolution. When individuals and groups become stuck in dysfunctional thinking or mental modeling, functional fixedness exists. This kind of habitual, reactive, and stagnant thinking restricts the ability of competing parties to evolve win-win options for the management of conflict. Stale, archaic, and often adversarial warfare images dominate the thinking of competing parties and lead to an "I'm gonna win at any cost" mentality which ensures that neither party will benefit in the end.

As we can see with the Eastern situation, Borman's images appeared to freeze. It was as if he sought to protect the sacred managerial prerogative that is the cornerstone of much corporate image-making and strategy. Apparently, he had difficulty envisioning a more collabourative approach to conflict resolution. His image-making seemed to become insular and he may have excluded sound advice that would have altered the dynamics of the conflict. The same is probably true of the union. Negotiators for flight attendants and mechanics probably bore and generated extremely negative images of Borman and the managerial team at Eastern.

In the imaginal scenarios that governed their negotiation choices and alternatives, the union representatives also decided that they wouldn't give in to Borman and his allies at any cost. What developed and was publicized was the adolescent "warmaking" of two groups that couldn't see beyond their mutually destructive and obsolete images to reframe alternatives in the best interests of both parties. In the end, both parties lost as Eastern was enveloped by Texas Airlines. It was the mental modeling of the two adversaries that spelled their mutual doom. This is often true in conflict situations, although it doesn't have to be this way. As noted earlier, there are at least three areas in which imaginal techniques can contribute to effective conflict resolution. We shall now provide examples of such applications.

CORRECTING DISTORTED PERCEPTIONS

In conflicts, competing groups distort their perceptions of themselves and their adversaries. Take a moment to think back to a recent conflict in which you were a part. This may have involved a conflict with another unit in your organization, a supplier, or a union. Recall and imagine the types of thinking that went on in your own group as you manipulated your images of your group and your conflicting group. If your group is like most groups in conflict, you probably developed highly positive, protective, and self-righteous images of yourself. You, in fact, altered perceptual reality so that you appeared in your collective mind's eye to be better than your competitors, but also more deserving of victory or favour and more in tune with positive motivations and agenda relative to the conflict. Your group developed an imaginal set that played out the theme: "We are really better than that other group."

Now realise that the other group was doing exactly the same thing. They, too, were building inaccurate imaginal sets of their own goodness in reference to your group. A second imaginal alteration that occurs during conflict is that while we are improving our self-images, we increase the amount of fault-finding and derogation of the other group. We may actually fantasize and invent shortcomings of our adversaries. We may generate rumors about them and attempt to "negativize" their image in our own eyes and in the eyes of others. Both of these activities are largely mental in nature and involve distortions of reality. Both tendencies are also extremely common in conflicting groups.

Finally, both activities make conflict harder to manage because these imaginal distortions contribute to greater adversarialism and pig-headed imagery between groups. While these distortions are detrimental to negotiations and conflict management, they can be overcome. Below is a script for use after a relaxation induction session that helps in this area:

Interpersonal Dynamics and Cooperative Strategies

As distortions of perception are corrected, room develops for a reframing of the interpersonal dynamics between the competing parties. In conflict situations, one cannot remedy the conflict by merely altering the mental modeling of perceptions between and within groups. Rather, this reframing must extend to the behavioural dynamics that govern interactions. As new attitudes are integrated through "re-envisionment" techniques, new behavioural mindsets can also evolve. The following script illustrates one approach to this.

As noted, changes of perceptions should be followed by changes in the actions and interactions between the teams. A first critical step here is to reframe current interactions in terms of future interactions of interdependency. While attitudinal changes may produce some behavioural changes, we must make certain that concrete behavioural strategies and new interpersonal dynamics are generated to reinforce new mental models within and between the groups. We wish to reiterate that first steps in the management of conflictual problems are to recreate and reframe the competing images of the involved parties. If these images are not revised, there is little likelihood that productive conflict management can evolve. In conflict situations especially, ideation (mental modeling) precedes and influences actions. Realistic and accurate modeling can reduce adversarialism that complicates the negotiation process.

SOLUTION IMPLEMENTATION

A final area where imaginal techniques are helpful in problem-solving is in the management of change within an organization. Employees resist change for many reasons including fear for personal security, disruption of the status quo, anxiety about reduced status and power, and fear that new changes will be too difficult to learn or manage. Generally, these barriers are largely perceptual in nature. While change may, in fact, disrupt routines, it is the perception of this disruption that leads to crippling resistances that thwart progress. Since resistance to changes or decisions is rooted in the perceptual mental models of employees, these models are amenable to alteration through the use of imaginal techniques.

Vital to managing resistances is ensuring employees recognize that resistances exist. This may be accomplished through the following script, which focuses on the introduction of advanced computerization in a firm. Now that you are relaxed and attentive, you are going to explore general reactions you have to the introduction of the new computer systems. As you know the decision has been made to acquire and introduce the TM-650 system. This system will improve many of our operations and will allow for quicker and more accurate decision making throughout our firm. The decision to acquire and implement this system was an organizational one based on giving us a greater competitive edge. Reflect for a moment on your reactions to the process that was used to make this decision. Are there things that bothered you about how the decision evolved? If so make some mental notes of these factors. We will discuss them later. Do not edit your thinking or your reservations.

Now we are going to shift focus. Perhaps there were things about the decision that bothered you. That is okay. Keep those factors in mind for later reference; but, for the time being, you are going to project yourself into your job and evaluate how the new system will affect you in a number of key areas. The more that you can picture the impact of the system, the better you'll be able to identify the positive and negative reactions that you have to the system.

First, take a moment to think about your job and your job's function in the recent past. What things do you like about your job? What things do you dislike? Take a moment to weigh the pros and cons of your job. Now focus your attention on only the information processing aspects of your position. How have you traditionally dealt with information processing problems and channels? What do you like and dislike about the ways in which information is used within your unit? Imagine yourself drawing up a balance sheet of the positive and negative aspects of information management within your unit. That's good.

Now, envision the ways that you think the new computer system will impact your work and your job. Envision both the positive and the negative consequences. What makes you feel comfortable about this change? What makes you uncomfortable about the introduction of the system? What does this change mean to you personally and professionally? If you had your choice, how would you like to see this change handled — be specific, and come up with suggestions that can be discussed later.

Such a script can help employees focus on the resistances that they have to a new programmeme, and can give management clues as to how to best implement a change agendum within the firm. All too often, new technologies and methods are introduced without their impact on the personal and professional consequences of change being considered. When this is the case, management will face stalling, resistance, and even sabotage as new approaches are integrated into the existing organizational culture. To deal effectively with resistances, you must know what they are so that you can clarify the eventual consequences of change, while also helping your workers deal with the anxiety that comes up when change occurs.

A second example shows how you might help your employees come to terms with the personal relevance of change. This script would, of course, be presented after you and your employees had candidly looked at the issue of resistance and had consented to deal with resistance within the implementation programmeme. For the next few minutes, you are going to build a scenario of the future. You will be using your creativity and imagination to project the various impacts of the new system on different aspects of your work. By envisioning what you think the likely consequences of implementation will be, you can establish how you wish to respond positively to the new system as an individual and as a member of the team. Take a moment and relax. Open your mind to the future and place yourself in this organization one year from now.

As you think about your unit and your job one year from now, take a little time to study your impressions about several areas. Each of these areas may have changed in the future as a result of the system implementation. It is your task to project and predict what types of changes are likely in each of these areas. The clearer a picture you can build, the better. Let's see what your images tell you.

The first area you will scan is the area of personal relationships within your unit. Think of the people you work with at this time. Think about how they will react to the changes that are taking place with the introduction of the computer system. From your impressions of their current attitudes, how will they adjust over the next year to the new system? Who will be most amenable to change and who will tend to resent the change? How will your interactions with your personnel and colleagues be affected as a result of this change? Be as specific as you can in building this picture of future relationships after the introduction of the computer system. That's good.

Next, try to envision how the new system will impact your personal performance in the unit next year. How will your ability to lead be either improved or hampered by the system? Can you envision yourself as able to manage the new technology effectively? Try to build an image of competency. See yourself as able to adapt to the new system and as able to model new behaviours for your staff. The more that you can lead by example, the better for you. Your employees will follow your lead and will adapt attitudes about the system that are a reflection on your own. Build a comprehensive model of how you want to see the staff use the new system. Build an ideal scenario for application to your unit. That's good.

Again, such scripts won't eliminate resistances, but they can help get primary issues of concern on the table for discussion. Further, projective scripts can help personnel develop strategies for the introduction of a change agendum in the firm. In the imaginal realm, these scenarios can be manipulated safely and inexpensively so that problems are anticipated and dealt with in advance of their arising. As with all problem-solving, this ability to project and anticipate the dynamics of the problem increases the likelihood that the problem can be managed in an effective manner. Problem-solving fails when people go into problem events with habitual and reactive thinking. Effective efforts at problem-solving occur when personnel are able to move beyond reactivity. Imaginal techniques can, in fact, provide this opportunity to members of your firm.

A few of our ideas about imagery applications in organizational decision and problem-solving processes. Your ability to apply such technologies is only limited by your own creativity and willingness to experiment with non-traditional approaches to organizational effectiveness. As has been previously emphasized, creativity and effective problem-solving emerge from concerted practice in these skill realms. Commitment to the use of imaginal or envisionary technologies will not of itself solve your problems more easily. Rather, the introduction and use of these technologies gives you tools to use to enhance the efficacy of your personnel in the evermore complex discipline of decision making.

12

The Role of HRD in Corporate Social Responsibility

Various alternative dispute resolution (ADR) techniques and the reasons for their increased adoption at the workplace have been discussed. What follows are some examples of what some corporations are doing, as well as a guide with suggested clauses to enable an organization to initiate an ADR programmeme of its own. There is no single dispute resolution system appropriate for every organization and therefore creativity and experimentation are encouraged. This subject is so dynamic that many new developments and inventive approaches are sure to surface in the future.

Many corporations presently use some type of dispute resolution procedure. They include corporate open door policies, nonbinding employee grievance procedures, use of a corporate ombudsman, binding or nonbinding peer review of employee grievances, and similar policies that seek to resolve disputes at the workplace.

For example, Federal Express's Guaranteed Fair Treatment Procedure provides a system for employees to seek to resolve grievances through internal company appeal. Aetna Casualty and Life has a dispute resolution process that encourages the use of mediation prior to litigation. AT&T and United Airlines also use mediation programmemes. AT&T's mediation programmeme is incorporated into the AT&T-Communication Workers of America contractual grievance procedure. Rockwell International has an arbitration programmeme for its top management where both the employee and company agree to arbitrate all employment-related disputes. Bechtel will engage in discovery in litigation to identify relevant facts. Then, the company usually seeks to use ADR techniques to resolve the dispute.

ALTERNATIVE DISPUTE RESOLUTION MODELS

Major corporations have introduced ADR programmemes that have binding arbitration as the final step. Some of the more prominent programmemes are discussed here.

Northrup Corporation

The oldest binding nonunion arbitration model has been in use at the Northrup Corporation since 1945. This procedure provides for a formal grievance process ending with binding arbitration. An employee grievance that cannot be resolved informally is considered at the Administrative Office level. If denied, a Management Appeals Committee hears an appeal of the Administrative Office decision. After this decision, the employee may appeal to an arbitrator selected by both the employee and the company. The arbitrator's decision is binding on both parties.

Rockwell International Corporation Model

Since *Gilmer*, others have moved to implement internal ADR procedures culminating in mandatory arbitration. Rockwell International Corporation introduced a Mutual Agreement to Arbitrate Claims, which provides for mandatory arbitration of "all claims or controversies for which a court otherwise would be authorized by law to grant relief, in any way arising out of, relating to or associated with the Employee's employment with the Company, or its termination." The execution of this agreement is a prerequisite to employee receipt of certain corporate stock options which would otherwise lapse. While this policy is targeted at executives eligible for such options, Rockwell has also implemented predispute agreements to arbitrate for all new hires and on a voluntary basis for existing nonexecutive employees.

The Rockwell agreement contemplates arbitration for all claims held by the employee or employer except claims for workers' compensation benefits, unemployment compensation benefits, company claims for injunctive, or other equitable relief for unfair competition or unauthorized disclosure of trade secrets or confidential information, and employee pension or benefit plan claims where binding arbitration or other nonjudicial dispute resolution procedure is required.

The Rockwell arbitration procedure includes discovery between the parties. Each party has the right to take the deposition of one individual and any expert witness designated by another party. Parties are allowed to request the production of documents by any other party. Additional discovery may be allowed by the arbitrator upon a showing of substantial need. Thirty days before the arbitration hearing, the parties are obligated to exchange lists of witnesses and copies of exhibits intended for use at the hearing.

The arbitrator is selected from a list provided by the American Arbitration Association (AAA), The Rockwell procedure requires that the Model Employment Arbitration Procedures of the AAA apply from the time a notice of claim is given, except as modified by other language in the Mutual Agreement to Arbitrate. The arbitrator must apply the law of the state where the claim arose, as well as any applicable federal law. The Federal Rules of Evidence apply. The arbitrator has the authority to consider pre-hearing motions for dismissal and for summary judgment, pursuant to the standards set forth under the Federal Rules of Civil Procedure.

The Rockwell agreement also contemplates that each party will pay an equal share of the fees and costs of the arbitration. Where a statutory claim provides for payment of the prevailing party's attorneys' fees and costs, the arbitrator may award such reasonable fees and costs. Parties are permitted to file briefs; the arbitrator's award and opinion will be issued in the "form typically rendered in labour arbitrations."

Travellers Group

In September, 1992, the Primerica Corporation, which later merged into the Travellers Group, an organization with divisions offering a wide array of services including consumer financial, investment, and insurance services, implemented a procedure wherein pre-dispute agreements to arbitrate recognize arbitration as the exclusive forum for "the resolution of all employment disputes that may arise . . . under any federal, state or local statute, regulation, or common law doctrine regarding employment discrimination, conditions of employment or termination of employment.

The Travellers Group Arbitration Policy incorporates, to a large extent, the Model Employment Arbitration Procedures of the AAA. In addition, the policy permits limited discovery. Each party is entitled to propound one set of interrogatories pursuant to the Federal Rules of Civil Procedure; these interrogatories are limited to the identification of potential witnesses. The procedure also provides for one set of up to 25 Requests for the Production of Documents and allows up to two days of depositions of witnesses subject to the Federal Rules of Civil Procedure.

Under the Travellers Group procedure, the company pays all arbitration administrative fees in excess of $25. Should the arbitration proceed beyond one day, the incremental expenses of the additional days of hearing are borne equally by both parties.

Brown and Root

Brown & Root is an employer in heavy construction and related industries, headquartered in Houston, Texas. In June 1993 Brown & Root introduced a comprehensive employee dispute resolution programmeme. The Brown & Root dispute resolution programmeme provides four options: open door policy, conference, mediation, and arbitration. Option One, the open door policy, "guarantees that all doors are open to you within Brown & Root". It is a voluntary process that allows the employee to talk with his or her immediate supervisor or to a higher level of management without fear of retaliation.

The employee is encouraged to resolve the problem at the lowest possible level, but can take the complaint as far up the chain of command as the employee deems necessary. The employee is given guidance in using this open door policy through a toll-free employee telephone hot line. In addition to the employee hot line, the Brown & Root programmeme also provides a programmeme administrator who will assist an employee in use of the dispute resolution programmeme, including use of all options.

The dispute resolution programmeme also recognizes that where a dispute involves a "legally protected right," an employee is provided the opportunity of obtaining a legal consultation with the attorney of his or her choice. The legal consultation is treated similarly to benefits under the Brown & Root medical plan, with the employee paying a deductible and a co-payment. Brown & Root then pays the balance of the costs. The maximum annual benefit of this programmeme is $2,500 per employee. In the example in the Brown & Root dispute resolution manual, an employee would pay a deductible of $25 and then 10 percent of the balance of the legal bill, with Brown & Root paying the remaining 90 percent of that cost. The programmeme administrator must approve all payments under the legal consultation plan.

Option Two, the conference, is a meeting at Brown & Root where the employee and a company representative meet with a representative from the company's dispute resolution programmeme to discuss the dispute and choose a process for resolution. The goal of the conference is to help the employee and the company agrees on a way to settle the dispute and choose a person to help resolve the dispute. The employee's options at this conference include: loop-back to the chain of command; use of an informal process, such as informal mediation; and direct access to an outside process.

The outside processes are Options Three and Four, and involve mediation through the auspices of a professional, neutral, third party selected through the American Arbitration Association. Under Option Three, the employee must pay a $50 processing fee to obtain outside mediation. The company pays any costs in excess of this fee. The employee is provided the number and address of the American Arbitration Association to request mediation.

When a dispute has not been resolved through Options One, Two, or Three, either the employee or the company may seek arbitration under Option Four. The company does not require an employee to proceed through each of the options in sequence to reach Option Four arbitration. However, the company emphasizes that these multiple steps are designed to maximize the possibility of resolution. When Option Four is reached, the outside dispute resolution processes involve use of professional neutrals provided through the AAA. To request arbitration, the employee must pay a $50 processing fee; the company pays all costs that exceed $50.

Once again, the employee is provided the phone number and address of the AAA to request arbitration. The employee is allowed to move to Option Four directly from Option Two when the dispute involves a legally protected right. Thus, when the dispute does not involve an identified, legally protected right, arbitration is not provided under the Brown & Root dispute resolution programmeme.

The Brown & Root programmeme also recognizes that employees are allowed to consult a lawyer or other advisor of the employee's choice. Here, Brown & Root will pay the major part of the legal fees pursuant to the legal consultation plan. Employees are not required to hire a lawyer to participate in arbitration. Where an employee elects not to bring a lawyer to arbitration, the company participates without a lawyer.

Effective June 1, 1993, the four-option programmeme has been the exclusive means of resolving workplace disputes for legally protected rights at Brown and Root. The company manual states, "That means, if you expect to continue your job at Brown & Root after that date, you will agree to resolve all legal claims against Brown & Root through this process instead of through the court system. Use of Options One and Two of the programmeme for cases not involving legal rights is voluntary."

The Burlington Northern Railroad work force consists of approximately 3,800 exempt employees and 28,000 scheduled employees covered by a collective bargaining agreement. The company and its employees were familiar with the arbitration process as a result of the Interstate Commerce Commission's regulatory approval of mergers and the arbitration procedures covering scheduled employees under the Railway Labour Act.

As a result of numerous reorganizations in the mid- 1980s and the Age Discrimination Employment Act of 1967 lawsuits spawned by these reorganizations by terminated exempt employees, the company recognized that a better way was needed to resolve discrimination disputes. The company's internal complaint procedure was revised to include an arbitration policy that addressed only termination disputes. This policy was implemented by a letter from senior management announcing the new procedure. The letter also advised employees to insert a new page addressing this new procedure into their employee.

While the company may mediate a termination dispute prior to arbitration, there is no formal written agreement or procedure addressing this process. If mediation is not successful or not used, arbitration is invoked. This procedure provides that the parties will select an arbitrator; if they cannot agree, the AAA will select the arbitrator and administer the arbitration process.

The Continental Airlines discipline and appeal process provides an employee appeal procedure for nonmanagement, nonunion employees. The procedure, found in the company's policy and procedures manual, provides that the internal appeal procedure is the "sole remedy for any employee who believes that he/she has been treated unfairly." As opposed to the Brown & Root or Burlington Northern models, which provide for arbitration of only statutory or termination disputes, this procedure provides a binding dispute resolution procedure for any employee complaint.

Where the dispute cannot be resolved at earlier steps of the process, the procedure calls for an initial, informal hearing before a hearing manager appointed by the management employee who received the appeal from the employee. If the employee disagrees with the result, he may appeal to a board comprised of two management employees appointed by the company and two peers selected by the employee from an employee council. This hearing is also informal and no transcript is taken. Nevertheless, the decision of the board is final and binding.

Where the board deadlocks, a list of three outside arbitrators is submitted to the employee by the labour relations department. The employee chooses an arbitrator from among these three persons. This arbitrator's decision is final and binding. The company pays the arbitrator's expenses. This procedure has been challenged by employees in federal court on two occasions. Both times, the dispute resolution process was upheld and the award of the board was honoured by the court. In both cases, the court relied on the plaintiff's voluntary participation in the procedure, through the issuance of a final decision, to preclude later judicial review of any claim.

BINDING PRE-DISPUTE AGREEMENT TO ARBITRATE

The appropriate procedures or standards for introduction of a predispute agreement to arbitrate have not been directly addressed by the courts or Congress. In *Gilmer*, the Supreme Court noted that it would consider underlying due process factors when reviewing the appropriateness of arbitration. Footnote three of the *Gilmer* decision suggests that the waiver of the right to a judicial forum may be subject to the waiver requirements of the Older Workers Benefit Protection Act (OWBPA). However, *Gilmer* did not provide any other guidance.

The recent report of the Commission on the Future of Worker Management Relations (Dunlop Commission) addressed the growing importance of private employer grievance procedures that end in binding arbitration. As part of its original charge, the Dunlop Commission was asked to consider what could or should be done to increase the extent to which workplace conflicts are resolved directly by those involved, rather than by resorting to administrative agencies, such as the National Labour Relations Board, the EEOC, or the courts.

The final report noted that there was an explosion of employment related disputes and that at present there was a staggering caseload before the EEOC. The commission recommended "encouraging experimentation and use of private dispute resolution systems that meet high quality standards for fairness, provided these are not imposed unilaterally by employers as a condition of employment." According to the commission, low-wage employees who seek to remain in their jobs do not appear to be able to use the litigation system to resolve their statutory complaints.

The commission then set forth standards under which private arbitration may serve as a legitimate form of private enforcement of public employment law. These standards include a neutral arbitrator with knowledge of the law at issue, fair cost sharing, the right to independent representation if the employee wants it, and remedies equal to those available through litigation.

The OWBPA was passed by Congress and signed by President Bush in 1990. The OWBPA sets forth a threshold standard for ascertaining whether a waiver and release of an age discrimination claim was "knowing and voluntary." The criteria under this law provide guidance as to what Congress believes is a "knowing and voluntary" waiver by an employee.

Those criteria state that a waiver may not be considered knowing and voluntary unless at a minimum:

the waiver is written in a manner calculated to be understood by the individual or average individual eligible to participate; the waiver specifically refers to rights or claims under the OWBPA; additional consideration for an age discrimination waiver is provided; the employee is advised in writing to consult with an attorney; the employee is allowed 21 days to consider whether to sign; and the employee is allowed 7 days to revoke the executed agreement.

The OWBPA places the burden of proof on the employer to prove in any subsequent litigation that the waiver was knowing and voluntary. However, the law governing agreements to arbitrate, the Federal Arbitration Act (FAA), places the burden on the person seeking to avoid the arbitration clause. It is unclear which approach will prevail.

In addition to Congress's definition of "knowing and voluntary" under the OWBPA, the interpretive statement for the OWBPA, issued by Senator Dole, also indicates that the alternate dispute resolution contemplated by Section of the 1991 Act must be "knowing and voluntary."

While many of the practices and procedures associated with the implementation and administration of pre-dispute agreements to arbitrate will be influenced by subsequent legislative and court decisions, there are several advantages to immediate introduction of this procedure. A procedure introduced now can be amended after additional legal guidance has been provided. The main advantage of immediate implementation of a binding arbitration procedure is that there is a legal presumption in favour of enforceability under the FAA and *Gilmer*. Thus, with an agreement in hand, should one party later seek to avoid the contemplated arbitration, they may be required to exhaust the internal grievance procedure first through arbitration or spend considerable legal fees seeking to avoid arbitration.

Another advantage to the immediate implementation of a pre-dispute procedure ending in binding arbitration is that when a party seeks to avoid arbitration, the other party can seek to renegotiate the pre-dispute agreement, thus converting the pre-dispute agreement into an enforceable postdispute agreement to arbitrate. For example, an attorney representing an employee subject to a pre-dispute agreement to arbitrate may be obligated to exhaust the employee's internal remedies before filing suit in federal court. Thus, arbitration will occur, subject to the parties' disagreement as to the finality of the decision. Counsel may recognize the substantial legal costs associated with petitioning a court to obtain a stay of arbitration or with arbitrating and then attacking the arbitration process. Thus, employee counsel may agree to convert the pre-dispute agreement into an acceptable post-dispute agreement, incorporating certain additional terms and conditions of arbitration favoured by the employee.

Company counsel may agree to the alteration of certain portions of the pre-dispute arbitration agreement in return for consent to a clearly enforceable post-dispute arbitration agreement. Any agreement to arbitrate should be knowing and voluntary. In adopting a procedure for prospective hires, the employment application should state that the applicant agrees to submit any claim or dispute arising from hire or refusal to hire, actual employment, or termination from employment, to arbitration. Prior to hire, the applicant should also be presented with a pre-dispute agreement to arbitrate that incorporates the OWBPA guidelines. Alternatively, an employer could request an applicant to execute such an agreement and return it prior to making an offer of employment.

One unresolved issue is whether an employer can require a prospective employee to execute a pre-dispute agreement to arbitrate as a condition of employment. The law is not clear. Some would argue that such an agreement is, *a fortiori,* a contract of adhesion. A separate issue is whether employers may implement, as a condition of employment, a pre-dispute procedure for current employees. The issue of whether an employer can require such an agreement as a condition of employment, either for new hires or existing employees, is unresolved. The National Labour Relations Board opposes any arbitration agreement that requires an employee to waive the right to access to the board in favour of arbitration where acquiescence to arbitration in lieu of board procedures is a condition of employment. Another open issue is whether consideration is necessary to support such agreement, and the amount and type of valid consideration.

Regarding the issue of the type of consideration necessary to support the enforcement of an arbitration agreement, the courts have found adequate consideration in various situations. For example, the Eleventh Circuit Court of Appeals has held that "the consideration exchanged for one party's promise to arbitrate must be the other party's promise to arbitrate at least some specified class of claims."

The Michigan Court of Appeals has found that a securities industry agreement to arbitrate is not a contract of adhesion and that the unilateral implementation of an internal arbitration procedure is binding on current employees, because the continued employment of the employee consisted of adequate consideration to support enforcement of the agreement. The Michigan Court has also found that an employee is bound by a preexisting arbitration procedure in an employee where the employee accepted employment. In general, most courts will consider a mutual promise to arbitrate or the hiring of an individual as sufficient consideration.

One author argues that, because the Supreme Court has yet to decide whether arbitration agreements contained in employment contracts are enforceable under the FAA, an agreement to arbitrate should be separate from an employment contract. It is argued that the arbitration agreement should state that the agreement is not an employment contract and that the employee is employed at will. The agreement should state that it is not intended to add to or create any employment rights or to imply that any employment rights exist beyond those otherwise imposed by law. An employer takes a risk when providing for arbitration in an employee personnel manual. This risk is that the manual will not be treated as contractually binding or may be interpreted by a court to create unintended contractual obligations.

Other contractual provision, or other enforceable promise to the contrary, an employer should be allowed to introduce a new dispute resolution process. The employer should seek to obtain employee acceptance of the arbitration model through employee communication and education. If the process is properly marketed it should result in a majority of employees accepting the process. Anecdotal evidence to date supports this approach.

For those employees who refuse to agree, the employer is placed in a difficult situation. Since it is not clear that the employer can require the agreement as a condition of employment, the employer may prefer to allow the development of a bifurcated process whereby certain employees agree to arbitrate all disputes, while others may litigate in court. In each dispute, a party may deem a dispute's locus to be preferable in arbitration or court, depending on the facts. Thus a bifurcated process does not necessarily cause greater economic exposure to the employer. A bifurcated process also will allow an employer to measure the experience of the arbitration model vis-à-vis courtroom litigation.

The design of particular pre-hearing procedures and rules of conduct at arbitration is as important as the general agreement to resolve a dispute by arbitration. One of the major benefits of arbitration is that the parties can agree on a particular procedure tailored to the needs of each disputant that covers the inception of a dispute through the arbitration hearing. The process should be carefully crafted, with regard for each party's due process rights. Since most arbitration procedures and written agreements will be drafted and proposed by an employer, it is critical that an employer does not overreach in the agreement.

An appropriately drafted agreement to arbitrate should address many of the particular aspects of the investigation and presentation of each party's case. The agreement should spell out in detail the pre-hearing dispute resolution process and procedure.

The agreement should address the following issues:

- The scope of disputes subject to binding arbitration, specifically those issues excluded from arbitration, such as, workers' compensation and unemployment;

- The time limits for presenting or maintaining an issue within the grievance procedure and at arbitration;
- The levels of management afforded an opportunity to resolve the dispute prior to arbitration;
- The point at which the final management decision is issued;
- The time limits after the final management decision within which one must request arbitration;
- Whether other procedures such as mediation or peer review can be voluntarily or mandatorily invoked by either party prior to arbitration;
- The existence and extent of pre-hearing summary judgment procedures;
- The existence and extent of discovery;
- Sanctions on parties;
- Apportionment of costs and/or attorneys' fees;
- All of the parties who are required to be sued in this forum (all company supervisors, agents, subsidiaries, and so forth); and all other procedures that seek to resolve or clarify the issue prior to a hearing.

The agreement should also address how the arbitrator will consider prehearing motions to dismiss or for summary judgment and the procedures governing them. An arbitration agreement should also pay careful attention to how the arbitrator will be selected. The parties should have considered and agreed upon the panel from which to select an arbitrator. Since the arbitrator is obligated to honour the "four corners" of the agreement to arbitrate, careful attention should be placed on all procedures that either party believes are important to govern the arbitration procedure.

For example, the parties may wish to address the following issues:

- The apportionment or sharing of certain costs;
- The award of prevailing party attorneys' fees and costs;
- The appropriateness of a transcript and who will pay for it; the site of the hearing;
- The procedure for company release of witnesses;
- Issues regarding the subpoena power of the arbitrator;
- The effect of a witness or party's failure to appear;
- The use of telephone testimony or affidavits;
- The applicability of federal or state rules of evidence and procedure;
- Whether an expedited arbitration procedure for claims under a certain dollar amount will be available;
- The number of arbitrators;
- Whether the arbitration is a closed or open proceeding; and
- Other issues dealt with in the model procedures set.

Even where the arbitration agreement clearly identifies all major procedures, the agreement should also state the rules that apply in the absence of specific reference in the agreement. Such a default provision must be provided. The Employment Dispute Resolution Rules of the AAA, the Final Report on Model Rules for the Arbitration of Employment Disputes by the Committee on Labour and Employment Law of the Bar Association of the City of New York, or the employment dispute resolution rules of the Center for Public Resources are recommended in lieu of specific language in the agreement to arbitrate.

When these rules are referenced, both parties to the agreement should ensure that the present version of the rules referenced and each model rule in itself is acceptable. These rules should be referenced by date or edition so that a new edition does not automatically supplant the rules selected. An employer needs to consider how non-meritorious claims will be handled in the arbitration process. In particular, the employer may want to provide for both parties to adjudicate the claim by submission of documents and position statements to the arbitrator in lieu of a hearing. This procedure avoids convening a hearing where there is no basis for the claim in law or fact.

Also, the employer may want to provide a procedure wherein after initial discovery is complete the parties are permitted to petition the arbitrator for summary judgement on the pleadings similar to summary judgment motions under Rule 56 of the Federal Rules of Civil Procedure or under a summary judgment procedure tailored by the employer. The employer must recognize that the selection of the organization that will administer the procedure is an important decision.

Various organizations offer such services and all should be carefully investigated before one is selected. One organization, J.A.M.S./ENDISPUTE, has stated that it will not accept cases where the arbitration agreements do not allow for full remedies, reasonable discovery, the right to counsel, and other safeguards. J.A.M.S./ENDISPUTE also will administer only those agreements that provide the remedies of punitive damages and attorney fees. The selection of the arbitrator is as important as the design of the process and the selection of the organization that will administer the procedure.

Some of the issues that were addressed in these rules, and which must be addressed in any procedure include:

- The availability and scope of pre-hearing discovery,
- The procedure for selecting the arbitrator,
- The costs of the arbitration,
- The scope of authority and remedial powers of the arbitrator, including the arbitrator's power to award attorneys' fees, and
- Whether the proceedings or decisions of arbitrators should be confidential.

Some of the more interesting elements of the model procedure include the requirement of a voluntary exchange of detailed statements of position, a presumptive right to one deposition with application for cause to the arbitrator for additional depositions, disclosure of the employee's personnel file documents and all documents related to the personnel decision at issue, costs to be handled per traditional litigation standards except for the arbitrator's fee, a cap on the payment of the arbitrator's fees by the employee in the amount of two days' gross salary, full remedial powers for the arbitrator identical to the powers of the court including the right to order an attorneys' fees award, and provisions for confidentiality of the proceedings and awards.

Furthermore, the model rules require that any and all counterclaims must be maintained at the arbitration. The model rules do not require a transcript but do require that the hearing be recorded by audio tape so that any procedural irregularities do not escape judicial review. The rules provide that a proceeding must be initiated within 180 days of the time an employee has been notified or otherwise learns of the employer's action that is challenged. The rules allow for representation by nonlawyers and follow the same order of presentation as the courts, with the plaintiff going first. Finally, the rules provide for the use of expert witnesses and the disclosure of the expert's testimony in advance. Where substantial need exists, a party can obtain the right to depose the expert witness.

Many arbitration agreements are simple, one page documents. They set forth that all disputes and controversies arising out of the employment relationship are subject to arbitration, and reference a particular set of rules governing the conduct of arbitration (usually the Model Rules of Arbitration set forth by the AAA or other third-party administrator for the particular type of dispute or industry). For example, the AAA rules recommend the following language to resolve future disputes:

Any controversy or claim arising out of or relating to this contract, or the breach thereof, shall be settled by arbitration in accordance with the Employment Dispute Resolution Rules of the American Arbitration Association, and judgment upon the award rendered by the arbitrator(s) may be entered in any court having jurisdiction thereof.

The following language can be used to resolve existing disputes:

We, the undersigned parties, hereby agree to submit to arbitration under the Employment Dispute Resolution Rules of the American Arbitration Association the following controversy: We further agree that the above controversy be submitted to [one] [three] arbitrator(s) selected from the panels of arbitrators of the American Arbitration Association. We further agree that we will faithfully observe this agreement and the rules, and that we will abide by and perform any award rendered by the arbitrator(s) and that a judgment of the court having jurisdiction may be entered upon the award.

Except as otherwise provided in this agreement, the company and the employee hereby consent to the resolution by arbitration of all claims or controversies for which a court otherwise would be authorized by law to grant relief, in any way arising out of, relating to, or associated with, the employee's employment with the company, or its termination (claims), that the company may have against the employee or that the employee may have against the company or against its officers, directors, employees or agents in their capacity as such or otherwise.

The claims covered by this agreement include, but are not limited to, claims for wages or other compensation due; claims for breach of any contract or covenant, express or implied; tort claims; claims for discrimination, including but not limited to, discrimination based on race, sex, religion, national origin, age, marital status, handicap, disability, or medical condition; claims for benefits, except as excluded in the following paragraph; and claims for violation of any federal, state, or other governmental constitution, statute, ordinance or regulation.

Exclusion of Matters

The parties may also wish to specifically identify what is excluded:

Except for disputes, claims or grievances concerning [state all excludable matters, i.e., workmens' compensation, unemployment, claims not involving a claim of legal right], any dispute, claim, or grievance arising out of or relating to this agreement shall be submitted to arbitration pursuant to the terms and conditions of this agreement.

The parties may also wish to exclude certain matters, for example:

Claims Not Covered by this Agreement

This agreement to arbitrate does not apply to or cover claims for workers' compensation benefits or compensation; claims for unemployment compensation benefits; claims by the company for injunctive or other equitable relief for unfair competition or the use or unauthorized disclosure of trade secrets or confidential information; and, claims based upon an employee pension or benefit plan the terms of which contain an arbitration or other nonjudicial dispute resolution procedure, in which such case the provisions of such plan shall apply.

In sum, it is imperative that a broad dispute and controversies clause be included as the first part of any agreement to arbitrate. The clause should clearly specify the type of disputes covered and identify those disputes within this definition that are excluded. Employers must pay careful attention to whether they want to provide the right to arbitrate all disputes or only disputes involving a claim of a legal or statutory right. Employers must also make sure that they address whether the arbitration agreement includes an employee cause of action against a supervisor as an individual defendant.

Other Clauses

Once the arbitration clause tailored to the parties' needs has been included, the parties are free to address all arbitration procedures and practices. This is the opportunity to carefully craft the arbitration process to meet particular needs. The following is a suggested list of possible clauses to be included in any arbitration agreement, either pre-dispute or post-dispute.

Initiation of Arbitration

Arbitration under an arbitration provision in a contract shall be initiated in the following manner:

The initiating party (hereinafter claimant) shall, within the time period, if any, specified in the contract(s), give written notice to the other party (hereinafter respondent) of its intention to arbitrate [identify the dispute], which notice shall contain a statement setting forth the nature of the dispute, the amount involved, if any, the remedy sought, and the hearing locale requested, and shall file at any regional office of the AAA three copies of the notice and three copies of the arbitration provisions of the contract, together with the appropriate filing fee unless the parties agree to some other method of fee advancement.

The AAA shall give notice of such filing to the respondent or respondents. A respondent may file an answering statement in duplicate with the AAA within ten days after notice from the AAA, in which event the respondent shall at the same time send a copy of the answering statement to the claimant. If a counterclaim is asserted, it shall contain a statement setting forth the nature of the counterclaim, the amount involved, if any, and the remedy sought. If a counterclaim is made in the answering statement, the appropriate fee provided in the schedule shall be forwarded to the AAA with the answering statement. If no answering statement is filed within the stated time, it will be treated as a denial of the claim. Failure to file an answering statement shall not operate to delay the arbitration.

The AAA Employment Dispute Resolution Rule 3 states:

Cases may be initiated by joint submission in writing or in accordance with provisions in a personnel manual or employment agreement, and filed together with the appropriate filing fee as provided herein.

Time Limitations

It is within the power of the parties to establish their own time limitations for the seeking of relief or other mandated action. This is where the various procedural steps of the dispute resolution process should be carefully and explicitly detailed. For example:

Any dispute or claim arising under this agreement must be presented to [name of in-house programmeme administrator], by [writing or other method], within [number of days] of [the incident giving rise to the claim]. Should the parties be unable to resolve this dispute, either party must file a demand for arbitration with [name of in-house or other administrator of arbitration process] by [writing or other method], within 30 days of [denial of complaint by supervisor or other predetermined final step]. Any proceeding under this procedure must be brought within one year of the act or omission giving rise to the controversy.

Federal or State Rules of Civil Procedure

The parties may wish to provide that all discovery or other pre-arbitration proceedings are to be conducted pursuant to the Federal Rules of Civil Procedure as continuously amended and/or current local court rules of the United States District Court or particular state court Rules of Procedure. In particular, the parties may wish to preserve those parts of the Federal Rules of Civil Procedure that address discovery and pre-trial motions. An attractive option to many employers may be the inclusion of the right of a party to file a motion to dismiss or summary judgment with the arbitrator.

Duration of the Hearing

Both parties may wish to set a time frame for the arbitration hearing within which all evidence must be heard. For example, parties may agree that each party will have up to one full hearing day for the presentation of their positions, with the arbitrator permitted to determine appropriate hearing time for rebuttal.

Stenographic Costs

The parties should agree to the procedure for stenographic costs in the arbitration agreement. For example:

The parties hereby agree that all costs of stenography will be assumed by the party requesting such record. Should both parties seek a stenographic record, the costs shall be split equally between them. In any event, where one party has obtained a stenographic record, the other party should be allowed to copy the record at the requesting party's cost.

There shall be no stenographic record of these proceedings unless either party requests it. In the event a party requests a stenographic record, that party shall bear the cost of such a record. If both parties request a stenographic record, the cost shall be borne equally by the parties.

The cost of the stenographic record, if any is made, and all transcripts thereof, shall be prorated equally among all parties ordering copies, unless they shall otherwise agree, and shall be paid for by the responsible parties directly to the reporting agency.

Location of Arbitration Hearing

The parties may wish to identify a particular location where arbitration hearings will be conducted. The parties may mutually agree on the locale where the arbitration is to be held. If any party requests that the hearing be held in a specific locale and the other party files no objection thereto within ten days after notice of the request has been sent to it by the AAA, the locale shall be the one requested. If a party objects to the locale requested by the other party, the AAA shall have the power to determine the locale and its decision shall be final and binding.

An alternative clause may be:

The parties hereby agree that all disputes arising from this arbitration agreement will be heard in [state, city, or exact location]. The parties should identify how the hearing will be scheduled.

Attorneys' Fees

The parties may wish to waive any attorneys' fees award provisions of a particular law in the agreement to arbitrate. For example:

The parties hereby agree that the arbitrator's award shall not include provision of any attorneys' fees or costs to either party. Such attorneys' fees or costs shall be assumed solely by the respective parties.

Alternatively, the parties may prefer to empower the arbitrator to award prevailing party attorneys' fees as permitted under the statutes at issue. The failure to do so may be evidence of employer overreaching. For example:

The parties shall share equally the fees and costs of the arbitrator. Each party will deposit funds or post other appropriate security for its share of the arbitrator's fee, in an amount and manner determined by the arbitrator, ten days before the first day of hearing. Each party shall pay for its own costs and attorneys' fees, if any. However, if any party prevails on a statutory claim which entitles the prevailing party to attorneys' fees, or if there is a written agreement providing for fees, the arbitrator may award reasonable fees to the prevailing party in accordance with such statute or agreement.

Tripartite Panel

The parties may wish to use a three-person (tripartite) panel in lieu of the selection of a single arbitrator. In this situation, each party is allowed to appoint one arbitrator. The two arbitrators selected then select a third arbitrator. For example:

Any claim or controversy arising under this arbitration agreement shall be referred to three arbitrators. One arbitrator will be appointed by each party and a third will be appointed by the two arbitrators heretofore selected. An award in writing signed by any two of the arbitrators shall be final. If either party shall refuse or neglect to select an arbitrator within 30 days after the other has appointed an arbitrator, and written notice is served upon that party requesting the appointment of an arbitrator, the arbitrator so appointed by the first party shall have power to proceed to arbitrate and determine the matters of disagreement as if that arbitrator were appointed by both parties for that purpose. The award of that arbitrator in writing, signed by the arbitrator, will be final.

A tripartite panel is not recommended because it is more expensive, less procedurally streamlined, and may be more predisposed to encourage a challenge of the award where there is a two-to-one split. For example, AAA rules provide: If the arbitration agreement does not specify the number of arbitrators, the dispute shall be heard and determined by one arbitrator, unless the AAA, in its discretion, directs that a greater number of arbitrators be appointed.

If the parties have not appointed an arbitrator and have not provided any other method of appointment, the arbitrator shall be appointed in the following manner: immediately after the filing of the demand or submission, the AAA shall send simultaneously to each party to the dispute an identical list of names of persons chosen from the panel.

Each party to the dispute shall have ten days from the transmittal date in which to strike any names objected to, number the remaining names in order of preference, and return the list to the AAA. If a party does not return the list within the time specified, all persons named therein shall be deemed acceptable.

From among the persons who have been approved on both lists, and in accordance with the designated order of mutual preference, the AAA shall invite the acceptance of an arbitrator to serve. If the parties fail to agree on any of the persons named, or if acceptable arbitrators are unable to act, or if for any other reason the appointment cannot be made from the submitted lists, the AAA shall have the power to make the appointment from among other members of the panel without the submission of additional lists.

Successor Arbitrator

Parties may wish to anticipate situations where the initial arbitrator or arbitrators selected cannot complete the hearing. For example:

In the event that any arbitrator dies, or refuses to act, or becomes incapable, incompetent, or unfit to act before hearings have been completed, or before an award has been rendered, a successor arbitrator may be appointed by the party pursuant to the selection procedures set forth in this agreement. A *de novo* hearing is not necessary unless either party, or the new arbitrator requests one.

or

If for any reason an arbitrator is unable to perform the duties of the office, the AAA may, on proof satisfactory to it, declare the office vacant. Vacancies shall be filled in accordance with the applicable provisions of these rules. In the event of a vacancy in a panel of neutral arbitrators after hearings have commenced, the remaining arbitrator(s) may continue with the hearing, and determination of the controversy, unless the parties agree otherwise.

Arbitrator Powers Clause

Parties may wish to set forth a clause specifically identifying and possibly limiting the powers of the arbitrators. In general, these clauses establish that the arbitrators' powers are all inclusive. For example:

The arbitrator shall have full power to give such directions and to make such orders as he shall deem fit and just.

Clause Regarding the Death of a Party

The parties may wish to specifically agree that an arbitration and all underlying claims are terminated by the death of a party. Here it should be noted that the death of a party revokes an arbitration agreement unless the agreement or submission or a statute expressly provides otherwise. Thus, if parties intend to ensure that arbitration will continue after death, it should be specifically stated.

Arbitration as a Condition Precedent to Any Court Action

For those employers who wish to ensure that the arbitration process is fully utilized by an employee prior to that employee's resort to court, the following clause may be of assistance:

The parties agree that a condition precedent to the commencement of court proceedings of any nature arising out of any disputes from this agreement shall first be submitted to arbitration as set forth herein.

Provision that Judgment May be Entered on Award

The parties may wish to specifically provide that the arbitrator's award may be entered in the highest court of the particular state or federal jurisdiction. For example:

Both parties agree that the judgment upon the arbitration award issued in this proceeding may be entered in the highest court of the state or federal jurisdiction.

This provision is particularly helpful where one of the parties is a nonresident and subsequent difficulty may arise regarding the power of the court to enter judgment on the award.

Award of Attorneys' Fees for Challenge to the Arbitration Agreement

Since arbitration is designed as an expedient, less expensive process than courtroom litigation, the parties may wish to introduce a cost-shifting provision in the situation where either party unsuccessfully challenges the legality of the arbitration agreement or unsuccessfully appeals an arbitrator's award beyond the arbitrator's jurisdiction. For example:

Both the parties agree that, should either party to this agreement seek to avoid arbitration prior to its inception by resort to federal or state court process or by refusing to arbitrate, should the party seeking to avoid arbitration fail to prevail, the attorneys' fees of the other party spent in defence of this arbitration provision or the compelling of arbitration shall be awarded to that party.

The parties agree that should either party appeal the arbitration award and opinion or any part thereof beyond the arbitrator, should that party fail to prevail in their appeal, all attorneys' fees and costs expended by the other party shall be paid for by that appealing party.

Reconsideration by the Arbitrator

Parties may wish to specifically obligate an arbitrator, upon request, to reconsider the award and opinion or request for rehearing within so many days of issuance.

Within 30 days of the date of issuance of an arbitrator's opinion and award, or any part thereof, either party may petition the arbitrator for reconsideration or rehearing of the matter.

Time Limits for Issuance of an Arbitrator's Award and Opinion

Parties may wish to obligate an arbitrator to issue a decision within so many days of the close of the hearing. For example:

Within [number] days of the close of the hearing, the arbitrator shall issue an opinion and award in this matter. Should the arbitrator fail to issue this opinion and award within the time frame set forth above, both parties are released from all costs associated with the arbitration.

The Award

- The award shall be made promptly by the arbitrator, and, unless otherwise agreed by the parties or specified by law, no later than 30 days from the date of closing of the hearing or, if oral hearings have been waived, from the date of the AAA's transmittal of the final statements and proofs to the arbitrator.
- The award shall be in writing and shall be signed by a majority of the arbitrators. Unless the parties agree otherwise, any opinion shall be in summary form. It shall be executed in the manner required by law.
- The arbitrator may grant any remedy or relief that the arbitrator deems just, equitable, and within the scope of the agreement of the parties, including, but not limited to, specific performance of a contract. The arbitrator shall, in the award, assess arbitration fees, expenses, and compensation as provided herein in favour of any party and, in the event any administrative fees or expenses are due the AAA, in favour of the AAA.
- If the parties settle their dispute during the course of the arbitration, the arbitrator may set forth the terms of the agreed settlement in an award. Such an award is referred to as a consent award.
- The parties shall accept as legal delivery of the award the placing of the award or a true copy thereof in the mail, addressed to a party or its representative at the last known address, personal service of the award, or the filing of the award in any manner that is permitted by law.

Release Time for Witnesses

Parties should consider how release of witnesses will be performed. This is especially important where a company anticipates a problem allowing numerous company employees to testify at a hearing. For example:

The parties hereby agree that should any witnesses be under the control of the opposing party that party will release those witnesses for testimony. All costs of said witnesses are to be assumed by the party presenting the witness.

Telephone Testimony

Parties may wish to control the costs of the arbitration by allowing for telephone testimony by a non-party witness, subject to either party's right to veto this testimony in favour of person-to-person confrontation. For example:

Both parties hereby agree that the telephone testimony of a witness may be taken upon consent of the parties. Should either party request to confront the witness in person, no telephone testimony will be permitted. Should either party initially consent to telephone testimony and subsequently revoke this consent, the objecting party must assume all costs of all parties related to the revocation of consent.

Postponements

To expedite a hearing and ensure appropriate preparation the parties may wish to penalize postponement requests by use of a fee shifting device. For example:

Should either party request postponement of a hearing, to the extent that any fees or costs are incurred by the opposing party as a direct result of such postponement request, those fees and costs shall be paid by the party requesting postponement.

The parties agree that should either party request a postponement that prevents the close of hearing which in the arbitrator's opinion would have otherwise occurred at the time of the postponement request, should the opposing party consent to the postponement request, the party requesting postponement shall be responsible for all attorneys' fees and costs and arbitration fees associated with the postponement or reconvening of the hearing. Should a party oppose said postponement request, the arbitrator may, but is not required to, award similar fees and costs where consent is granted.

The AAA Rules recommend:

The arbitrator, for good cause shown, may postpone any hearing upon the request of a party or upon the arbitrator's own initiative and shall also grant such postponement when all of the parties agree.

Filing of Briefs

Parties should specify whether briefs are permitted. Parties not incorporating state or federal rules of procedure may wish to set time limits for the filing of briefs. For example:

Either party may file a brief at the time of the hearing or any time prior thereto. Either party may file a reply to any brief not later than five days after the close of hearing. In all other situations, either party may file a reply brief within ten days after receipt of an opposing party's brief. Where a brief is filed with the arbitrator, a copy of said brief shall be filed concurrently with the opposing party. The arbitrator may alter the time periods for the filing of any briefs or reply briefs.

Admissibility of Affidavits

The admissibility of affidavits is often a point of contention in arbitrations. The parties may wish to expedite a hearing by anticipating this issue. For example:

The arbitrator may, in his sole discretion, admit as evidence any affidavit or declaration concerning the matters in difference, provided that a copy of any said document has been previously served to all opposing parties at least three days prior to the time at which the affidavit is offered into evidence. The burden is on the party seeking to admit said affidavit to establish appropriate service. The party against whom the affidavit is offered into evidence is permitted to seek to subject that affiant to cross-examination. Should that affiant be unavailable for cross-examination, the affidavit may not be admitted, absent admissibility pursuant to the Federal Rules of Evidence.

AAA Rules recommend:

The arbitrator may receive and consider the evidence of witnesses by affidavit, but shall give it only such weight as the arbitrator deems it entitled to after consideration of any objection made to its admission. If the parties agree or the arbitrator directs that the documents or other evidence be submitted to the arbitrator after the hearing, the documents or other evidence shall be filed with the AAA for transmission to the arbitrator. All parties shall be afforded an opportunity to examine such documents or other evidence.

Failure of a Party to Attend Hearing

Where a party fails to attend the arbitration hearing, the parties may wish to carefully consider how to handle this incident. Parties may provide that a hearing will be held in the absence of any such party. However, this provision may run afoul of due process requirements. In the alternative, parties may wish to provide that if a party fails to attend, that party must pay all fees and costs associated with that day's scheduled hearing and all opposing party's attorneys' fees and costs associated with the failure to attend.

Furthermore, one may wish to consider the placement of that demand for arbitration on an inactive roster for 60 days. At the end of the 60 days, if not rescheduled for hearing, the parties may provide that the claim is deemed dismissed with prejudice and barred from relitigation by all applicable limitations. For example:

In the event of either party or his witness failing to attend before the arbitrator, after [number] days' written notice given to such party by the arbitrator, the arbitrator may proceed with the arbitration in the absence and without further notice to such party or witness,

or

In the event of either party or his witness failing to attend before the arbitrator, after [number] days written notice given to such party, the hearing will be placed on an inactive roster for 60 calendar days. Should that party fail to appear or request rehearing in writing to the arbitrator, the arbitration demand is deemed to have been abandoned and the arbitrator is required to dismiss said arbitration claim with prejudice. The limitations period will bar any reprosecution of said arbitration demand.

or

Should either party fail to produce a witness, the party may elect to continue the proceeding absent said witness or the party may request that the arbitrator rule on the record as established to date by that party. In any event, the opposing party shall have the full right to present their witnesses in full testimony and shall not be prejudiced by the opposing party's failure to produce a witness.

AAA Rules recommend:

Unless the law provides to the contrary, the arbitration may proceed in the absence of any party or representative who, after due notice, fails to be present or fails to obtain a postponement. An award shall not be made solely on the default of a party. The arbitrator shall require the party who is present to submit such evidence as the arbitrator may require for the making of the award.

Use of Consultants

Unless expressly authorized by the parties, arbitrators may not consult or employ counsel, accountants, or other experts. Thus, the parties may wish to consider permitting the arbitrator to seek the advice of outside counsel, accountants, or other experts. For example:

The arbitrators may submit to [name of consultant] whom they may select any [identity of submission] arising in the course of the arbitration, and may accept such opinion as conclusive.

For example, AAA Rules recommend:

An arbitrator finding it necessary to make an inspection or investigation in connection with the arbitration shall direct the AAA to so advise the parties. The arbitrator shall set the date and time and the AAA shall notify the parties. Any party who so desires may be present at such an inspection or investigation. In the event that one or all parties are not present at the inspection or investigation, the arbitrator shall make a verbal or written report to the parties and afford them an opportunity to comment.

Procedure for Arbitrator Selection

Under AAA procedures, the AAA may offer prospective parties to arbitration a list of commercial or labour-management arbitrators. The parties may wish to set forth additional procedures for the selection of such arbitrators to include the particular type of panel from which the arbitrators will be selected, the procedure for striking the arbitrators, and whether either party may initially reject an arbitration panel. For example:

The parties agree that a single arbitrator will be selected from a panel of [labourmanagement] or [commercial] arbitrators supplied by the American Arbitration Association. Either party may reject the full panel within 10 days of receipt by requesting a new panel from the AAA.

or

The parties will select an arbitrator from the panel by mutual agreement or by alternate striking of arbitrators until one arbitrator remains. Where alternate striking is used, a coin flip or any other procedure may be used where the parties can agree on who will make the first strike.

Here, AAA Rules recommend:

If the arbitration agreement does not specify the number of arbitrators, the dispute shall be heard and determined by one arbitrator, unless the AAA, in its discretion, directs that a greater number of arbitrators be appointed. If the parties have not appointed an arbitrator and have not provided any other method of appointment, the arbitrator shall be appointed in the following manner: Immediately after the filing of the demand or submission, the AAA shall send simultaneously to each party to the dispute an identical list of names of persons chosen from the panel. Each party to the dispute shall have ten days from the transmittal date in which to strike any names objected to, number the remaining names in order of preference, and return the list to the AAA.

If a party does not return the list within the time specified, all persons named therein shall be deemed acceptable. From among the persons who have been approved on both lists, and in accordance with the designated order of mutual preference, the AAA shall invite the acceptance of an arbitrator to serve. If the parties fail to agree on any of the persons named, or if acceptable arbitrators are unable to act, or if for any other reason the appointment cannot be made from the submitted lists, the AAA shall have the power to make the appointment from among other members of the panel without the submission of additional lists.

Confidentiality

A major advantage of arbitration is that it is a private process. The parties may wish to bind themselves and the arbitrator to strict confidentiality concerning the facts of the matter at issue. The parties may also wish to agree on who will be allowed to attend the proceeding and whether the proceeding will be considered closed to the public. Finally, if confidentiality is valued, an appropriate sanction should be identified for breach of this provision. For example:

Both parties recognize that any claim, dispute, or arbitration under this agreement is considered confidential. In this regard, the dispute or claim at issue, the arbitration proceedings, and the arbitration award and decision may be disclosed solely to a parties' attorney, potential witnesses, accountant, spouse, and only after each of those persons have executed a confidentiality agreement as set forth [an appropriate confidentiality agreement should be attached] in this agreement. Both parties agree that any breach of this confidentiality clause will relieve the other party from all payment obligations of any kind due to that party plus a damages award in the amount of [dollar amount to be set by the parties].

AAA Rules recommend: The arbitrator shall maintain the privacy of the hearings unless the law provides to the contrary. Any person having a direct interest in the arbitration is entitled to attend hearings. The arbitrator shall otherwise have the power to require the exclusion of any witness, other than a party or other essential person, during the testimony of any other witness. The arbitrator shall determine whether any other person may attend the hearing.

Confidentiality—Request of an Award Only

The award shall be in writing and shall be signed by the arbitrator. If either party requests, the arbitrator shall issue an opinion in writing, which shall set forth in summary form the reasons for the arbitrator's determination. All awards shall be executed in the manner required by law.

Both parties are permitted to request that, pursuant to confidentiality considerations, an award without an accompanying opinion be issued. Should either party request that an award only be issued for this reason, the arbitrator is required to honour that confidentiality request unless [parties to determine standards to waive confidentiality].

Default Provision

Even where the parties have a tailored procedure, parties should establish a default set of procedural rules. For example:

To the extent that any procedural issues are not addressed by the parties herein, the parties stipulate that the Employment Dispute Resolution Rules of AAA shall govern.

Requirement of Enumerated Claims and Damages

The parties may wish to require enumeration of all claims and damages sought at the time of filing or amendment. For example:

At the time of filing of a demand for arbitration, the party filing such demand is required to specifically set forth the basis of all statutory claims. A failure to specifically identify a claim by reference to statute, case law, or common denomination, bars that party from raising that claim or claims at hearing. The filing of an arbitration demand does not toll or otherwise suspend the running of time for purposes of compliance with contractual time limitations set forth herein.

A party seeking relief must file at the time of a demand for arbitration or relief, whichever is earlier, an itemized statement of claims specifically identifying the amount of relief requested pursuant to each legal claim and the denomination of such claimed relief by punitive, compensatory, back pay, front pay or other.

Waiver of Defects

This clause ensures that the parties have had a full and fair hearing and minimizes the possibility that they may later claim otherwise.

At the close of the arbitration, both parties agree that they will be queried by the arbitrator as to whether they have any objections to the conduct of the arbitrator or the arbitration proceedings. At that time, both parties will be requested to waive any claim of defects or to stipulate that said objections have been cured and that an arbitration opinion and award shall issue without regard to any above stated objections.

For example, AAA Rules recommend: Any party who proceeds with the arbitration after knowledge that any provision or requirement of these procedures has not been complied with and who fails to state objections thereto in writing, shall be deemed to have waived the right to object.

Attorneys' Fees

It is further agreed that the arbitrators may, in their sole discretion, award attorneys' fees to the prevailing party.

Waiver of Procedures

Any party who proceeds with the arbitration after knowledge that any provision or requirement of these procedures has not been complied with, and who fails to state objections thereto in writing, shall be deemed to have waived the right to object.

Apportionment of Expenses

The cost and expenses of the arbitration shall be borne and paid as the arbitrators by their award direct (or shall be paid by the parties in equal share).

Deposit for Arbitrators' Fees and Costs

At any time during the proceeding the arbitrator(s) may request that both parties deposit a security amount satisfactory to the arbitrator. Unless both parties are required to make said security deposit, this request may not be made by the arbitrator. For example, AAA Rules recommend:

The AAA may require the parties to deposit in advance of any hearings such sums of money as it deems necessary to cover the expenses of the arbitration, including the arbitrator's fee, if any, and shall render an accounting to the parties and return any unexpended balance at the conclusion of the case.

Representation by Counsel

Any party may be represented by counsel or by any other authorized representative. A party intending to be so represented shall notify the other party and the AAA of the name and address of the representative at least three days prior to the date set for the hearing at which that person is first to appear. When such a representative initiates an arbitration or responds for a party, notice is deemed to have been given.

Interpreter Clause

Both parties, subject to the arbitrator's power to resolve any disagreements, shall make the necessary arrangements for the services of an interpreter upon the request of one or more of the parties, who assume the cost of such service.

Oaths

The arbitrator has the discretion to require witnesses to testify under oath administered by any duly qualified person, or if required by law, or demanded by either party, shall do so. The AAA Rules recommend:

Before proceeding with the first hearing, each arbitrator may take an oath of office and, if required by law, shall do so. The arbitrator may require witnesses to testify under oath administered by any duly qualified person and, if it is required by law or requested by any party, shall do so.

Order of Proceeding

The AAA Rules recommend: A hearing shall be opened by the filing of the oath of the arbitrator, where required; by the recording of the place, time, and date of the hearing, and the presence of the arbitrator, the parties, and their representatives, if any; and by the receipt by the arbitrator of the statement of the claim and answering statement, if any. The arbitrator may, at the beginning of the hearing, ask for statements clarifying the issues involved. In some cases, part or all of the above will have been accomplished at the preliminary hearing conducted by the arbitrator pursuant.

The complaining party shall then present evidence to support its claim. The defending party shall then present evidence supporting its defence. Witnesses for each party shall submit to questions or other examination. The arbitrator has the discretion to vary this procedure but shall afford a full and equal opportunity to all parties for the presentation of any material and relevant evidence. Exhibits, when offered by either party, may be received in evidence by the arbitrator.

The names and addresses of all witnesses and a description of the exhibits in the order received shall be made a part of the record. There shall be no direct communication between the parties and a neutral arbitrator other than at oral hearing, unless the parties and the arbitrator agree otherwise. Any other oral or written communication from the parties to the neutral arbitrator shall be directed to the AAA for transmittal to the arbitrator.

Expedited Arbitration for Claims Involving Less Than $50,000

The AAA Rules provide for expedited arbitration of claims for less than $50,000. These procedures are set forth below:

Unless the AAA in its discretion determines otherwise, the Expedited Procedures shall apply in any case where no disclosed claim or counterclaim exceeds $50,000, exclusive of interest and arbitration costs. Parties may also agree to use the Expedited Procedures in cases involving claims in excess of $50,000.

The parties shall accept all notices from the AAA by telephone. Such notices by the AAA shall subsequently be confirmed in writing to the parties. Should there be a failure to confirm in writing any notice hereunder, the proceeding shall nonetheless be valid if the notice has, in fact, been given by telephone.

Appointment and Qualifications of Arbitrator: The AAA shall appoint one neutral arbitrator from its Panel of Arbitrators who has familiarity with the employment field, who shall hear and determine the case promptly. The parties will be given notice by telephone by the AAA of the appointment of the arbitrator, who shall be subject to disqualification for the reasons specified in "Cost of Arbitration". Within seven days, the parties shall notify the AAA, by telephone, of any objection to the arbitrator appointed. Any objection by a party to the arbitrator shall be confirmed in writing to the AAA with a copy to the other party or parties.

Date, Time, and Place of Hearing: The arbitrator shall set the date, time, and place of the hearing. The AAA will notify the parties by telephone at least seven days in advance of the hearing date. A formal notice of hearing will also be sent by the AAA to the parties.

The Hearing: Generally, the hearing shall be completed within one day, unless the dispute is resolved by submission of documents, upon the agreement of all parties. The arbitrator, for good cause shown, may schedule an additional hearing to be held within seven days.

Time of Award: Unless otherwise agreed by the parties, the award shall be rendered not later than 14 days from the date of the closing of the hearing.

Designation of Witnesses

At least 30 days before the arbitration, the parties must exchange lists of witnesses, including any expert, and copies of all exhibits intended to be used at the arbitration.

Enforcement

The decision of the arbitrator may be enforced under the terms of the Federal Arbitration Act or under the law of any state. If the decision is not completely enforceable, final, and binding, it shall be enforced and binding on both parties to the extent permitted by law. Even if a party of this procedure is held to be void or unenforceable, the remainder of the procedure will be enforceable and any part may be severed from the remainder, as appropriate.

Administrative Conference, Preliminary Hearing, and Mediation Conference

At the request of any party or at the discretion of the AAA, an administrative conference with the AAA and the parties or their representatives will be scheduled in appropriate cases to expedite the arbitration proceedings. There is no administrative fee for this service.

In large or complex cases, at the request of any party or at the discretion of the arbitrator or the AAA, a preliminary hearing with the parties or their representatives and the arbitrator may be scheduled by the arbitrator to specify the issues to be resolved, to stipulate to uncontested facts, and to consider any other matters that will expedite the arbitration proceedings. Consistent with the expedited nature of arbitration, the arbitrator may, at the preliminary hearing, establish the extent of and schedule for the production of relevant documents and other information, the identification of any witnesses to be called, and a schedule for further hearings to resolve the dispute. There is no administrative fee for the first preliminary hearing.

With the consent of the parties, the AAA at any stage of the proceeding may arrange a mediation conference under its mediation rules, in order to facilitate settlement. The mediator shall not be an arbitrator appointed to the case. Where the parties to a pending arbitration agree to mediate under the AAA's rules, no additional administrative fee is required to initiate the mediation.

Qualifications of Neutral Arbitrator

- Arbitrators serving under these rules shall have familiarity with the employment field.
- Any neutral arbitrator appointed shall be subject to disqualification for the reasons stated in paragraph C of this section. If the parties specifically so agree in writing, the arbitrator shall not be subject to disqualification for those reasons.
- No person shall serve as a neutral arbitrator in any matter in which that person has any financial or personal interest in the result of the proceeding. Prior to accepting appointment, the prospective arbitrator shall disclose any circumstance likely to prevent a prompt hearing or to create a presumption of bias. Upon receipt of such information, the AAA will either replace that person or

communicate the information to the parties for comment. Thereafter, the AAA may disqualify that person and its decision shall be conclusive.

- The term "arbitrator" in these rules refers to the arbitration panel, whether composed of one or more arbitrators.

Majority Decision

All decisions of the arbitrators must be by a majority. The award must also be made by a majority, unless the concurrence of all is expressly required by the arbitration agreement or by law.

Interim Measures

The arbitrator may issue such orders for interim relief as may be deemed necessary to safeguard the subject matter of the arbitration, without prejudice to the rights of the parties or to the final determination of the dispute.

Closing of Hearing

The arbitrator shall specifically inquire of all parties whether they have any further proofs to offer or witnesses to be heard. Upon receiving negative replies or if satisfied that the record is complete, the arbitrator shall declare the hearing closed.

If briefs are to be filed, the hearing shall be declared closed as of the final date set by the arbitrator for the receipt of briefs. If documents are to be filed and the date set for their receipt is later than that set for the receipt of briefs, the later date shall be the date of closing the hearing. The time limit within which the arbitrator is required to make the award shall commence to run, in the absence of other agreements by the parties, upon closing of the hearing.

Reopening of Hearing

The hearing may be reopened on the arbitrator's initiative, or upon application of a party, at any time before the award is made. If reopening the hearing would prevent the making of the award within the specific time agreed on by the parties in the contract(s) out of which the controversy has arisen, the matter may not be reopened unless the parties agree on an extension of time. When no specific date is fixed in the contract, the arbitrator may reopen the hearing and shall have 30 days from the closing of the reopened hearing within which to make an award.

Waiver of Oral Hearing

The parties may provide, by written agreement, for the waiver of oral hearings in any case. If the parties are unable to agree as to the procedure, the AAA shall specify a fair and equitable procedure.

Extensions of Time

The parties may modify any period of time by mutual agreement. The AAA or the arbitrator may for good cause extend any period of time established by these rules, except the time for making the award. The AAA shall notify the parties of any extension.

Serving of Notice

Each party shall be deemed to have consented that any papers, notices, or process necessary or proper for the initiation or continuation of an arbitration under these rules; for any court actions in connection therewith; or for the entry of judgment on an award made under these procedures may be served on a party by mail addressed to the party or its representative at the last known address or by personal service, in or outside the state where the arbitration is to be held, provided that reasonable opportunity to be heard with regard thereto has been granted to the party.The AAA and the parties may also use facsimile transmission, telex, telegram, or other written forms of electronic communication to give the notices required by these rules.

Release of Documents for Judicial Proceedings

The AAA shall, upon the written request of a party, furnish to the party, at its expense, certified copies of any papers in the AAA's possession that may be required in judicial proceedings relating to the arbitration.

Interpretation and Application of Procedures

The arbitrator shall interpret and apply these procedures as they relate to the arbitrator's powers and duties. When there is more than one arbitrator and a difference arises among them concerning the meaning or application of these rules, it shall be decided by a majority vote. If that is not possible, either an arbitrator or a party may refer the question to the AAA for final decision. All other procedures shall be interpreted and applied by the AAA.

Signature Clause

Employee acknowledges that he or she has carefully read this agreement, that he or she understands its terms, that all understandings between the employee and the company relating to the subjects covered in this agreement are contained in it, and that he or she has entered into this agreement voluntarily and not in reliance on any promises or representations by the company other than those contained in this agreement itself.

Employee further acknowledges that he or she had an opportunity to discuss this agreement with his or her personal legal counsel and has used that opportunity to the extent he or she wishes to do so.

[Employee Name]	[Company Name]
Signature of Employee	Name of Company Official
____________________	____________________
	Title of Company Official
Date:____________________	

Consideration

Each party's promise to resolve claims by arbitration in accordance with the provisions of this agreement, rather than through the courts, is consideration for the other party's like promise.

Not an Employment Agreement

This agreement is not, and shall not be construed to create, any contract of employment, express or implied.

One of the leading in-house ADR programmemes mandating arbitration as a condition of employment was introduced by the Primerica Corporation in September 1992. This programmeme has been modified since its introduction. For example, when first introduced it provided for a procedure ending in arbitration for all employment disputes. Now, it applies solely to those disputes that involve a legal cause of action.

When this programmeme was introduced, Primerica was far ahead of other organizations in developing a workplace due process model that avoided the courtroom in favour of arbitration. The vision of Primerica's executives and legal counsel has been rewarded with a dispute resolution process that is now one of the model programmemes in industry.

Primerica merged into the Travellers Corporation; the new organization is called the Travellers Group. The Primerica ADR programmeme has now been introduced throughout the Travellers Group.

Travellers Group is committed to fair and equitable employment practices. We recognize that misunderstandings or conflicts can and do arise in the course of daily business relationships. While most situations resolve themselves naturally, there are times when an employee may wish to seek review of an employment related action or decision. The Dispute Resolution Procedures is an impartial process by which employees may request resolution of any employment-related concern.

PROCESS

Step 1. Employees are encouraged to first discuss informally any concern they have with their immediate manager prior to initiating a formal review. However, if this discussion is not successful from the employee's point of view, the review should be submitted in writing within thirty (30) days of the incident to their manager with a copy to their Human Resources representative. The manager and Human Resources representative have twenty (20) working days to investigate the claim and respond to the employee:

Step 2. If the employee is not satisfied with the response in Step 1, he/she may submit an appeal to the next level manager within ten (10) working days of receiving an answer from Step 1, with a copy to the Manager, Human Resources within his/her subsidiary. At the conclusion of the discussion relating to the dispute, the parties shall agree that all the facts have been brought forward. A written response is given to the employee within twenty (20) working days after the discussion.

Step 3. If the employee is not satisfied with the response in Step 2, he/she may submit an appeal to the next level manager within ten (10) working days of receiving an answer from Step 2, with a copy to the Vice President, Human Resources within their subsidiary.

The third level of appeal is with the Division/Regional/Department Manager and the Vice President, Human Resources within the subsidiary. The Vice President, Human Resources will consult with the Senior Vice President, Human Resources, Travellers Group. This step is the final level of appeal in the internal Dispute Resolution Procedure. After this meeting, the employee will receive a written response within twenty (20) working days.

If the dispute is still not resolved, the employee is entitled to request aribtration in accordance with the Travellers Group Employment Arbitration Policy.

Termination

An employee may appeal a termination within thirty (30) days. The appeal will automatically progress to Step 2 of the process.

Field Operations

At times it may be impractical to arrange face-to-face meetings within the specified time limits of the programmeme. In these circumstances, the Vice President of Human Resources may make modifications to the process as necessary.

Exceptions

The existing procedures for reporting alleged incidents of sex discrimination (including sexual harassment), racial discrimination, age discrimination, disability discrimination and other illegal forms of discrimination will remain in place to provide the maximum confidentiality and privacy. Such complaints should be sent directly to the Vice President, Human Resources of each subsidiary.

The internal Dispute Resolution Procedure is a sequential process which stops wherever the individual bringing forward a perceived problem accepts a decision at one of the interim steps. Decisions concerning terminations, promotions and disciplinary actions are typical types of issues raised. This process ensures prompt confidential resolution of such issues. Employees who wish to avail themselves of the process will not be subject to any retaliatory action by management. No disciplinary action or other management decision will be postponed as a result of the presentation of a dispute by the employee.

EMPLOYMENT ARBITRATION POLICY STATEMENT OF INTENT

Travellers Group and its affiliates (referred to collectively as "Travellers Group") value each of its employees and look forward to good relations with, and among, all employees. Occasionally, however, disagreements may arise between an individual employee and Travellers Group, or between employees in a context that involves Travellers Group. Travellers Group believes that the resolution of such disagreements will be best accomplished by internal dispute review and, where that fails, by arbitration conducted under the auspices of the American Arbitration Association.

For these reasons, Travellers Group has adopted this Employment Arbitration Policy ("the Policy"). The Policy applies to all persons employed by Travellers Group on the date of its adoption and all employees joining Travellers Group after that date.

This Policy does not constitute a guarantee that your employment will continue for any specified period of time or end only under certain conditions.

Employment at Travellers Group is a voluntary relationship for no definite period of time, and nothing in this Policy or any other company document constitutes an express or implied contract of employment for any definite period of time. This policy does not constitute, nor should be construed to constitute, a waiver by the Travellers Group of its rights under the "Employment-at-will" doctrine; nor does it afford an employee or former employee any rights or remedies that the employee or former employee does not otherwise have under applicable law.

Scope of the Policy

The Policy makes arbitration the required, and exclusive, forum for the resolution of all employment disputes based on legally protected rights (i.e., statutory, contractual or common law rights) that may arise between an employee or former employee and the Travellers Group or its affiliates, officers, directors, employees and agents (and which are not resolved by the internal dispute resolution procedure), including claims, demands or actions under Title VII of the Civil Rights Act of 1964, the Civil Rights Act of 1866, the Age Discrimination in Employment Act, the Rehabilitation Act of 1973, the Americans with Disabilities Act, the Employee Retirement Income Security Act of 1974, and all amendments thereto, and any other federal, state or local statute, regulation or common law doctrine, regarding employment discrimination, conditions of employment or termination of employment.

The Policy does not require that Travellers Group institute arbitration nor is it required to follow the steps of the dispute resolution procedure before taking disciplinary action of any kind, including termination; however, if an employee disagrees with any such disciplinary action, and believes that such action violated his or her legally protected rights, he or she may institute proceedings in accordance with the Policy.

ARBITRATION RULES AND PROCEDURES

The following rules and procedures are based on, and largely incorporate, the Employment Dispute Resolution Rules of the American Arbitration Association ("AAA"). Travellers Group has modified and expanded these rules and procedures in certain respects. In particular, provisions regarding fees and costs have been modified to provide that many of the costs typically shared by the parties will be borne by Travellers Group, In addition, provisions permitting limited discovery have been added to insure equal access to relevant information.

Initiation of Arbitration Proceeding

Arbitration may be initiated by a written demand for arbitration submitted to the Senior Vice President, Human Resources, Travellers Group together with a check payable to the AAA for the requisite administrative fee as provided in the AAA's fee schedule. The fee schedule is available from the Human Resources Department. Employees, however, whose total compensation for the previous calendar year was $150,000 or less (or former employees whose total compensation for the last calendar year they were a Travellers Group employee was $150,000 or less) need only submit a check for $50 payable to the Travellers Group.

The demand shall set forth the claim, including the alleged act or omission at issue and the names of all persons involved in the act or omission. Within ten (10) business days of receiving such demand, Travellers Group shall file the demand with the appropriate office of the AAA, together with the applicable administrative fee as provided in the AAA's fee Schedule. The employee or former employee will be required to sign a submission agreement.

Appointment of Neutral Arbitrator

The AAA shall appoint one neutral arbitrator from its Panel of Arbitrators, unless one party requests that a panel of three (3) arbitrators be appointed. In the event a panel of arbitrators is appointed, all decisions of the panel must be by a majority and the use of the word "arbitrator" in these Rules shall refer to the panel.

The arbitrator shall be appointed in the following manner:

- Immediately after the filing of the demand, the AAA shall submit to each party an identical list of proposed arbitrators;
- Each party shall then have ten (10) business days from the mailing date of the list to cross off any names to which the party objects, number the remaining names in order of preference and return the list to the AAA;

- If the party does not return the list within the time specified, all persons on the list shall be deemed acceptable; and
- The AAA shall invite arbitrators remaining on the list in the order of preference, to the extent the order of preference of the parties can be reconciled by the AAA.

In the event the parties fail to agree on any of the persons named, or if an acceptable arbitrator is unwilling to act, the AAA may issue additional lists or, at its option, make the appointment from among other members of its panel of arbitrators without submitting additional lists.

Qualifications of Neutral Arbitrator

No person shall serve as a neutral arbitrator in any matter in which that person has any financial or personal interest in the result of the proceeding. Prior to accepting appointment, the prospective arbitrator shall disclose any circumstance likely to prevent a prompt hearing or to create a presumption of bias. Upon receipt of such information, the AAA will either replace that person or communicate the information to the parties for comment. Thereafter, the AAA may disqualify that person and its decision shall be conclusive. Vacancies shall be filled in accordance with Rule number 2.

Vacancies

The AAA is authorized to substitute another arbitrator if a vacancy occurs or if an appointed arbitrator is unable to serve promptly.

Date, Time and Place of Hearing

The arbitrator shall set the date, time, and place of the hearing, notice of which must be given to the parties by the AAA at least ten days in advance, unless the parties agree otherwise.

Representation

Any party may be represented by an attorney, a non-supervisory co-worker or by him or her self. If the employee or former employee chooses not to be represented by an attorney, Travellers Group shall waive its right to be represented by an attorney unless such person is or was licensed to practice law in any jurisdiction in the United States.

Attendance at Hearing

The arbitrator shall maintain the privacy of the hearings unless the law provides to the contrary. Any person having a direct interest in the arbitration is entitled to attend hearings. The arbitrator shall otherwise have the power to require the exclusion of any witness, other than a party or other essential person, during the testimony of any other witness. The arbitrator shall determine whether any other person may attend the hearing.

Postponement

The arbitrator, for good cause shown, may postpone any hearing upon the request of a party or upon the arbitrator's own initiative, and shall also grant such postponement when all of the parties agree thereto.

Oaths

Before proceeding with the first hearing, each arbitrator may take an oath of office and, if required by law, shall do so. The arbitrator may require witnesses to testify under oath administered by any duly qualified person and, if it is required by law or requested by any party, shall do so.

Stenographic Record

There shall be no stenographic record of these proceedings unless either party requests it. In the event a party requests a stenographic record, that party shall bear the cost of such a record. If both parties request a stenographic record, the cost shall be borne equally by the parties.

Proceedings

The hearings shall be conducted by the arbitrator in whatever manner will most expeditiously permit full presentation of the evidence and arguments of the parties. Normally, the hearing shall be completed within one day. In unusual circumstances and for good cause shown, the arbitrator may schedule an additional hearing to be held within five business days.

Arbitration in the Absence of a Party

Unless the law provides to the contrary, the arbitration may proceed in the absence of any party or representative who, after due notice, fails to be present or fails to obtain a postponement. An award shall not be made solely on the default of a party. The arbitrator shall require the party who is present to submit such evidence as the arbitrator may require for the making of the award.

Discovery

Each party shall be entitled to propound and serve upon the other party one set of interrogatories in a form consistent with the Federal Rules of Civil Procedure and which shall be limited to the identification of potential witnesses. Each party shall be entitled to propound and serve upon the other one set of Requests for the Production of Documents in a form consistent with the Federal Rules of Civil Procedure and which shall be limited in number to twenty-five (25) Requests (including sub-parts, which shall be counted separately).

Evidence

The arbitrator shall be the judge of the relevance and materiality of the evidence offered, and conformity to legal rules of evidence shall not be necessary.

Evidence by Affidavit and Filing of Documents

The arbitrator may receive and consider the evidence of witnesses by affidavit, but shall give it only such weight as the arbitrator deems it entitled to after consideration of any objection made to its admission. All documents to be considered by the arbitrator shall be filed at the hearing. There shall be no post-hearing briefs.

Closing of Hearing

The arbitrator shall ask whether the parties have any further proofs to offer or witnesses to be heard. Upon receiving negative replies, or if satisfied that the record is complete, the arbitrator shall declare the hearing closed and the minutes thereof shall be recorded.

Reopening of Hearing

The hearing may be reopened on the arbitrator's initiative, or upon application of a party, at any time before the award is made. The arbitrator may reopen the hearing and shall have fourteen (14) days from the closing of the reopened hearing within which to make an award.

Waiver of Procedures

Any party who proceeds with the arbitration after knowledge that any provision or requirement of these procedures has not been complied with, and who fails to state objections thereto in writing, shall be deemed to have waived the right to object.

Time of Award

The award shall be made promptly by the arbitrator unless otherwise agreed by the parties or specified by law. The arbitrator shall be instructed to make the award within thirty (30) days of the hearing or as soon as possible thereafter.

Award

Form

The award shall be in writing and shall be signed by the arbitrator. If either party requests, the arbitrator shall issue an opinion in writing, which shall set forth in summary form the reasons for the arbitrator's determination. All awards shall be executed in the manner required by law.

Scope of Relief

The arbitrator shall be governed by the rule of law of the state where the employee worked as well as taking note of applicable Federal law as submitted by the parties and shall be bound by Travellers Group policies and procedures. Furthermore, the arbitrator shall have no authority to alter or otherwise modify the parties' at will relationship or substitute his or her judgment for the lawful business judgment of the Travellers Group management. The arbitrator shall have the power to award, in appropriate circumstances, money damages in an amount sufficient to compensate the aggrieved party for such direct injury as the arbitrator determines such party has suffered.

The arbitrator shall have the authority to order reinstatement of employment to a former employee only if money damages are insufficient as a remedy. Unless expressly provided for by applicable statute, the arbitrator shall not have the authority to award punitive damages, attorney's fees or injunctive relief of any nature. The arbitrator shall not have the authority to make any award that is arbitrary and capricious or to award to Travellers Group the costs of the arbitration that it is otherwise required to bear under this Policy.

Delivery of Award to Parties

Parties shall accept as legal delivery of the award the placing of the award or a true copy thereof in the mail, addressed to a party or its representative at the last known address via certified mail, return receipt; personal service of the award; or the filing of the award in any manner that is permitted by law.

Enforcement

The decision of the arbitrator may be enforced under the terms of the Federal Arbitration Act (Title 9 U.S.C.) and/or under the law of any state. If the decision is not completely enforceable, final and binding, it shall be enforced and binding on both parties to the extent permitted by law. Even if a part of this procedure is held to be void or unenforceable, the remainder of the procedure will be enforceable and any part may be severed from the remainder, as appropriate.

Judicial Proceedings and Exclusion of Liability

- Neither the AAA nor any arbitrator in a proceeding under these procedures is a necessary party in judicial proceedings relating to the arbitration.
- Parties to these procedures shall be deemed to have consented that judgment upon the arbitration award may be entered in any federal or state court having jurisdiction thereof.

Expenses

In order to make these arbitration procedures available to all employees, Travellers Group or its affiliate shall pay 100 percent in excess of fifty dollars ($50) of any administrative fee required by the AAA for those employees whose total compensation for the previous calendar year was $150,000 or less (or former employees whose total compensation for the last calendar year they were a Travellers Group employee was $150,000 or less.) The expenses of witnesses for either side shall be paid by the party requiring the presence of such witnesses. Each side shall pay its own legal fees and expenses.

All other expenses (except Postponement Fees or Additional Hearing Fees) of the arbitration, such as required travel and other expenses of the arbitrator (including any witness produced at the direction of the arbitrator), and the expenses of a representative of AAA, if any, shall be paid completely by Travellers Group and affiliates. If the arbitration proceeding continues more than one day, the incremental expenses of the additional days shall be borne equally by the parties. This allocation of expenses may not be disturbed by the arbitration award.

Serving of Notice

Any parties, notices, or process necessary or proper for the initiation or continuation of an arbitration under these procedures; for any court action in connection therewith; or for the entry of judgment on an award made under these procedures may be served on a party by mail addressed to the party or its representative at the last known address or by personal service, in or outside the state where the arbitration is to be held, provided that reasonable opportunity to be heard with regard thereto has been granted to the party. The AAA and the parties may also use facsimile transmission, telex, telegram, or other written forms of electronic communication to give the notices required by these procedures, provided that such notice is confirmed by telephone or subsequent mailing to all affected parties.

Time Period for Arbitration

Any proceeding under this procedure must be brought within one year of the act or omission giving rise to the controversy. This time period may be extended, however, by any circumstance that would otherwise toll the applicable statute of limitations, but in no event shall the time for initiating an arbitration be extended beyond two years.

Interpretation and Application of Procedures

The arbitrator shall interpret and apply these procedures insofar as they relate to the arbitrator's powers and duties. All other procedures shall be interpreted and applied by the AAA.

MEDIATION

The parties may wish to require mediation as a precondition to arbitration. Alternatively, they may wish to identify mediation and offer it, but not require it.

The AAA Rules recommends the following language to cover future disputes:

If a dispute arises out of or relates to this contract, or the breach thereof, and if said dispute cannot be settled through negotiation, the parties agree first to try in good faith to settle the dispute by mediation under the Employment Mediation Rules of the American Arbitration Association before resorting to arbitration, litigation, or some other dispute resolution procedure.

The AAA Rules recommend this language for existing disputes:

The parties hereby submit the following dispute to mediation under the Employment Mediation Rules of the American Arbitration Association.

(The clause may also provide for the qualifications of the mediator(s), method of payment, locale of meetings, and any other item of concern to the parties.)

The AAA's Employment Mediation Rules state:

Employment Mediation Rules

- *Agreement of Parties* — Whenever, by provision in an employment dispute resolution programmeme, or by separate submission, the parties have provided for mediation or conciliation of existing or future disputes under the auspices of the American Arbitration Association (AAA) or under these rules, they shall be deemed to have made these rules, as amended and in effect as of the date of the submission of the dispute, a part of their agreement.
- *Initiation of Mediation* — Any party to an employment dispute may initiate mediation by filing with the AAA a submission to mediation or a written request for mediation pursuant to these rules, together with the appropriate administrative fee contained in the Administrative Fees.
- *Request for Mediation* — A request for mediation shall contain a brief statement of the nature of the dispute and the names, addresses, and telephone numbers of all parties to the dispute and those who will represent them, if any, in the mediation. The initiating party shall simultaneously file two copies of the request with the AAA and one copy with every other party to the dispute.
- *Appointment of Mediator* — Upon receipt of a request for mediation, the AAA will appoint a qualified mediator to serve. Normally, a single mediator will be appointed unless the parties agree otherwise or the AAA determines otherwise. If the agreement of the parties names a mediator or specifies a method of appointing a mediator, that designation or method shall be followed.
- *Qualifications of Mediator* — No person shall serve as a mediator in any dispute in which that person has any financial or personal interest in the result of the mediation, except by interest in the result of the mediation, except by the written consent of all parties. Prior to accepting an appointment, the prospective mediator shall disclose any circumstance likely to create a presumption of bias or prevent a prompt meeting with the parties. Upon receipt of such information, the AAA shall either replace the mediator or immediately communicate the

information to the parties for their comments. In the event that the parties disagree as to whether the mediator shall serve, the AAA will appoint another mediator. The AAA is authorized to appoint another mediator if the appointed mediator is unable to serve promptly.

- *Vacancies* — If any mediator shall become unwilling or unable to serve, the AAA will appoint another mediator, unless the parties agree otherwise.
- *Representation* — Any party may be represented by persons of the party's choice. The names and addresses of such persons shall be communicated in writing to all parties and to the AAA.
- *Date, Time, and Place of Mediation* — The mediator shall fix the date and the time of each mediation session. The mediation shall be held at the appropriate regional office of the AAA, or at any other convenient location agreeable to the mediator and the parties, as the mediator shall determine.
- *Identification of Matters in Dispute* — At least 10 days prior to the first scheduled mediation session, each party shall provide the mediator with a brief memorandum setting forth its position with regard to the issues that need to be resolved. At the discretion of the mediator, such memoranda may be mutually exchanged by the parties.

  At the first session, the parties will be expected to produce all information reasonably required for the mediator to understand the issues presented. The mediator may require any party to supplement such information.
- *Authority of Mediator* — The mediator does not have the authority to impose a settlement on the parties but will attempt to help them reach a satisfactory resolution of their dispute. The mediator is authorized to conduct joint and separate meetings with the parties and to make oral and written recommendations for settlement. Whenever necessary, the mediator may also obtain expert advise concerning technical aspects of the dispute, provided that the parties agree and assume the expenses of obtaining such advice. Arrangements for obtaining such advice shall be made by the mediator or the parties, as the mediator shall determine.

  The mediator is authorized to end the mediation whenever, in the judgment of the mediator, further efforts at mediation would not contribute to a resolution of the dispute between the parties.
- *Privacy* — Mediation sessions are private.

  The parties and their representatives may attend mediation sessions. Other persons may attend only with the permission of the parties and with the consent of the mediator.
- *Confidentiality* — Confidential information disclosed to a mediator by the parties or by witnesses in the course of the mediation shall

not be divulged by the mediator. All records, reports, or other documents received by a mediator while serving in that capacity shall be confidential, The mediator shall not be compelled to divulge such records or to testify in regard to the mediation in any adversary proceeding or judicial forum.

The parties shall maintain the confidentiality of the mediation and shall not rely on, or introduce as evidence in any arbitral, judicial, or other proceeding:

- Views expressed or suggestions made by another party with respect to a possible settlement of the dispute;
- Admissions made by another party in the course of the mediation proceedings;
- Proposals made or views expressed by the mediator; or
- The fact that another party had or had not indicated willingness to accept a proposal for settlement made by the mediator.

- *No Stenographic Record* — There shall be no stenographic record of the mediation process.
- *Termination of Mediation* — The mediation shall be terminated:
  - By the execution of a settlement agreement by the parties;
  - By a written declaration of the mediator to the effect that further efforts at mediation are no longer worthwhile; or
  - By a written declaration of a party or parties to the effect that the mediation proceedings are terminated.
- *Exclusion of Liability* — Neither the AAA nor any mediator is a necessary party in judicial proceedings relating to the mediation.

  Neither the AAA nor any mediator shall be liable to any party for any act or omission in connection with any mediation conducted under these rules.
- *Interpretation and Application of Rules* — Mediator shall interpret and apply these rules insofar as they relate to the mediator's duties and responsibilities. All other rules shall be interpreted and applied by the AAA.
- *Expenses* — The expenses of witnesses for either side shall be paid by the party producing such witnesses. All other expenses of the mediation, including required traveling and other expenses of the mediator and representatives of the AAA, and the expenses of any witness and the cost of any proofs or expert advice produced at the direct request of the mediator, shall be borne equally by the parties unless they agree otherwise.

13

Legal Reasoning—Business Jurisdiction in India

LEGAL ASPECTS

An indispensable part of a successful business environment in any country is its legal aspects. They reflect the policy framework and the mind set of the Governmental structure of that country. They ensure that every company is functioning as per the statutory framework of the country. Every enterprise must take into account this legal set up while framing the basic aims and objectives of its company. This is because, it is necessary for efficient and healthy functioning of the organisation and helps it to know about the rights, responsibilities as well as the challenges that it may have to face.

In India, Companies Act, 1956 is the most important law regulating all aspects of a company. It contains provisions relating to formation of a company, powers and responsibilities of the directors and managers, raising of capital, holding company meetings, maintenance and audit of company accounts, powers of inspection and investigation of company affairs, reconstruction and amalgamation of a company and even winding up of a company.

All the transactions of a company are regulated by the Indian Contract Act, 1872. It lays down the general principles relating to the formation and enforceability of contracts; rules governing the provisions of an agreement and offer; the various types of contracts including those of indemnity and guarantee, bailment and pledge and agency. It also contains provisions pertaining to breach of a contract.

The other major legislations are:- the Industries (Development and Regulation) Act 1951; Trade Unions Act; the Competition Act, 2002; the Arbitration and Conciliation Act, 1996; the Foreign Exchange Management Act (FEMA),1999; laws relating to intellectual property rights; as well as laws relating to labour welfare.

LEGAL ENVIRONMENT IN INDIA

A business operates its over all activities in environment where legal framework provides a protection to the business for its right and similarly business is also accountable for its duties towards various stakeholders. Constitutional Law of India is the source, root, stem, spirit and guiding factor for creating, maintaining and observing legal environment in the country. The chapter III conferred certain rights known as fundamental rights (Article 12 to 35) that cannot be taken or reduced by government without due procedure of law and a citizen approaching High Court or Supreme Court can challenge such violation of law.

The constitution of India provides that citizens can enjoy fundamental rights. But when they enjoy them, they should not damage similar rights of the rest of the citizens and national integrity. The right to approach directly the apex court is also a fundamental right. To strike balance between this two extreme is difficult ask, as the government need to take care of over all and sustainable growth.

Implementing this chapter has many time created conflicts with the subsequent chapter that empowers government by prescribing directive principles. Directive Principles in chapter IV has equal footing, which directs State to take such measure to see welfare of common mass.

However it is important to know that one can't approach apex court that can compel government to act accordingly. The government can create exceptions to the general rule, and during conflict, the apex court has delivered judgments harmonizing spirit of both chapters. Article 19 of the Constitution Law of India conferred fundamental right of citizen to operate any business activity in the country, but this right is not absolute per se, the government can bring restrictions within the provisions of other part of The Constitutional Law of India.

Articles 38 and 39 of the Constitution empowers the State should strive to promote public welfare by securing and protecting a social order in which socio-economic justice shall inform all institutions of national life, and ensure that the ownership and control of material resources are so distributed as to subserve the common good.

The operation of the economic system should not result in the concentration of wealth and means of production to the common detriment. Monopolistic & Restrictive Trade Practice Act was enacted in year 1969 (MRTP Act) to observe the directions cited in The Constitutional Law of India.

Business, Consumers, Economy and Competition

Profit generated through goods sold or services provided to the consumers are what business aims at. The government plays tutelage role and keeps balance that business survives and grows, consumers get goods and services at competitive rate and national economy also prospers and sustains.

Striking balance between these two extreme require long-term policy and public confidence in government actions. The three players i.e. consumers, business and government is interconnected and dependent on each other.

Therefore if there exists healthy competition amongst the all players, all segment of the society benefits in long term.

Dictionary meaning of 'compete' is to try to be more successful than someone or something else, strive against others where strive means to try hard, struggle etc. while 'competitive' means wanting very much to win or be more successful than other people. Modern economic legislation is becoming more complex. It has to take on giant MNCs thriving to drive out small firms from the market. Competition between two un-equal may create situation where small one may whither away in long run.

Main areas of competitiveness may be classified as physical competitiveness, intellectual competitiveness, and systemic competitiveness means - attitudes and mindsets that are necessary to fostering a competitive instinct. Thus government should provide conducive environment that business compete in a fair way and becomes constant innovative force to create and adopt new ideas in producing goods and delivering service.

It should also see that in global economy, the benchmark for efficiency and effectiveness is globally competitive. It is something that business should see that they achieve higher benchmark and becomes global leader by establishing higher benchmark.

World Development Report, 2000-01 states, markets work for the poor because poor people rely on formal and informal markets to sell their labor and products, to finance investment, and to insure against risks. Well functioning markets are important ingenerating growth and expanding opportunities for poor people.

Here "Well-functioning" implies markets that work efficiently and without distortions i.e. competitive markets where everyone has the opportunity to participate. However, "competition" is often less understood and easily distorted by the players in the market, even when there are a large number of them. It is therefore that governments enact competition laws to regulate the distortions.

Competition Policy

Government measures affecting the behaviour of enterprises and the structure of industry are encompassed by competition policy. It covers the broad spectrum of economic policies that have a bearing on competition in the economy, such as trade policy, sectoral regulation, privatization etc. At the heart of competition policy in many countries is a competition or anti-trust law, which sets down the legal principles and institutions that govern the behavior of firms in competitive markets including restrictive trade practices, merger scrutiny, provisions to deal with cartels etc.

Competition law can therefore be seen as a legal tool that allows competition principles to be enforced in the governance system. Governmental measures that directly affect the behavior of enterprises and the structure of industry constitute competition policy. While the law is a piece of legislative enactment to regulate the marketplace, which can be enforced in a court of law, it covers a whole raft of public policies and even approaches.

It is upon economic theory that the need for competition law is founded, Economic theory demonstrates that overall welfare is greatest when there is 'perfect competition' in markets. Perfect competition is a theoretical concept and it is not achieved in the real world. However, the closer the market gets to perfect competition, the greater the gains in welfare.

This is because competition directs resources in the economy to their most productive uses, and motivates firms to adopt the most efficient processes of production. Competition also ensures that the benefits of improved efficiency do not just lead to increased profits for firms, but reach the consumer as well. That when a company is a monopoly, it receives higher profits at the expense of its customers is demonstrated by economic theory.

These theoretical foundations are backed up by evidence of the way competition policy and law operates in the real world. Competition laws are regularly used to reduce the power of monopolists and to make sure they provide goods and services at fair prices; to make it possible for more efficient rivals to enter markets dominated by a few large firms; and to prevent firms from cooperating with each other to raise prices at the same time or to restrict their supply.

Competition also motivates firms to develop new products that will meet consumer needs ahead of their rivals, which contributes to dynamism and growth in the economy and helps firms as well as consumers by ensuring that upstream and downstream businesses operate fairly.

Paradigm Shift in Legal Environment and Reforms

The economic policies India followed for several decades after independence were based on the 'command and control regime'. However, in the 1980s, it became clear that many of policies had ceased to serve their objectives.

This resulted in the country embarking on the path of economic reforms, which started, more particularly, around 1991. The wide ranging reforms covered areas such as trade policy, industrial policy, reservations for public sector, privatization of state owned enterprises, etc. One of the objectives of reform is to allow level-playing field to business entity so as to increase efficiency, maintain global standards that, through healthy competition, may benefit consumers and economy as well as business entity itself.

Role of the Union Government in Reforms

National Common Minimum Programme (NCMP) of the UPA Government quote:

It will not support the emergence of any monopoly that only restricts competition. All regulatory institutions will be strengthened to ensure that competition is free and fair. These institutions will be run professionally.

It also aims on with two objectives: First- the corporate should be given hassle-free environment so that they are able to face the competition effectively and contribute to the national economy in the best possible way.

Second- The conduct of the companies should be fully transparent and they must strike proper balance between the interests of the company on one hand and interests of shareholders, depositors and other stakeholders, on the other.

The appointment of a bureaucratic to head the Competition Commission was provided for by the National Democratic Alliance Government while introducing the CCI. But the apex court stayed this and the Center was asked to consider amendments to the Act. The validity of The Competition Law and authority created under the law was put to test in The Supreme Court.

The Supreme Court allowed the Center to bring amendments to the Competition Commission Act as suggested by it, viz. that the Chairperson of the Competition Commission of India (CCI) would be an expert and not a judge, and only the chief of an appellate tribunal would be a judicial person. A three-judge Bench, comprising the Chief Justice, R.C. Lahoti, Justice G.P. Mathur and Justice P.K. Balasubramanyan, was disposing of the petitions filed by advocates Brahma Dutt and R. Gandhi challenging the constitutional validity of the Act. It was said by the bench leaving the issues open that the court could consider the questions raised in the petitions after the Center carried out the amendments proposed by it.

The UPA Government too endorsed the stand of its predecessor and informed the Supreme Court that only a technical expert and not a judge would be the Chairperson of the Competition Commission. In its fresh proposals, the Center, while reiterating that the CCI needed to be a body of experts, said that if at all a judge was included in the CCI, it would be on the strength of his expertise in the field and not because of his judicial background.

It said the CCI, apart from the Chairperson, should have a maximum of six members (a total of seven members). It, however, said there would be an Appellate Tribunal to hear appeals against the orders of the Commission and that this Tribunal would be headed by a sitting or retired Supreme Court judge or a Chief Justice of a High Court.

The other two members would be experts in competition and related matters. The Center also agreed to amend the controversial provision relating to the execution of the orders of the CCI by the High Courts and substituted the High Courts with civil courts. In another modification, the Government said that the CCI would be divested of its power to detain a person in civil prison in the event of contravention of the provisions of the Act. Only after the amended Act was put in place could the legality or otherwise of the provisions be tested. It was the contention of the Bench.

Competition, Consumers and Supreme Court

Prize Chits and Money Circulation Scheme (Banning) 1978 Act - Network marketing.

Whether this multi level marketing is legal or not? - Held, multi-level Marketing results in exploitation of personal influence of each and every distributor or his close relative. Monopolies and Restrictive Trade Practices Act, s. 36A - Allotment of flats - Demand of extra amount - Relief sought to restrain respondent from canceling allotment of apartments in D.L.F. Beverly, Park, Gurgaon for non payment of extra amount demanded from appellants.

Supreme Court of India observed Telecom Regulatory Authority of India Act, 1997 - Ss. 18 and 14 - Govt. permitted the Fixed Service Providers to offer WLL with limited mobility - appellants Cellular Mobile Service Providers challenged the decision of the Govt. - appeal against the decision of the Telecom Disputes Settlement and Appellate Tribunal - whether from the judgment of the tribunal, the contentions raised by the appellants can be held to be a substantial question of law, which requires interference with the order of the tribunal?

Held, the conclusion of the tribunal that nothing should be allowed to stand in the way of pursuing the objective of increasing teledensity in the country and that the decision being a policy decision, is not liable to be interfered with by the tribunal, cannot be sustained inasmuch as the main grievance of the cellular operators was to the effect that the tribunal did not consider several materials placed before it on the question of level playing field nor has it given any positive finding on that.

Non-consideration of relevant materials on the issue regarding level playing field and absence of any finding by the tribunal on that score vitiate its ultimate decision and would constitute a substantial question of law within the meaning of Section 18 of the Act, on account of which the Supreme Court can interfere with the decision of the Peico Electronics and Electricals and Another vs. Union of India and others.

Restrictive Trade Practice: MRTP Act, s. 2(o) (ii) - further finding that the impugned trade practice has the effect of imposing on the consumers' unjustified costs or restrictions - required. Held on facts, irrespective of the termination of the Agreement between appellant and R-2, the appellant should take steps to amend a similar clause existing in other agreements of similar nature with the dealers.

Also held, commission exceeded its jurisdiction in giving a direction not to give effect to the letter terminating the Agreement and to restore the supplies to the complainant - cannot be sustained in the absence of a finding that the termination of Agreement was contrary to the provisions of the Act or it is a device to circumvent the provisions of the Act so as to perpetuate the restrictive trade practice - cease and desist order.

Star India Private Limited vs: Siti Cable Network Limited and Others Monopolistic and Restrictive Trade Practices Act, 1969 - ss. 10 r/w 36B, 12A - Appellants not permitting the complainants and their associates from using the latest technology in telecommunication. Hindustan Ciba Geigy vs. Union of India and others (SUPREME COURT OF INDIA)Date of Judgment: 20/11/

2002Monopolies and Restrictive Trade Practices Act, 1969 - S. 36A - whether under Section 36A of the Act, causation of loss or injury to the consumer of goods or service is sine qua non for initiation of a proceeding there under - Held, an inquiry can be initiated against the notice not only when it adopts one or more practices specified therein but also thereby it must cause loss or injury to the consumers. A manifest error was therefore committed by the Commission in holding that the actual loss or injury need to be caused to the consumers.

Colgate Palmolive (India) Limited vs: Monopolies and Restrictive Trade Practices Commission and others (SUPREME COURT OF INDIA) M.R.T.P. Act - S. 36A - Interpretation of - held, for holding a trade practice to be an unfair trade practice, it must be found that it had caused loss or injury to the consumer - Causation or loss or injury is a sine qua non for invoking the principles of Section 36A of the M.R.T.P. Act.

The Commission committed a manifest error in holding that the actual loss or injury is not an essential ingredient of the unfair trade practice. A literal meaning should be assigned to a statute unless the same leads to anomaly or absurdity. It is a well established principle of law now.

The Supreme Court considered that in a price-fixing conspiracy, the conduct is illegal and no further enquiry was needed on intent or anti-competitive effect. It pointed out:

The critical analysis in determining whether a particular activity constitutes a per se violation is whether the activity on its face seems to be such that it would always or almost always restrict competition, and decrease output instead of being designed to increase economic efficiency and make the market more rather than less competitive. Hindustan Development Corporation, 1993, 3 SCC 499). These unhealthy trends will henceforth attract severe penalties.

Supreme Court directed under Central Excise Act, the deposit of refundable indirect tax that can't trace the real payee into special account created for over all welfare of consumers.

The doctrine of 'unjust enrichment' has given new direction to the practical way when one become unjust rich at expense of others, but could not refund such amount to actual person, such person were directed to deposit in special account under the trusteeship of government, and shall be utilized for benefit of consumers. Similar judgment was delivered to banking institutes to deposit amount accumulated due to rounding off in welfare of physically challenged people.

New Dimensions to Competition Policy

Competition policy is used as and instrument for achieving efficient allocation of resources, technical progress and consumer welfare and of regulating concentration of economic power detrimental to competition. It has different objectives in different countries but some major themes stand out. In most of the countries, it aims at promoting competition by discouraging anti-competitive behavior.

Freedom of trade, freedom of choice, access to markets, and achievement of economic efficiency to maximize consumer welfare is the other commonly expressed objectives of competition policy. The role of competition policy has also expanded in the last two decades to include regulation of government intervention in the marketplace.

Significant advantages to business and consumers may result fro introduction of a comprehensive competition policy. For business, such a policy means fairness as it acts against anti-competitive practices that can drive efficient and well-run companies out of business. It ensures consistency because it is applied by a single authority working to a single set of published rules and a reduction in regulation since it is proactive, efficient and effective which avoids the need to commit manpower and time to devising new rules when new products or markets emerge.

For consumers, lower prices and improved services result from an effective competition policy and law. An improvement in the coverage of competition law and a reduction in the time taken to remove barriers to competition mean a lot for the consumer, in particular the poor.

While opportunities for anti-competitive behavior may be limited in many sectors most of the time by fierce competition between firms, market conditions are constantly changing. It cannot be guaranteed that a particular market will remain very competitive and hence less vulnerable to anti-competitive practices in the long term. Competition policy by being comprehensive, provides a readymade, consistent framework for dealing with anticompetitive behaviour in any sector of the economy.

Free and fair competition is one of the pillars of an efficient economy. Competition stimulates innovation and productivity and leads to optimum allocation of resources in the economy. However, some enterprises undermine the market by resorting to anticompetitive practices for individual gain. For example, they may form cartels, or big companies may abuse their dominant position. Such practices, if not checked, can completely nullify or frustrate the gains from competition.

FORCES REINFORCING HEALTHY COMPETITION

There are certain internal as well as international forces working to strengthen the competition in business environment.

Internal Forces

The corporate sector also experienced global competitive environment and presented their voice at different forums. It also realized that to be globally competitive is the only mantra to survive and grow, not for merely businesses but economy as a whole need to be so. In a keynote address Reliance doyen Mr. Mukesh Ambani said: by setting the goal of global leadership before us, we are committing ourselves to climb the Everest of global economy.

The task is hazardous, but not impossible to achieve. In my view, competitiveness is critical for a successful assault on this high peak. Our attitude to competitiveness is a barometer of our self-confidence, and efficiency is the most crucial component of competitiveness. Faced with ruthless global competition, we have to worship the goddess of efficiency with unflinching dedication.

He further said: Let us not be afraid of international efficiency. Let us not shy away from global competitiveness. To protect low quality and high cost would induce consumers to procure foreign products in a clandestine manner. A strong Indian economy is the most dependable defence of our national interests. We should be satisfied only when it is ready to withstand global competition. When it makes inroads in foreign markets on its own merit and develops global brands.

International Forces

Many countries have their own competitive laws. And these competitive laws deal with anti-competitive agreements among firms engaged in the same lines and firms with vertical integration. Mexican Competition Law seeks to protect Free Market Participation through elimination of monopolies and monopolistic practices. Anti-Trust laws have been popular in the US.

The core objective of competition policy in most countries is to maintain a healthy degree of rivalry among firms in markets for goods and services. South Africa, the Netherlands and the UK have come out with laws radically altering competition regulations. There has been a divergence of views on competition policy in Europe and the US. American law focuses on the consumer whereas in Europe, industry gets the focus. But in both regions, it is distrust of concentration of economic power that competition policy is based on.

WTO acts as a catalyst for creating borderless globally competitive business environment. India as signatory of WTO convention took lead in drafting its environment to suit its duty as such signatory of WTO convention.

NEW DIMENSIONS AND LEGAL REFORMS

The MRTP Act was amended in 1991 and the Government realized that pre-entry restrictions under the MRTP Act on the investment decision of the corporate sector outlived its utility, and became a hindrance to the speedy implementation of industrial projects. The Act was restructured with focus on curbing monopolistic restrictive and unfair trade practices.

Ten years after this amendment, the Government realized that the whole setup had become an anachronism, and a committee was set up to suggest ways and means to promote competition. On the basis of the S. V. S Raghavan Committee report, the Government came out with a new tax law styled the Trade Related Competition Bill.

Amongst the first changes to be made were amendments to the MRTP Act to delete certain restrictive provisions that created pre-investment barriers. Since then, there has been a more competition-friendly regime, with greater freedom for business entities that has released the energies of the private sector and resulted in a more dynamic and faster growing economy. The forces of competition have brought benefits both for the business sector as well as for the consumers.

Competition Law

The Competition Law focuses on the firm's structure, not size and this is where the Competition law is different from the MRTP Act. The MRTP Act lists 14 offences. The Competition Law will recognize only four such offences. The MRTP Act's role was only advisory. The proposed competition commission can initiate suo motu proceedings and levy penalties. The Competition Law does not consider the firm's dominance per se detrimental to competition. Frowning upon dominance, the MRTP Act laid down an arithmetical test.

It is only abuse of dominance that the Competition Law frowns upon. It seeks to regulate agreements that control production, supply, markets, technical developments or investment in provision of services. All such agreements are considered anti-competitive and penalty can be levied. The recent experience with cement cartels is an example of price rigging under agreements to share markets. Sources of production by way of geographical allocation of market will be considered anti-competitive.

Agreement arrived at between enterprises that directly result in bid rigging or collusive tendering is prohibited by the Competition Law. The Act defines bid rigging as agreements between enterprises or persons engaged in identical or similar manufacturing, trading or provision of service that has the effect of eliminating or reducing competition for bids, or adversely affecting/manipulating bidding. Apart from these guidelines, other restrictive trade practices will fall under the rule of reason test before the Competition Commission of India (CCI).

Registration of agreements was mandatory under the MRTP Act, but the Competition Law has no such requirement. A combination is sought to be regulated beyond a threshold limit. The Government appointed the MRTP Commission's Chairman. A Collegium consisting of the Chief Justice, the Finance and other Cabinet Ministers, the Cabinet Secretary and the RBI Governor, will select the CCI chairman. An important difference lies in the fact that the Competition Law leaves unfair trade practices to consumer fora and not to the CCI.

The MRTP Act had definition of unfair trade practices u/S 36A that lists out various modes and possibilities of Unfair Trade Practice. The Competition Law will take care of cartelization that imposes unjustified cost on the consumers. Cases such as Sumitomo Corporation and others that quoted identical prices pursuant to a global tender floated by the Steel Authority of India will be easier to deal with under the new law.

The requirement of pre-merger notifications is dispensed with by the Competition Law. There will be a separate Bench of the CCI styled as the Merger Commission to deal with mergers. This part of the Law requires disposal of the case within 90 days. If there is no order, it will be presumed the merger has been approved. There is also possibility of power sharing conflict with SEBI, another body dealing with takeover bids of substantial shareholding of any listed company in India.

The Competition Law also seeks to regulate predatory pricing though it is not clear how the Commission will determine pricing below the cost. There is bound to be some overlap between the functions of the High Court and the CCI when it comes to cases involving mergers, acquisitions and amalgamations.

The CCI is also expected by the Competition Act to promote competition through advocacy. This is in line with the thinking of the OECD. The OECD had pointed out that in every member-country where significant reform efforts have been undertaken, the competition agencies have been active participants in the reform process. Advocacy can include persuasion behind the scenes and publicity outside. This part of the Act appears to suggest that the CCI should interact through the media to promote competition.

Objectives of Competition Law

Protecting the interests of consumers is one of the objectives of the Competition Law. They purchase the products of other firms as their inputs, and the price and quality of these inputs partly determine their own competitiveness and profits that they are able to make.

Another objective is stimulating efficiency and competitiveness across the economy. Competition helps to achieve efficient allocation of resources and stimulates dynamism through the free entry and exit of firms into markets, raising productivity.

At the same time Competition Law aims in preventing unfair competition. Businesses have a strong interest in ensuring that their competitors do not have an unfair advantage, and that their suppliers and customers are also operating in competitive markets. A large proportion of complaints of anticompetitive practices in firms are raised by other businesses. Competition policy relates to poverty reduction through these routes.

Many sectors, like water and electricity that are prone to anti-competitive behavior, affect the poorest most. These take up a much higher proportion of the budget of poorer households. Furthermore, the poor benefit by the indirect route of economic growth and job creation. Of course, many other policies need to be in place if the poor are to benefit from economic growth, but under the right conditions it will help them.

Competition Law & Business

Competition policy is sometimes used as a weapon for businesses to use against each other. Rulings of the competition authority are seen as a redistribution of profits between businesses at different stages in the production chain or between horizontal competitors. However, it is the consumer who can and should be the ultimate beneficiary of competition law and policy.

For the consumer to truly benefit, several requirements have to be met, both in the provisions of the law itself as well as an active well-organized and informed consumer movement.

Elements of Competition Culture

A competition culture promotes a well-regulated market; efficient allocation of resources and efficient production processes in the economy. It stimulates firms to compete with one another in price, quality and through the innovation of new products. It ensures that the benefits of this efficiency do not just accrue to firms, but lead to greater value and choice for consumers, environmental protection and sustainable development. It is made up of a number of elements, of which laws form only one part. All stakeholders have a role to play in creating this culture of competition. Among the most important elements are:

Active Consumers

Consumers can be the key beneficiaries of competition policy. But in order for them to reap these benefits, they need to take an active part in implementation of the law.

This can be done by identifying product markets of concern, providing information to the competition authorities and perhaps bringing cases against offending businesses. Despite their numbers, consumers are often not well organized. When raising the profile of consumers, it is extremely important to strengthen consumer organisations and representative groups.

Responsible Business

For a competition culture to thrive, businesses need to respect certain standards of behavior. This does not just mean refraining from cartelisation and the restrictive business practices that competition law is concerned with, but also maintaining standards of transparency, corporate governance, accounting practices and combating corruption as well as respecting social and environmental regulations. At the heart of fair competition is this respect for rules.

Sensitized Media

That public awareness and support necessary for competition laws to be implemented effectively has be noted above. The media has an extremely important role to play both in drawing attention to particular concerns and helping competition institutions and officials to demonstrate their role and public support when dealing with other public and private sectors institutions.

Institutional Cooperation

In any country, there are a large number of institutions that influence the competition culture. All these institutions and the people that work in them need to be sensitive to competition concerns and to cooperate with each other. Otherwise, the competition culture is in danger of being over-run by a bureaucratic culture and rent-seeking behavior.

TECHNOLOGY, IPRS AND PATENT

Technology, it goes without saying, has come out to be the most important driver of economic growth and development. Already computer engineers are caught up with designing complex engineered systems. Genetic engineers are galvanized by the promise of designing organisms to carry out industrial processes. Cell biologists are concerned with regeneration of tissues. Medical biologists are motivated by the prospects of controlling aging and making life immortal.

Tissue engineers are thrilled by the prospect of reconstructing human beings. Astronauts are assiduous about expeditions beyond the solar system. Physicists are passionate about building molecular computers and neural networks. India cannot remain captive to mediocrity when the world is setting out to capture new waves of disruptive technologies. Intellectual Property Right has taken ride in knowledge economy over other tangible property. Copyright, Patent, Design, Trademark and related IPRs are now synonyms of essential assets in the financial statements of corporate.

The aim of the Patent Act's being amended by the Indian government was to protect interest of the researchers and to make WTO TRIPS compliance. The introduction of pharmaceutical patents and the consequent threat to an internationally renowned generic industry that has, thus far, ensured the supply of affordable drugs catapulted this legislative effort to international significance, of an extent never before witnessed in the annals of intellectual property law making in India.

The 2005 Act attempts to balance out competing interests of a variety of stakeholders, including domestic generic medicine producers, the domestic research and development community, foreign multinational pharmaceutical companies, civil society groups concerned with access to medicines and (last, but certainly not least), intellectual property lawyers.

Although this delicate balancing deserves some applause, an unfortunate fall-out has been the hasty introduction of provisions that go against the grain of time tested patent law principles and are likely to provide excellent fodder for litigation. Some of the main changes brought about by the 2005 Act are highlighted by this note. Besides this, this not reflects on some of their broader implications.

It is the outcome of above discussion that on the passage of time path of socialistic pattern by government changed into capitalistic pattern, influenced by global forces and well supported by judicial interpretation that has drastically changed mindset of consumers and changed direction of doing business by taking care of consumers and society.

Recent judgments related to above Acts and relevant issues, e.g. restricting competition, welfare of consumers, marketing and unfair trade practices, abolishing unnecessary restrictions on manufacturers that are imposed by government, restrictive and monopolistic practice have influenced corporate to think otherwise. The positive aspect of competition is its use as weapon to improve quality and thereby winning confidence of customers, building brand image, increasing market share. If they satisfy their important stakeholders, i.e. consumer, the business survives and excels.

This is possible by improving quality of the product and complying legal obligation attracts more consumers for longer period. That gives them an edge in marketing, because loyalty of consumer consumes less market expenses and consumers perceive law-abiding business as good business. Finally competition improves quality of the product and service using optimum resources is seen as corporate social responsibility.

The perception and mind set has been changed due to increased literacy and awareness. Society expects that as business also consume common resources of the society and hence it should return a part of the fruit for social cause. The word consumer has been expanded by new judicial doctrine of unjust enrichment and created welfare fund for class of consumers from penny of millions of consumers.

Index